THE RIGHT TO THE CITY

THE RIGHT
TO THE
CITY

POPULAR CONTENTION IN
CONTEMPORARY BUENOS AIRES

Gabriela Ippolito-O'Donnell

University of Notre Dame Press

Notre Dame, Indiana

Published in the United States of America

Library of Congress Cataloging-in-Publication Data

Ippolito-O'Donnell, Gabriela.
The right to the city : popular contention in contemporary
Buenos Aires / Gabriela Ippolito-O'Donnell.
    p.   cm. — (From the Helen Kellogg Institute for International Studies)
Includes bibliographical references and index.
ISBN-13: 978-0-268-03179-4 (pbk. : alk. paper)
ISBN-10: 0-268-03179-7 (pbk. : alk. paper)
1. Buenos Aires (Argentina)—Politics and government—20th century.
2. Democratization—Argentina—Buenos Aires. 3. Political participation—
Argentina—Buenos Aires. 4. Urban poor—Political activity—
Argentina—Buenos Aires.   I. Title.
JS2328.B82I66   2011
320.982'11—dc23
2011036534

CONTENTS

———————

PART IV. THE POLITICS OF SIGNIFICATION

TABLES

———

FIGURES

GRAPHS

MAPS

———

ACKNOWLEDGMENTS

———————————

Many friends and colleagues from the northern and southern hemispheres and from both east and west of the Atlantic provided support and encouragement at different times of this study. I especially thank Verónica Montecinos, Carlos Acuña, David Lehmann, and Juan Méndez. I am indebted to Sarah Radcliffe at Cambridge, who helped me discover the importance of political geography for better understanding social movements. Mariana Sousa provided able assistance on statistical analysis. Two anonymous readers at Notre Dame Press greatly contributed by providing constructive criticisms and suggesting improvements to the book's organization. I am thankful to Stephen Little for clearing the way to publishing this book and to Elisabeth Magnus for copyediting my prose. They have both shown great professionalism all along. The production of this book was skillfully managed by Rebecca DeBoer, Elizabeth Sain, and Wendy McMillen at Notre Dame Press, and Judy Bartlett of the Kellogg Institute for International Studies.

I would like to express very special thanks to Scott Mainwaring, my former advisor at the University of Notre Dame. This book builds upon our early discussions of popular movements in Latin America. He always stimulated and respected my ideas.

I also appreciate the financial support provided by the Inter-American Foundation, the North-South Center of the University of Miami, and the Helen Kellogg Institute for International Studies at the University of Notre Dame in the United States.

Above all, this study was made possible because some remarkable people in a poor neighborhood of Buenos Aires found intriguing my interest in their acting together. I thank them all for sharing with me their experiences of participation.

I am thankful to my mother, Alicia, my sister Patricia, and my stepdaughter, Julia, for their enduring support and love. My friend since childhood, Fabiana Groppa, has been a constant source of confidence and much-needed fun during the crucial final steps of this project

Finally, the most important acknowledgment of all goes to Guillermo O'Donnell. He has taught me that academic life is not just a profession to make a living or get prestige; it is a struggle by way of thinking how to improve the life of others and make the world a better place for all. A lifetime of gratitude to him, lover, mentor, and husband.

Gabriela Ippolito-O'Donnell
Buenos Aires, April 2011

ABBREVIATIONS

CGDs *concejos de gestión democrática*
(councils for democratic administration)

CGPs *centros de gestión y participación*
(centers of city administration and participation)

CGT Confederación General del Trabajo
(General Confederation of Labor)

CMV Comisión Municipal de la Vivienda
(Municipal Housing Commission)

CVL Comisión de Vecinos de Villa Lugano
(Villa Lugano Neighborhood Committee)

JCN Junta Coordinadora Nacional
(National Coordinating Board, faction of the Radical Party)

NSMT new social movements theory

OS optimal scaling

PRN Proceso de Reorganización Nacional
(dictatorship, 1976-83)

RMT resource mobilization theory

SFs *sociedades de fomento*
(nongovernmental neighborhood associations)

UBs   *unidades básicas*
      (Peronist Party local headquarters)

UCD   Unión del Centro Democrático
      (Union of the Democratic Center)

UCR   Unión Cívica Radical
      (Radical Civic Union)

Introduction

Beginning in the early 1980s, throughout Latin America democratically elected governments took over from military dictatorships, inaugurating the longest period of democratic rule the region has ever enjoyed. Students of "transitology" (Stark and Bruzst 1998) have argued that, even though in most countries of the region factors from "above" precipitated the collapse of authoritarianism (a military fiasco, intraelite confl cts, etc.), it was in the end the "resurrection of civil society"—the outburst of citizen participation and popular mobilization—that played "the crucial role of pushing the transition further than it would otherwise have gone" (O'Donnell and Schmitter 1986: 56). The optimism that accompanied the transition processes in the region led many scholars and activists to stress the democratizing impact of urban popular organizations and movements and their role as vehicles for social and political change. However, after the initial wave of popular mobilization, it became evident that the demands and collective strategies of the urban poor were quite heterogeneous and their political and organizational practices, with few exceptions, not too democratic. It also became apparent that the workings of democratic institutions and public policies toward the poor often played an important role in demobilizing them. The collective action of the urban poor became uncertain and ephemeral—and has mostly remained so. While the emergence of urban popular movements and their role during the transition have been widely documented, the effects of their cyclical nature on the quality of democracy and on people's well-being have not.

With this in mind, this book aims at contributing to the study of democratization "from below" by focusing on the dilemmas and opportunities urban popular organizations and movements face in their attempts at acting collectively to improve their living conditions and gain fair access to urban space in the city of Buenos Aires, the capital of Argentina.

Like the opening of Chinese boxes, the study of the organizational capabilities of the urban poor entails unpacking a series of nested themes. Several theoretical concerns inform this study.

The fi st concern refers to the role of civil society in democratization. For some decades now, scholars and policy makers have disagreed on the effects of an active civil society on the quality of democracy. Does participation in relatively autonomous civic associations have positive consequences for community life, individual well-being, and democracy? Some authors are convinced this is true. The idea that participation and organization at the grassroots have positive effects on the life of the community and the individual is not at all new in the social sciences (Portes 1998). For example, de Tocqueville attributed the vitality of democracy in the United States to the proliferation of civic associations and widespread participation, and Durkheim believed that group life was an antidote to anomie and self-destruction. In a similar vein, Putnam (1993) argued that by participating at the grassroots level people accumulate a crucial asset to improve individual and community life: social capital. An active associational life fosters trust and cooperation among citizens, which in turn promote democratic stability and government effectiveness. Criticisms of Putnam's social capital theory are numerous. Most of them focus on two aspects. First, research has shown that not all kinds of associations have a positive effect on democracy (Armory 2004). Second, when associations do have a positive effect, it is often on the stability rather than the expansion of democracy (Foley and Edwards 1996).

This perspective on the impact of associational activities on democracy and people's well-being is somewhat different from Putnam's. As Foley and Edwards (1996) remind us, while Putnam's "organized civil society" model is good for regime stability, the political experience of many newly democratized countries in Latin America and eastern Europe suggests that a "rebellious civil society" is necessary for pushing democratization forward. Furthermore, as Tilly (2004: 6) has stressed, political contention, or "politics in which people make concerted claims bearing on each other's interests," is at the root of most democratization processes. Indeed, not all episodes of political contention lead to democratization, but in most advances of democratization contention has been in one form or another present. Confl ct, as Barrington Moore Jr. has shown in *Social Origins of Dictatorship and Democracy* (1966), is a common feature in the history of most stable democracies. Similarly, I argue that in principle a *contentious* civil society is a necessary (but not a sufficient) condition for the expansion of democracy and citizenship rights.

A second theoretical concern refers to the quality of democracy and the effectiveness of citizenship rights among the urban poor. A main assumption of this study is that, not only by voting but also through various channels of collective action and associational activities, the urban popular sectors are a fundamental actor in the expansion of democracy. Voting is a basic right of citizenship, but it is just one such right. Other rights of citizenship are equally important, and without them the effectiveness of voting is at stake. Even a narrow (procedural) defi ition of democracy needs to include other rights, such as the rights of associational autonomy and of free expression. O'Donnell (2004) has referred to these rights as the "surrounding freedoms" of the political regime, without which the act of voting is less than meaningful. The effectiveness of these other rights of citizenship has been largely overlooked by mainstream studies of democratization, which have focused primarily on the dynamics of voting.

There are, however, some exceptions. As Fox (1994) has argued, the effectiveness of the right of associational autonomy is of foremost importance for those disadvantaged members of society who have only this resource to make their voices truly heard in the political process. If one accepts O'Donnell's (2004) defi ition of democracy as based upon the idea of citizens as agents (beings endowed with practical reason and moral discernment), the violation of the right of associational autonomy—as happens, for example, under clientelism—infringes on the very conception of human agency on which democracy is based and negatively affects the quality of democracy.

But why is the study of the dynamics of (contentious) collective action important with regard to the urban poor? This is the third concern of this study. Amartya Sen defi ed "development as freedom" as the "expansion of the capabilities of people to lead the lives they value—and have reason to value" (1999: 18). This expansion depends upon the elimination of oppression and the provision of some basic services. As Peter Evans (2002: 56) persuasively argues in his reply to Sen, the expansion of individual capabilities depends on *collective capabilities:* "In practice, my ability to choose the life I have reason to value often hangs on the possibility of my acting together with others who have reason to value similar things."

For the less privileged, Evans concludes, "attaining development as freedom requires collective action." It follows that "fostering the expansion of such means of collective action is central to the expansion of freedom" (2002: 56). This is why it is important to know about the dynamics of urban popular contention and the dilemmas and opportunities that organizations and movements face in their struggles for better living conditions, the achievement of development as freedom, and the expansion of democracy through the gaining of fair access to urban space.

The last concern of this study is to uncover the relevance of geography, space, and territory to the dynamics of contention among the urban poor. As I discuss in chapter 1, geography has been until recently quite absent from the study of popular movements and organizations, especially among social scientists. This is even truer for the study of urban popular movements in Latin America, where emphasis has been lately placed on indigenous and agrarian movements (Perreault 2008). I argue that geography is a constitutive part of urban popular collective action and the emergence of spatial agency, defi ed as the reshaping of urban space by reclaiming it, the ultimate goal of most mobilization attempts at the grassroots level. While my approach for explaining the dynamics of popular contention builds upon well-established theories in the field of social movements and collective action, it places geography at the center of the analysis and, in doing so, generates new implications for the understanding of the nature of mobilization in an urban setting. To put it briefly, in complex and sometimes unexpected ways geography strongly conditions the chances of the urban poor to mobilize around their most urgent demands.

METHOD AND SOURCES

In this book I use qualitative and survey data to analyze what factors—spatial, economic, politico-institutional, organizational, and subjective—account for the emergence in the 1980s, and the collapse in the 1990s and up to the present, of a wave of grassroots popular organization in Villa Lugano, a poor neighborhood located in the south of Buenos Aires City. These factors are crucial for explaining the organizational weakness and concomitant cyclical patterns of collective action of the urban poor and their negative consequences for the alleviation of poverty and inequality, as well as for the prospects of deepening democratization.

To do so, this book adopts the form of an analytic narrative. As Bates et al. (1998: 3) have argued, the use of analytic narratives points to the conviction that theory linked to data is more powerful than either one alone. Narratives of this sort stress the relevance of stories, details, and context. They are analytic in the sense that by describing events in detail they facilitate explanation. According to Bates et al. (1998), analytic narratives use "thick" descriptions for "thin" reasoning. By interviewing people, participating in meetings, reading local newspapers, and consulting archives, I sought to understand actors' preferences, their perceptions and evaluations of their situation, the opportunities they saw as possible alternatives, the information they had access to, the expectations they formed, the strategies they pursued, and the constraints that precluded their chosen course of action.

Case Selection

Social scientists have developed a series of rules for deciding what case or set of cases should be included in a well-designed research study.[1] However, in many instances social scientists are "chosen by" their cases: it is true that more often than not case selection comes out of either fascination with and/or ethical commitment to the explanation of a particular event (Bates et al. 1998). Back in the early 1980s, as a junior researcher at CEDES (Centro de Estudios de Estado y Sociedad), I conducted my fi st fieldwork in Villa Lugano, a poor neighborhood in southern Buenos Aires. I was assigned to this particular neighborhood (one among several included in a broad comparative project on grassroots organization) by chance, because I lived close by. This experience exposed me early on to the deep (and increasing) spatial inequality of Buenos Aires, a city often perceived as rather well integrated. It also showed me that in spite of extreme material hardship many poor people would keep on participating in and working for their community instead of withdrawing into apathy or turning to illegal activities or violence. As soon as I set foot in Villa Lugano I had the urge to explain why Buenos Aires, in spite of its contentiousness, is in many ways a deeply divided city. For this reason this book is, above all, an attempt to show that the successes and failures of popular collective action in Buenos Aires are inevitably intertwined with its unjust landscape.

Even though I decided to focus on one neighborhood, Villa Lugano, this is not a "neighborhood study." As Clifford Geertz (1973) has said, anthropologists do not so much study "villages," whether tribes, towns, or neighborhoods, as study "*in* villages." I have chosen Villa Lugano, fi st, because after sharing the experiences of political participation and the hopes and despairs of many of its residents I have felt ethically impelled to give voice to their experience, and second, because it clearly reflects many of the political, cultural, and economic changes that have affected the urban popular sectors so deeply in the last decades in Argentina.

Despite the great expectations raised by Argentina's transition to democracy in 1983, the country has since experienced periods of hyperinflation, economic adjustment, neoliberal restructuring, and welfare state retrenchment that have led to increasing heterogeneity of the popular sectors and impoverishment of important parts of the middle class. Falling wages, unprecedented levels of unemployment and poverty, and increasing violent crime, inequality, and illegal immigration from neighboring countries have dramatically reinforced (in a historically homogeneous country) patterns of spatial segregation and social discrimination; these, in turn, have raised levels of intra- and intergroup hostility and changed patterns of social cleavages. Furthermore, a deepening divide between the haves and have-nots and, as importantly, increasing social fragmentation among the poor themselves are transforming social identities as well as changing the nature of collective action and participation, presenting new challenges to the democratizing efforts of civil society movements and organizations, especially those of the urban poor.

Data

The data I use in this study are both qualitative and quantitative. From 1985 to 1988, I conducted participant observation in various grassroots organizations of Villa Lugano. I attended weekly meetings, rallies, and visits to city officials. During this period I also conducted about a dozen interviews with local leaders and city officials. In 1994, I returned to Villa Lugano to conduct a second round of thirty in-depth interviews with grassroots activists and residents. At this time, I also applied a survey (N = 506) of Villa Lugano residents to learn about their political orientations. I then returned yearly to Villa Lugano and repeated interviews with leaders up through 2005. I have taped and transcribed all in-depth interviews. Content analysis of the local press (newspapers and magazines) covers the years 1983–95.

OUTLINE OF THE BOOK

In Chapter 1, I defi e contentious collective action and review the main theoretical approaches to this topic. Following recent trends in the literature, I adopt a synthetic approach to explain the dynamics of contention, but one that stresses the relevance of geography and territory. Chapter 2 historically reviews the forms and traditions of participation and contention used by the lower classes in the city of Buenos Aires. The aim of this chapter is to provide background on how collective action has played out in the city. These practices of collective action help explain some of the long-term obstacles to acting collectively that the urban poor face. Chapter 3 presents the physical landscape of contention, the geographical aspects of Buenos Aires that I argue play a crucial role in the formation of popular identities. Chapter 4 tells the story of people who dared to use their right of association to improve their neighborhood and reclaim urban space. Chapter 5 explores the political culture of the urban poor in Villa Lugano. It is based on in-depth interviews and survey data. Chapter 6 contains a statistical analysis of the survey data presented in chapter 5. The aim of this chapter is to explore political cleavages among the urban poor and their effects on the discursive practices of popular movements. Chapter 7 deals with the most robust fi ding in this study: social hostility among the urban poor. I argue that social hostility is a place-based phenomenon and the ultimate factor in the decline of popular contentious collective action. In the Conclusion I return to the nested themes and review the various factors involved in explaining the dynamics of contention among the urban poor in contemporary Buenos Aires.

PART I

Politics in Space

CHAPTER 1

Contentious Politics in Space

The study of contentious politics is a broad field of research. It includes "all situations in which actors make collective claims on other actors, claims which, if realized, would affect the actors' interests, when some government is somehow party to the claims" (McAdam, Tarrow, and Tilly 1997: 143). This defi ition encompasses a variety of collective action events—from revolutions to strikes, urban riots, and banditry—all having in common their contentiousness. Indeed, collective action can take many forms, but "it becomes contentious when it is used by people who lack regular access to institutions, act in the name of new or unaccepted claims and behave in ways that fundamentally challenge others" (Tarrow 1994: 2).

To explain the dynamics of contentious collective action, scholars have emphasized either rationalist, structural, or cultural factors. Rationalist approaches have built upon individualistic rational choice models (Olson [1965] 1982) and organizational-resource mobilization theories (Zald and McCarthy 1987). Structuralist approaches are best represented by institutionalist "political opportunity structure" models (Lipsky 1970; Lowi 1971; Eisinger 1973; Tarrow 1989) and the macroeconomic "new social movement" theory (Offe 1985). Culturalist approaches build around a somewhat fragmentary body of literature, including the work of social historian E. P. Thompson (1971) on the moral economy of the crowd, Melucci's (1980, 1988) version of new social movement theory, and Goffman's (1974) concept of "framing."

While most studies of collective action fall into one or another approach, recent trends in the field of contentious politics call for a synthetic model to better integrate rationalist, structural, and cultural factors (McAdam, Tarrow, and Tilly 1997). In what follows, I survey the main theories in the study of contentious collective action and briefly discuss their influence on the study of popular mobilization in Latin America. Building upon these theories, I adopt a synthetic approach of contentious collective action—one that places geography as a central factor for explaining the dynamics of urban popular contention. Following Tarrow (1994: 6), I stress that while changes in political opportunities create the incentives that may trigger episodes of popular collective action, the sustainability, magnitude, and duration of these actions depend on organizing people through social networks and discursively mobilizing them around symbols drawn from repertoires of contention and cultural frames of meaning. Yet I add that, to make sense of the dynamic interrelation of these factors (opportunities, organization, and discursive practices), we should turn to the geography or *landscape of contention*: in subtle and unexpected ways, geography in its material and symbolic aspects brings new implications to well-established theories of collective action and social movements. As Tilly asserts (1998: 5), thick representations of spatial dynamics may open the field for resolution of the main difficulties that analysts of political contention face, the inconsistencies among structuralist, rationalist, and culturalist accounts of political processes.

The review of the main theories of collective action and social movements that follows illustrates the way my approach builds upon but also differs from them.

DECONSTRUCTING THE CROWD: FROM COLLECTIVE VICIOUSNESS TO INDIVIDUAL SELFISHNESS

Early studies of contentious collective action focused on individual psycho-sociological characteristics to explain the mobilization of the popular classes. In the 1950s, a burgeoning literature argued that certain states of mind (not structural conditions, institutional or economic) predisposed some individuals to engage in social protest: individuals with authoritarian personalities (Hoffer 1951), who felt alienated or anomic (Kornhauser 1959), felt frustrated and deprived (Gurr 1970), or for a variety of reasons were attracted to new social norms (Smelser 1963) qualified as potential rebels. The roots of this approach, in particular of considering anomie and deprivation as preconditions for popular mobilization, owed much to political events in Europe during the interwar period: the emergence of authoritarian movements (fascism and Nazism) reinforced the perception of the deviant character of the masses and, as a consequence, of their propensity to support antidemocratic forces from either the left or the right (Adorno et al. 1950; Hoffer 1951; Arendt 1968; Fromm 1969; Reich 1970; Germani 1978). Few dissenting voices postulated the mobilization of popular sectors as crucial for the expansion of freedom and equality, while most approaches portrayed the popular classes as a "vicious crowd," whose collective action, guided by dysfunctional psychological predispositions, was inherently irrational.

In the late 1950s and early 1960s, these views came under attack. The work of the social historian George Rudé (1964, 1980) on popular riots involving urban crowds in France and Great Britain during the eighteenth and nineteenth centuries challenged the argument that protest and contentious politics were nonrational (or irrational). In contrast to earlier studies, Rudé depicted protesters as rational actors motivated by common goals, and protest as often expressing an embryonic sense of class solidarity. Rudé's research was supported by E. P. Thompson's (1971, 1975) analysis of the moral economy of the English crowd. For Thompson (1971) events of popular contention (e.g., grain seizures) were not the expression of an irrational and deprived crowd; to the contrary, they were forms of collective bargaining manifested in the form of a riot.[1] Poor people rebelled, not simply when they were starving or deprived but when they perceived that the customary norms of interclass reciprocity (the moral economy) were being violated. The work of British social historians came out in a period of general political demobilization in the aftermath of the Second World War, during which fears of the consequences of social protest had faded away. Some scholars even labeled this period as the "end of ideology" (Bell 1960; Lipset 1960).

In the 1960s, a new wave of popular mobilization gave renewed emphasis to the study of social movements worldwide. Contentiousness began to be seen as a normal feature of the political system. In this context, a series of new models to explain collective behavior emerged. In spite of their diversity, these models, as I discuss below, were responses to criticism of earlier models that had made the mere existence of "material deprivation" a sufficient precondition for collective action and had viewed protest as irrational behavior.[2]

RATIONALIST MODELS OF COLLECTIVE ACTION

Rational Choice Theory: The Individual Perspective

With the publication in 1965 of Mancur Olson's seminal book *The Logic of Collective Action,* a new paradigm emerged in the United States for the study of protest and social movements. Drawing on the field of microeconomics, Olson's model of collective action starts with the assumption that individuals are rational and that participation, contentious or otherwise, is a calculated decision based upon an assessment of the risks and rewards involved. Focusing the analysis on interest groups, Olson asked under what conditions rational and self-interested individuals will engage in collective action to pursue a collective good. Rational and self-interested individuals, Olson concluded, will not engage in collective action except when selective incentives motivate them; they also will not incur the costs of participation if they can "free-ride," that is, if they know that there are other individuals willing to take those costs for them. Thus stated, the likelihood of collective action depends upon the availability of selective incentives (rewards) and the possibility of effectively punishing nonparticipants if they free-ride. Under this assumption, the role of would-be organizers is to provide potential participants with those incentives and/or impose sanctions on free riders.

Olson's microeconomic model meant (in theoretical terms) that grievances were not a sufficient condition for the emergence of collective action or social protest. However, some scholars have correctly pointed out that even though Olson's model may explain why aggrieved people do not participate, it leaves unexplored why people do participate, even when lacking selective incentives (Oliver 1984; Klandermans and Tarrow 1988; Tarrow 1989). Furthermore, contradicting Olson's assumptions (that rational individuals will free-ride to avoid the costs of participation), empirical research has shown that people's motives to participate vary significantly, marginal utility being just one motive among others. Some people engage in collective action because they somehow understand Olson's dilemma: if everybody free-rides the collective good will never be achieved (Oliver 1984). Case studies also show that sometimes people engage in collective action because the collective good at stake is so valuable that even a slight chance of success is enough to motivate participation (Oberschall 1980); because they are motivated by feelings of loyalty to their community, obligation, and a need to maintain their own self-respect (Fireman and Gamson 1979); or because they are ideologically committed to a cause they consider to be just (Carden 1978). In turn, Hirschman (1982) questioned Olson's assertion that participation involves only costs and risks; participation in itself may generate material as well as less tangible benefits, such as the achievement of various kinds of solidarity independently of an instrumental goal. Furthermore, Olson's model, despite its great influence on the study of collective action, focuses on economic associations. As Tarrow (1994) has argued, several of Olson's assumptions apply only to economic associations, not to popular contentiousness or social movements. Basically, Olson's model left unanswered the question of why, despite risks and costs, people still participate in collective action and participation and how such action is coordinated and sustained. As I discuss next, resource mobilization theory (hereafter RMT) was developed in part to answer the difficulties posed by Olson's model.

Resource Mobilization Theory: An Organizational Perspective

In the 1970s, under the influence of (and in response to) Olson's model, a new perspective for the study of social movements and popular protest emerged in the United States: RMT. Its main contribution was "to argue that discontent is at best secondary in accounting for the emergence of insurgency, that organizational resources and the changing power position of the aggrieved, not sudden increases in their grievances, are the major factors leading to the outbreak of disorders" (Jenkins 1979: 224).

At the core of RMT is the argument that since material deprivation is present in all societies in many forms and at all times, its mere presence cannot explain the upsurge of contentious collective action and popular protest (Klandermans and Tarrow 1988). Availability of resources seems to be the crucial variable for explaining these phenomena (McCarthy and Zald 1973, 1977; Jenkins 1983). Scholars who have contributed to RMT have emphasized different aspects of protest, drawing on rational actor approaches (Popkin 1979), organization theory (Wilson 1961; Zald and Ash 1966), and leadership approaches (McCarthy and Zald 1973). But in spite of differences in emphasis, they share the premise that movement participants' actions are rational responses to perceived costs and rewards. By doing so, RMT scholars have adopted Olson's approach of paying close attention to the incentives, cost-reducing mechanisms, and career benefits that may or may not lead to collective behavior (Zald and McCarthy 1987; Oberschall 1973). Klandermans and Tarrow (1988) summarize the three defi ing elements of RMT as follows: (1) Influenced by rational choice models, RMT scholars focus on the cost-benefit calculations of participation (Oberschall 1973; Klandermans 1984); (2) a movement's organization is crucial because it lowers the costs of participation (Morris 1984), helps in recruiting participants (Oberschall 1973), and may increase the chances of success (Gamson [1975] 1990); and (3) the expectation of success plays a very important role among incentives for participation (Oberschall 1980; Klandermans 1984; Marwell and Oliver 1993).

RMT studies have focused primarily on two basic mobilization resources: organization and leadership. Organization, from this perspective, is one of the most valuable resources available to protesters. For Zald and McCarthy (1987: 20), a social movement organization is "a complex, or formal, organization that identifies its goals with the preferences of a social movement or a countermovement and attempts to implement those goals." Formal organizations compete with others and with nonorganized informal actors. Even though RMT scholars have extensively researched the relationship between organizational processes and protest, there is neither consensus on the effects of organizations on movements nor a general model of movement organization (Tarrow 1989).[3]

Leadership does help trigger protest and direct it toward institutional behavior. But not all authors agree with this assertion of RMT. While Eric Hobsbawm (1959) forcefully argued that lack of leadership makes rebellion "primitive" and ephemeral, Piven and Cloward (1979) stressed that leaders often deprive participants of their most effective resource: their spontaneous power to disrupt. In their view, grassroots leaders were crucial for organizing the unorganized at the onset of protest; later in the movement's history, however, leaders (especially those at the top) tended to divert protest from its original purposes and goals. In contrast to Piven and Cloward, Wilson (1961) argued that black leaders in the civil rights movement tended to escalate their demands to mobilize followers, something that made it difficult for them to negotiate with elites because of the risk that followers would defect. Piven and Cloward's (1979) criticism was aimed at the image of the "professional organizer," one of the core ideas of RMT. On their part, McCarthy and Zald (1973: 1215) developed the concept of movement entrepreneurs "who defi e, create and manipulate grievances and discontent that are always present in any society." Even though this proved a useful concept, some authors have argued that it does not grasp the complexity and manifold effects of different types of leadership on movement success: charismatic leaders, agitators, leaders with different social backgrounds, and outsiders (like nonpeasant leaders in peasant movements) may have different impacts on protest dynamics (Tarrow 1989).

STRUCTURALIST APPROACHES

New Social Movements Theory

In the 1970s, western European countries experienced the emergence of non-class-based social movements. Youth, women's, environmental, antinuclear, and human rights movements rapidly spread and challenged the boundaries of traditional institutional politics (Offe 1985; Melucci 1988). A new paradigm, the new social movements theory (hereafter NSMT), explained the emergence of these unconventional movements as a consequence of changes in macrostructural factors: the crisis of advanced capitalism and of the welfare state in a context of declining pluralist-democratic politics (Berger 1979; Offe 1985). The NSMT paradigm stressed the differences between new non-class-based and old labor-based movements in terms of followers, strategies, and predominant values. New social movements were formed by new and declining middle classes, held antimodernist values, used unconventional strategies, and promoted decentralized, nonhierarchical small organizations and direct democracy. Postmaterialist values seemed to come from a rejection of material society (Inglehart 1977) and reactions to a stalled welfare state (Klandermans and Tarrow 1988). One of the most influential authors writing within NSMT, Claus Offe, foresaw in these movements the emergence of a new paradigm of political action that would replace the one based upon the old postwar political consensus. According to Offe (1985: 846), NSMT shared an important analytical insight with neoconservative projects: "The confl ct and contradictions of advanced industrial society can no longer be resolved in meaningful and promising ways through statism, political regulation, and the proliferating inclusion of ever more claims and issues on the agenda of bureaucratic authorities." On the basis of this realization, he argued, new social movements sought to politicize the institutions of civil society in ways that would not be constrained by the representative bureaucratic political institutions and thereby to reconstitute a civil society that would no longer be dependent upon ever more regulation, control, and intervention. To emancipate itself from the state, civil society, Offe concluded, was politicized through practices that belonged to an intermediate sphere between private pursuits and concerns on the one side and institutional, state-sanctioned modes of politics on the other.

NSMT has been criticized for focusing excessively on macrostructural factors to explain movement emergence, disregarding the processes by which consensus is generated at the base and individuals and groups are led to participate. As Klandermans and Tarrow (1988: 23) stressed, "It is a long way from the structural changes of advanced capitalism to the decisions of individuals and groups to participate in social movements." While RMT focuses on movements' internal resources to explain how social movements emerge, NSMT emphasizes features of society and the state at large that lead to participation, or why social movements emerge (Melucci 1988). According to Tarrow (1989, 1994), both approaches ignore the intervening variables of political structure (the "when" of social movements). To these I turn now.

Political Opportunity Structure: The Institutionalist Perspective

To explain the "when" of social movements, scholars in the United States attempted to link the rise of contentious collective action to macro political processes. The "political opportunity structure" paradigm developed out of a series of works including Lipsky's (1970) account of rent strikes, Lowi's (1971) study of urban politics, and Eisinger's (1973) research on urban protest in American cities. The main argument of this paradigm is that people engage in collective action in response to expanded political opportunities and then, by participating, create new ones for themselves and others. Political opportunities are features or dimensions of the political environment that either encourage or discourage people from acting collectively. Tarrow (1994: 85) defi es the political opportunity structure as "consistent—but not necessarily permanent or formal—dimensions of the political environment that provide incentives for people to undertake collective action by affecting their expectations about success or failure." By lowering the cost of participation, expanded political opportunities create incentives to act collectively (Tarrow 1994). Political opportunities can be considered resources external to individuals and groups. As a consequence, they are contingent and unequally distributed. However, research has shown that even disorganized and weak groups can sometimes take advantage of them (Tilly 1978; Tarrow 1994).

Eisinger (1973) was the fi st scholar to operationalize the concept of political opportunity and link it to the dynamics of popular collective action. Later works have basically extended and refi ed Eisinger's operationalization.[4] The most commonly cited dimensions of the political environment are

1. *Increasing access to institutions:* Access to participation is the fi st important incentive for collective action. Eisinger (1973: 15) pointed

out that the likelihood of protest is higher "in systems characterized by a mix of open and closed factors." Elections are one way to gain access and in democratic regimes are the most common one.

2. *Shifting alignments:* In democratic regimes, electoral instability seems to encourage collective action. According to scholars of social movements, the emergence of the American civil rights movement supports this hypothesis: the volatility of voting patterns in the South pushed the Democratic Party to seek the support of black voters, which in turn opened opportunities for the civil rights agenda (Tarrow 1994).

3. *Availability of influential allies:* Gamson (1975) has argued that the presence of influential allies is important not only for the emergence of collective action but also for its success. Kriesi (1991) also pointed out the crucial role played by the presence or absence of influential allies. Would-be protesters are encouraged to undertake collective action when they have allies at several key power posts that can help them avoid repression and might act as negotiators.

4. *Divided elites:* Intraelite cleavages also promote would-be protesters to engage in collective action. O'Donnell and Schmitter (1986) have shown that divisions between soft-li ers and hard-liners in authoritarian regimes provide openings for opposition movements and regime changes.

Long-Term Opportunities for Collective Action: The State-Building Perspective

While changes in political opportunities may trigger contentious events, structural features of the political system create more enduring opportunities and constraints for participation (Katznelson 1981; Tilly 1986; Tarrow 1994). For example, the type of state (democratic or authoritarian, centralized or federal), the prevalent forms of state repression, and the structure of the party system condition the dynamics of contentious collective action. Historically, the process of state building has created opportunities for collective action. Individuals and groups have not only resisted state formation but also forged links with the state to advance their goals. As Tilly (1986) argues, the expansion of national states radically changed the nature of protest from challenging private and local actors to holding public demonstrations before parliaments. Furthermore, the state classification of people as citizens, taxpayers, and soldiers laid the ground for the formation of new social identities and broader social coalitions.

Machine Politics

Katznelson (1981) and Bridges (1986) have shown that the prospects and strategies of collective action have been affected by the expansion of the right to vote and the formation of party machines. According to Bridges (1986), the early expansion of citizenship rights and the emergence of political parties and electoral machines transformed workers in the United States into Democrats and Republicans and, in so doing, precluded the emergence of worker solidarity and the eventual mounting of radical collective action at the local (residential) level. Expanding Bridges' argument, Katznelson (1981) argues that the early development of machine politics and the availability of city municipal resources established patron-client relationships between parties and lower-class residents in New York, thus generating a sharp split in workers' consciousness, language, and behavior regarding issues about work and residence. In contrast to English workers, who perceived society as being divided along class cleavages (not only at work but also at the political and community levels), Katznelson noticed that American workers perceived class as a cleavage only at work. At the residency level machine politics predominated, and workers became clients of the Democratic or Republican Party who competed among themselves for limited resources. As a result, the likelihood of urban popular contentious collective action became uncertain; this accounts, in his view, for the decline of the 1960s urban movements.

State Repression

State repression, or the threat of it, generates severe constraints for collective action (Tilly 1978). Above all, repression makes participation more costly. While under authoritarian rule expected repression hinders traditional and open forms of collective action, it creates incentives for more subtle forms of resistance. Scott (1990) vividly portrayed

how systematically repressed peasants in Southeast Asia developed unconventional resistance techniques, "or hidden transcripts," to under-
mine domination. Furthermore, even though under democratic states
open repression is the exception, the strategy of blocking the preconditions for collective action, notably by enforcing strict legal regulation
over protest and the right of association, is often effectively used (Tarrow 1994).

CULTURALIST APPROACHES

Popular Culture and Collective Action:
The Moral Economy Perspective

The most influential approaches stressing cultural factors come from
twentieth-century neo-Marxist social historians. Rudé (1964) was the
fi st to introduce beliefs, norms, and symbols as crucial factors to explain the behavior of the crowd. Within this approach, the pathbreaking
work of E. P. Thompson should also be singled out for his influence on
historians and social scientists alike. He rejected economistic views that
linked, automatically, the experience of hunger with the outbreak of
riots. Thompson argued that food riots had been too quickly explained
by simply pointing to the hunger of the workers and overlooking the
detailed and rich information on social norms and reciprocity rules for
a variety of groups that was available to social scientists. In response,
Thompson (1971, 1975, 1993) developed the concept of "moral economy" and employed it to explain popular contention in England during
the seventeenth and eighteenth centuries. The term *moral economy* refers to a constellation of norms, customs, mentalities, and rules of interclass reciprocity that order the social, political, and economic life of a
community. People rebel when they perceive that these customs are
being violated, not just when they are suffering material deprivation of
some sort. Rioting, Thompson stresses (1993), is not an obvious response to material need but a sophisticated pattern of collective behavior used as an alternative to other strategies of survival. At the core of
Thompson's work is the notion of legitimization: the women and men
in the crowds that he studied acted with the conviction of defending

traditional rights or customs, with the support of the majority of their community. This "popular consensus" was sometimes endorsed by local authorities, but, more importantly, it was strong enough to overcome fear and/or deference. Scott (1985) transplanted Thompson's moral economy concept to the study of peasant villages in Southeast Asia. He found out that peasants were more likely to rebel when they perceived that customary norms in the village were being violated by landlords. In agreement with Thompson's perspective, Scott pointed out that peasants rebelled when consensus on legitimate marketing practices and other community obligations was perceived to have been violated.

The Formation of New Collective Identities:
The Constructivist Perspective

Some scholars working within the paradigm of NSMT have emphasized the role of social movements as vehicles for cultural change. The work of Alberto Melucci (1980, 1988, 1996) and Alessandro Pizzorno (1978, 1986) points in this direction. Pizzorno (1978) employs a collective identity approach to interpret industrial confl ct in western Europe in the 1960s and 1970s. He argues that some types of collective actions can be made understandable only by focusing on whether they produce solidarity (instead of gains and losses) for the actors involved. The logic of collective action thus understood involves noninstrumental, nonstrategic rationality. Cost-benefit calculations cannot explain the actions of the new social movements of the 1960s and 1970s, which sought identity, solidarity, and autonomy. Pizzorno claimed that the ultimate goal of the new social movements was nonnegotiable, since it entailed the formation of the very subject who would eventually become the bearer of gains and losses while engaged in strategic bargaining. From this springs Pizzorno's assertion that for an actor to be able to calculate costs and benefits and act strategically, his identity must fi st be established. The logic of collective action is expressive, in the sense that con-fl ct emerges not out of a specific demand but out of new or nonrecognized actors' need to affirm their very existence.

Melucci (1988, 1996), while sharing the basic assumptions of NSMT (that new movements emerge out of the crisis of advanced capitalism

and the welfare state), stressed the cultural significance of social movements and their crucial role in the formation of new identities and solidarity. For this author, collective action was defi ed "by the presence of
solidarity": that is, by a system of social relations that linked together
and identified those who participated within it and by the presence of
a confl ct. He described collective identity as an interactive process
through which individuals and groups defi e the meaning of their actions. The process of identity construction is twofold: it entails the plu-
rality of orientations of the collective action actor itself, and its relationships with others. Collective identity formation emerges out of struggles
for recognition between and within groups; the process by which collective action is constructed also sets the parameters for cost-benefit calculations. Collective identity is an ongoing process but tends to crystallize
into forms of organization, systems of rules, and leadership relations
(Melucci 1996).

Repertoires of Contention: The Collective Memory Perspective

The publication of Charles Tilly's *The Contentious French* (1986) opened
another avenue for the cultural interpretation of collective action. After
reviewing four centuries of popular struggle in France, Tilly concluded
that protesters construe their strategies by using historically learned
routines of collective action. These routines are not invented anew by
leaders or activists; they belong to the realm of the collective memory of
the community and as such are culturally embedded and transmitted
(Kertzer 1988). Every civil society has a reservoir of collective action
strategies known by both would-be protesters and their potential oppo-
nents. Tilly has labeled these routines repertoires of contention: "the
whole set of means a [group] has for making claims of different kinds
on different individuals or groups" (1986: 4). These routines are, as
Stinchcombe suggested, "simultaneously the skills of the population
members and the cultural forms of the population" (1987: 1248).[5] Repertoires of contention change over time. Major shifts in routines of collective action depend upon changes in interest, opportunities, and organization, which in turn are contingent upon changes in state building
and capitalist development. Tilly (1995) identifies two basic repertoires
of contention, one traditional, the other modern. The traditional reper-

toire of contention was *"parochial* because most often the interests and interaction involved concentrated in a single community[;] . . . *bifur-cated* because when ordinary people addressed local issues and nearby objects they took impressively direct action to achieve their ends[;] . . . *particular* because the detailed routines of action varied greatly from group to group, issue to issue, locality to locality" (1995: 45). The most common routines of contention under the traditional repertoire were grain seizures, ritual shaming or charivari, and antiseignorial riots. But in the eighteenth century, as a consequence of the state's increasing penetration of society, the development of modern capitalism, and the concentration of large numbers of people in cities, a new repertoire of contention emerged. Routines of collective action became *"cosmopoli-tan* in often referring to interests and issues that spanned many lo-calities or affected centers of power whose actions touched many lo-calities[;] . . . *modular* in being easily transferable from one setting or circumstance to another[;] . . . *autonomous* in beginning on the claim-ants' own initiative and establishing direct communication between claimants and nationally-significant centers of power" (1995: 46). Pre-dominant modern routines of contention are the petition, the strike, the demonstration, the barricade, and the urban insurrection.

The Politics of Signification: The Collective Action Frames Perspective

In the mid-1980s, scholars in the United States began to criticize RMT and the political opportunity structure paradigm for their tendency to ignore the role of beliefs and ideas in mobilizing protesters. Snow and Benford (1988) addressed this issue by adopting and expanding Erving Goffman's concept of "framing." Goffman (1974: 21) referred to framing as a schema of interpretation "to locate, perceive, identify, and label" encounters with others. In the same vein, Snow and Benford defi e a collective action frame as an interpretative schema "that simplifies and condenses the 'world out there' by selectively punctuating and en-coding objects, situations, events, experiences, and sequences of actions within one's present or past environment" (1992: 137). Frames organize and provide guidance for individuals and collective action. Within this perspective movements are signifying actors: through their framing activities they give meaning and interpretation to different situations, and this, in turn, may mobilize potential followers. As Moore explains in his classic study of injustice, "Any movement against oppression has to develop a new diagnosis and remedy for existing forms of suffering, a diagnosis and remedy by which this suffering stands morally condemned" (1978: 88). Snow and Benford (1988) identify three aspects of movements' framing activities that affect consensus formation and action mobilization. The fi st is *diagnostic framing*: movements have to identify the problem of concern and attribute it to a cause, whether technological, political, economic, or moral. The second is *prognostic framing*: movements must not only identify a problem and fi d somebody responsible for it but also propose solutions, strategies, tactics, and specific targets. The third is *motivational framing*: movements need to provide a "vocabulary of motives" for participation, a moral justification for people to engage in collective action. The most common motivational framing relates to the fact that "if we do not do it nobody will."

Furthermore, "collective action frames serve as accenting devices that either underscore and embellish the seriousness and injustice of a social situation or redefi e as unjust and immoral what was previously seen as unfortunate but perhaps tolerable" (Snow and Benford 1992: 137). Movement framing varies according to target. Its mobilizing potential depends on the "resonance" of the frame. Building upon Rudé's assertion (1980) that the mobilizing potential of beliefs and ideas depends upon their interconnection with popular culture, Snow and Benford contend that the closer the frame is to the everyday life of the people called upon, the greater the chance of high resonance. If a frame has empirical validity (its diagnosis, prognosis, and motives seem plausible), experiential commensurability (it reflects a common problem and people agree on strategies), and narrative fidelity (the frame resonates with existing cultural traditions), then frame resonance will be high.

Frame Resonance, Democratic Beliefs, and Contentious Politics

As Tarrow (1994: 122) has stressed, along the same lines as Snow and Benford (1992), protest movements "are deeply involved in the work of 'naming' grievances, connecting them to other grievances, and constructing larger frames of meaning that resonate with a population's cultural predispositions and communicate a uniform message to power holders and others." One of the most relevant factors affecting the resonance of a frame is its narrative fidelity—that is, the frame's success in resonating with existing cultural traditions. As most students of cognitive frames of meaning have noticed, leaders and organizers do not construct, all on their own, the symbols to mobilize people. Rather, popular political culture and traditions of participation are the foundations that provide leaders with a reservoir of symbols to construct these frames. When frames of meaning incorporate widely held political beliefs, the odds of high resonance are increased. For example, the experience of the civil rights movement in the United States shows that the use of a language of "rights" derived its strategic importance from its embeddedness in American political culture (Tarrow 1994). Of course, popular political culture is far from being a system of homogeneous meanings. As a consequence, knowledge of popular political culture is crucial for leaders and movement core activists. Likewise, to evaluate the resonance of a frame of meaning we need to explore popular political culture and its main cleavages. In the case of protest movements, people's understandings of participation and democratic institutions are of particular interest. If in the realm of popular political culture people value participation, then a frame of meaning based upon the positive aspects of participation will have, *ceteris paribus,* high resonance. But if broadly shared beliefs in popular political culture value clientelism, quiescence, or delegative democratic practices—the delegation of authority to a powerful leader and the exclusion of citizens and other democratic institutions from the political process (O'Donnell 1994)—then a pro-participation frame of meaning will lack resonance in the target population. If most in the target population believe that the process of political representation ends at election time, as happens under delegative democracy, any attempts at mobilizing them for other goals will fi d little resonance. But if a target population believes that political representation also encompasses active citizen participation in public affairs *between* elections, a frame of meaning that stresses these aspects will have better odds of achieving high resonance. Likewise, the existence of a divided popular political culture with differing traditions of participation within the target population will pose a significant challenge to the framing activities of movements' organizers.

In sum, mounting contentious collective action requires a high-resonance frame of meaning rooted in popular political understandings of politics. The target population's adherence to a delegative or a participatory model of democracy, democratic institutions' legitimacy or lack of legitimacy as interlocutors in popular struggles, and the presence or absence of a tradition of rights embedded in popular culture are all potential cleavages that may affect the chances of constructing a high-resonance frame for one's movement. Thus the construction of a frame is a dynamic and strategic process that requires close knowledge of popular culture and traditions of participation. Needless to say, while movement organizers aim at constructing a high-resonance frame of meaning to mobilize potential followers, they also try to reconfi ure popular political culture by their discursive practices and collective action.

THE STUDY OF POPULAR CONTENTION AND SOCIAL MOVEMENTS IN LATIN AMERICA

Until the 1970s, studies of popular contention in Latin America focused primarily on labor and peasant movements and their role in regime change. In the 1940s and 1950s, populist regimes supported by workers (sometimes also peasants) emerged throughout the region.[6] This generated a wide range of interpretations of the character and effects of popular contentiousness. Early studies addressing these issues focused on structural and psychosociological factors to explain the mobilization of the lower classes and their support of populist regimes: the dislocations generated by rapid industrialization, urbanization, and massive migration to the cities had created an "available mass" of marginal, unorganized, deprived, and anomic people who became the natural clientele of charismatic leaders (Lipset 1960; Germani 1962, 1969). Influenced both by the literature on authoritarian movements of the interwar period in Europe and by theories of marginality, these studies characterized these masses as irrational and inherently antidemocratic.[7] Some scholars criticized this perspective and empirically refuted the

claim that the poor were apathetic and unorganized (Murmis and Portantiero 1971; Perlman 1976), while others stressed the crucial role
played by popular movements and populist regimes in the recognition
and expansion of social and political rights (Laclau 1979; Weffort 1980;
James 1988).

The demise of populist regimes and the inauguration in the region
of a period of bureaucratic-authoritarianism (O'Donnell 1972; Collier
1979) reinforced the emphasis on the study of labor and peasant movements and their role in the process of regime change. Not until the
1970s and under the influence of NSMT did the study of popular contention move away from an almost exclusive focus on labor and peasant
movements and begin to incorporate other forms of popular collective
action, such as movements of the urban poor, of shantytown dwellers,
and of various neighborhoods. As Lehmann (1990: 149) argued, these
new forms of political mobilization emerged not only in response to
repression but also as reactions to changes in the economic structure
and the role of the state. In the 1980s, the proliferation of nontraditional
movements (environmental, neighborhood, human rights, women's,
and youth movements) that accompanied the transition to democracy
in the region further expanded the scope and relevance of the field of
popular contention. NSMT, and particularly the new identity formation
perspective developed by Melucci, became the most influential framework of analysis among Latin American scholars.[8] Within this perspective, scholars stressed the newness of the emergent movements and
their potential for advancing democratization and social and political
change. The process by which new collective identities were formed
would challenge traditional politics and create a more egalitarian and
participatory social order. By the 1990s, the assessment of the democratizing impact of these movements had become more skeptical (Mainwaring 1987; Cardoso 1989; Lehmann 1990; Pásara et al. 1991). After
the initial wave of popular mobilization, it became apparent that because of differences not only in their material needs but also in their
political orientations, the urban poor typically had quite heterogeneous demands and collective strategies. Furthermore, the practices
of these movements were not always as democratic and transparent as
originally presumed, and in many cases clientelism replaced autonomous action. These factors contributed to making popular collective

action uncertain and ephemeral—a characteristic that has been repeatedly noted in studies of the United States and other mature democracies
(Piven and Cloward 1979; Katznelson 1981).

More recent studies have adopted a less romanticized view of the
dynamics and impact of popular contention as well as a more diversi-
fied theoretical and methodological approach (Haber 1996; Roberts
1997). By focusing on culturalist, political, or socioeconomic factors,
these studies draw attention to different dimensions of popular contention. Among the most influential recent works, Stokes (1995) asserts
the relevance of popular political culture to explain the emergence of
shantytown mobilization in contemporary Peru. Borrowing Gramsci's
concept of hegemony, Stokes argues that ideological subordination is a
major impediment for mounting contentious collective action in Latin
America. In her analysis of Argentina's human rights movement, Brysk
(1994) challenges what she calls "economistic" structural models of social movements and stresses the normative symbolic uses of protest.
Schneider (1995) focuses on the role of parties, in particular the key
role played by left- ing parties, to explain the dynamics of collective
action among Santiago de Chile shantytown dwellers. In response to
Schneider, Oxhorn (1995) suggests that parties are responsible for the
failure of Chile's *pobladores* to establish horizontal links with other
organizations and thus for the ephemerality of their mobilization.

This brief account suggests that diversity in emphasis has enriched
the study of contentious politics in Latin America. However, with the
exception of Escobar and Alvarez's (1992) edited volume, there have
been very few attempts to provide a synthetic approach to the study of
popular contention; and geography has seldom been considered as a
constitutive factor for explaining the dynamics and outcomes of urban
popular contention.[9] A fundamental reason for this lacuna is the fact
that since the mid-1990s most scholars of social movements in the region have turned their attention from urban grassroots movements
toward indigenous, gender, environmental, and transnational movements. In a way, the "urban," when explored, has been subsumed into
these other social categories. This is somewhat surprising in a worldwide and regional context of increasing and sustained urbanization: in
the 1960s 50 percent of the Latin American and the Caribbean population lived in cities; today 75 percent do (UN-Habitat 2006). Thus a syn-

thetic approach to popular contention that considers geography as a constitutive aspect is especially relevant.

POLITICS IN SPACE: TOWARD A POLITICAL GEOGRAPHY OF POPULAR CONTENTION

For quite some time geographers and social scientists have disagreed upon the relevance of geography (or context) to explain political outcomes. While geographers have insisted that "we can never satisfactorily explain what drives individual choices and action unless we situate the individuals in the social-geographical contexts of their lives" (Agnew 1996: 165), some social scientists have taken the extreme position that context should not count at all in the study of politics (King 1996). In spite of these contrasting views, in recent years the relevance of geography to explain political outcomes has come strongly to the fore among social scientists. Examples of the "spatial turn" in the social sciences are studies on the spatial unevenness of democratization (O'Donnell 1993), of economic reform in Latin America (Snyder 1999, 2001; Gibson, Calvo, and Falleti 1999), and of ethnic confl ct in the new republics of the former Soviet Union (Duffy Toft 2003). This spatial turn, however, has been largely absent from the field of contentious politics, as this chapter's review of the main theoretical approaches has shown. In his study of antinuclear activism in Boston, the political geographer Byron Miller (2000) reminds us that most processes of social mobilization involve interactions concerning space. Geography "not only defi es the constitution of social movement processes, it is also an 'object' of struggle" (xii). Yet "struggles over, and uses of, space, place, and scale are overlooked in most treatments of social movements" (xii). In the same vein, Sewell Jr. (2001: 51–52) asserts that "with rare exceptions, the literature has treated space as an assumed and unproblematized background, not as a constituent aspect of contentious politics that must be conceptualized explicitly and probed systematically."

The absence of geography in the study of contentious politics is surprising,[10] since a careful analysis of most contentious events shows that at least in the urban setting most successful strategies of mobilization rely on some kind of territorial networking. Physical proximity of participants plays a very important role in mobilization, as does symbolic proximity or the perception of belonging to the same "place."[11]

Geography always makes reference to a territory, rural or urban.[12] Any territory has a dual reality (Duffy Toft 2003). On one hand, it is a physical object that can be conquered, used, and divided. On the other hand, it has symbolic value for those who inhabit it and as such may become indivisible and a source of cleavages and intractable confl ct. This distinction between territory as a physical object and territory as a symbolic object is merely analytical, since these aspects are mutually embedded and usually reinforce each other. Settlement patterns, or the process by which people gain access to their homeland, turn a physical space into a symbolic place.

How can we make sense of the effects of geography or territory on contentious collective action? The distinctive role of spatial analysis is to differentiate between the compositional and contextual effects of a given outcome (O'Loughlin 2002). Compositional factors are sociostructural variables such as class, age, educational status, and income level, as well as some individual preferences such as religion, party identification, and union membership. Contextual factors refer to some kind of conventionally defi ed space such as neighborhood, school, area, or region. Territorial or place-based effects are those that cannot be canceled out by any compositional effects.

*   *   *

The argument in this book is that better integration between rationalist, structural, and culturalist perspectives is possible and desirable. Following recent trends in the study of contentious politics, I argue that opportunities, organization, and discourse are all important factors to explain the life cycle of social movements and collective action events.[13] In so doing, I employ three levels of analysis. The fi st level is that of political institutions. It involves exploring how changes in political opportunities (the political opportunity structure) help constrain or trigger waves of popular grassroots organization and collective action. I focus on three aspects at this level: (1) degree of openness or closure of state institutions, political parties, and elected bodies, with special attention to clientelistic practices at the local level; (2) instability of political party alignments; and (3) the availability of coalitions with various support groups. The second level is that of urban popular organizations. The aim is to learn about the issues, demands, and circumstances around which cleavages emerge and how these affect the dynamics of the organizations. At this level, I analyze three aspects emphasized by the resource mobilization approach: style of leadership, institutional dynamics, and internal solidarity (Zald and McCarthy 1987). The third level is that of discursive practices and individual perceptions and evaluations. The survey of neighborhood residents and the in-depth interviews that I designed explore the following dimensions: (1) whether various salient cleavages exist among the urban poor; (2) to what extent these cleavages are due to structural variables (such as history of migration, settlement patterns, socioeconomic status, type of employment, level of education, and gender) or political experience (such as participation in grassroots organizations, political parties, and unions); and (3) how these cleavages may affect the formation of frames of meaning.

In particular, my approach stresses the relevance of geography in its dual reality (material and symbolic) to better understand the dynamic interrelationship of the above-mentioned factors (opportunities, organization, and discourses). As I will show in the coming chapters, place-based effects at the various levels of analysis are crucial for explaining the nature and limits of popular collective action. By including geography and territory as independent factors in the analysis that follows, I map out the process by which the emergence of spatial agency (i.e., the reshaping of urban space by reclaiming it) may succeed or fail.

PART II

———

The Landscape of Contention

CHAPTER 2

Buenos Aires

A Contentious City

POPULAR CONTENTION IN THE CAPITAL

For all its cultural and artistic Parisian élan, Buenos Aires is a contentious city. The events that led to the fall of President De la Rúa and the collapse of the center-left coalition Alianza in December of 2001 showed dramatically the lethal effects of popular contention in the political, cultural, and fi ancial capital of Argentina. Indeed, though intense social protest occurred in many provinces throughout most of the 1990s, it was the contentiousness unleashed in Buenos Aires in December of 2001 that put an end to neoliberal economic restructuring and the political corruption that had made it possible.[1] Yet Buenos Aires City as a place of popular contention has been rather neglected in most recent studies of social protest movements, which have tended to focus on the city's periphery or on the provinces (Farinetti 1998; Auyero 2000, 2001; Delamata 2002).[2]

This is at odds with the social and political history of Buenos Aires City and its potential for effective mobilization. Well before becoming the capital of the republic in 1880, this city emerged as the main place of popular contention and participation in Argentina. In the two decades that preceded the federalization of the city, Buenos Aires' inhabitants—*porteños*—acted collectively, joined civic organizations, and used the print media to voice their discontent about the country, the city, and their own living conditions.[3] In so doing, they not only struggled to build up the city but also took the crucial fi st steps on the long road to citizenship. The social historian Hilda Sábato (2001) has documented the existence of a public sphere of politics in the two decades that preceded the federalization of Buenos Aires, between 1860 and 1880. Since then, this public sphere, comprising many associations and strategies of participation, has been a constant feature of Buenos Aires and has given the city its contentious profile. The account that follows of the main forms of popular participation (or the repertoire of contention) in Buenos Aires in the nineteenth and twentieth centuries aims at describing the popular traditions that make up the background of contemporary urban collective action in this city.

REPERTOIRES OF CONTENTION

When ordinary people band together to pursue their interests, they rely on strategies or routines of collective action that have historically developed and form part of their society's public sphere. Leaders and organizers do not fully create strategies of collective action; these come from learned conventions (Kertzer 1988). In a trial-and-error process, people use strategies of collective action and with time learn which are more successful and which need to be discarded (Tarrow 1998). Different groups have different collective memories of which strategy to use at what time. The repertoire of collective action that is available to people changes over time. Years of popular struggles bring about innovations in the way people bond and act together. As already noted, main changes in the repertoire are related to changes in interests, opportunities, and organization, which in turn are mainly related to the expansion of capitalism, the concentration of poor people in cities, and the process of nation-state building and its concomitant penetration in society (Tilly 1986). These changes alter the organization of everyday life in which routines of contention have been rooted. Tilly suggests that to go beyond descriptive chronicles of confl ct as a result of these macrostructural changes one must look at how the organization of everyday life has changed and study the institutions and protoinstitutions that mediate between ordinary citizens and the state (courts, mutual aid associations, charity associations, etc.).

Below I describe the development of a modular repertoire of contention among the urban poor in Buenos Aires from the late nineteenth century to the present. According to Tarrow (1998: 3), *modular* implies "the capacity of a form of collective action to be utilized by a variety of social actors, against a variety of targets, either alone or in combination with other forms." This repertoire is a constitutive part of a vital public sphere of politics. Looking into more than a century of popular contentiousness in Buenos Aires will help us better understand the nature and conditions of collective action and its sustainability among the urban poor.[4]

The Emergence of Contentious Popular Politics (1850–80)

In the second half of the nineteenth century Buenos Aires underwent important demographic changes. Whereas in the 1850s it had scarcely one hundred thousand inhabitants, it had four hundred thousand by 1887.[5] In 1860, three out of four adult males were immigrants. Industry, composed of small and medium-sized establishments, employed less than 20 percent of the labor force. Most men were employed in commerce, transportation, and the service sector. A high proportion of jobs were unskilled and unstable wage labor. The self-employed (associated with petty commerce and the service sector) were significant in number and embodied the upward mobility that characterized Buenos Aires society at the time (Sábato 2001).

In this context, elections were not the main channel of citizen participation, just one among other forms of political participation available. Even though suffrage had been universal (but neither compulsory nor secret) for adult males since 1821 in Buenos Aires and since 1853 in the whole country, only around 2 percent of the population regularly attended the polls (Botana 1979; Sábato and Palti 1990; Sábato 1992). Despite the low percentage of voting turnout, sociohistorical analysis of electoral practices at the turn of the century in Buenos Aires reveals the predominant forms of political participation available to the lower classes. Voters included the city's unskilled workers and, between the

1860s and 1870s, an increasing number of socially marginal men. Relevant for the study of contentious politics and the formation of repertoires of contention is the analysis of electoral mobilization strategies. Sources of the time describe voters in occupational terms, not as individuals, and as part of a collective force. These workers were mobilized not only to vote but also to participate in the violent acts that were common during election days. Violence never reached the level of rebellion, but polling days were defi itely violent. Controlled violence required organization. Until the 1870s, a two-party system formed by the Partido Autonomista and the Partido Federal dominated electoral competition. These parties created a fraudulent electoral system combining the mobilization and manipulation of the popular sectors. Using their control over the state, these parties sent out foremen and overseers who acted as political bosses, recruiting and organizing low-skilled workers employed in public works.

Clientelism or vote buying in exchange for a job became a regular feature of the political system. One important aspect of vote buying during this period was that it did not operate at the individual level, as in its more contemporary form, but was instead organized on a collective-labor basis (Sábato and Palti 1990; Sábato 2001). Thus, from early on in Buenos Aires, electoral practices including manipulation, clientelism, and violence kept many people from voting and skewed election results. Further, the popular sectors at the turn of the century did not perceive voting as the most effective strategy for influencing government; they used other strategies to participate in politics and voice their demands. Political parties, elections, and patronage networks did exist, but the expansion of the press and the proliferation of grassroots organizations were crucial in the formation of a public sphere and a culture of mobilization (Sábato 1992, 2001) that contributed to the early development of a modern and modular repertoire of contention.

Most scholars of contentious politics emphasize the crucial role played by print and associations in the emergence and diffusion of popular mobilization. This was also the case in Buenos Aires. After the fall of Rosas, the press underwent a huge expansion (Halperín Donghi 1985). Between 1860 and 1870 several dozen periodicals and news-

papers were published for the fi st time. Some of them are still alive
and very influential, like the newspapers *La Nación* and, to a lesser extent, *La Prensa*. Would-be leaders of the time searching for political
influence needed the press. Some politicians even had their own newspapers. An important characteristic of the press in this period was that
it tried to address a wide audience, not just intellectuals or political
elites. Leaders of immigrant communities used the press to address
issues within each ethnic community and to raise their voice outside
them (Sábato and Cibotti 1986). The press had the capacity to shape
public opinion.

This expansion of communications fostered the spread of associations, especially mutual aid societies, among immigrant groups, some
professionals (pharmacists, physicians), and workers. Associations became a very important component of an informal network of institutions linking an emergent civil society to the national state (Baily 1967;
Falcón 1986; Munck 1998). Together with the press, they helped create
a culture of mobilization. The most common way to voice a claim or
demand was by declaration or petition. The submitting of a declaration
or petition was not individual and private but collective and public.
Such actions were initiated by leaders or any of the aforementioned
associations and were supported by the press and other associations.
Most of the time, petitioning was accompanied by a public demonstration. Claims were varied, but demonstrations were aimed at showing the strength of public opinion in endorsing a demand before public
authorities.

There are many examples of demonstrations and petitions during
this period. One of the most successful was the 1878 petition against
new taxes on tobacco.[6] Demonstrations were well organized and usually
nonviolent.[7] Participants included immigrants and various groups of
workers and merchants. Public fi ures, such as politicians and editors,
often joined the protests. Of course, not all demonstrations were successful. The petition against new taxes on tobacco was successful because of changes in the political context. In 1878, a series of political
realignments within the party system took place. Parties experienced
splits and alliances were renewed. All in all, this type of episode revealed

the existence of a well-developed network of associations and communications that helped spread demonstrations. Rather than being class-based interpellations, demonstrations invoked the people, consumers, immigrants, workers by profession, women, and children as protagonists. The leaders were neither rich nor poor; rather, they tended to be journalist-intellectuals, lower-ranking politicians, and small merchants. Even though the elite relied on popular voting for election to public office, they did not overlook other forms of participation and worked to win over popular support. Public fi ures were often honorary members of associations and rarely missed invitations to attend their events. They were looking for broad support, not just votes, since many of those who regularly participated and led these organizations could not vote. Demands for inclusion in the electoral process would come later, after 1890.

State Expansion and Violence: General Strikes and Mobilization (1880–1912)

Between 1880 and 1912, under what historians refer to as the Oligarchic Republic, European immigration increased significantly.[8] An expanding modern capitalist economy based on exports of agricultural products was centered in Buenos Aires, mainly in the port. Most immigrants came to work in activities linked to the port, construction, and public works. As a consequence of rapid demographic changes, the society in Buenos Aires was highly heterogeneous, and social relations were very fluid. Informality and job insecurity were the rule for the masses of newly arrived immigrants. In this context, as one might expect, housing conditions deteriorated. The predominant form of housing arrangement was the *conventillo* (rooming tenement): many families were crammed together in small spaces with poor sanitation and little privacy.

In this fluid society, language acquired peculiar features. *Cocoliche*, a pidgin mix of Spanish and Italian, was the main language spoken by those living in *conventillos*. While the expansion of Argentine capitalism had created a vital but very heterogeneous society, the expansion and consolidation of the national state required building consensus and legitimacy (PEHESA 1982, 1983; Gutiérrez and Romero 1995). The state's penetration of civil society to create "order and progress" was very intense. A set of institutions and laws in the areas of labor discipline, registration of births and marriages, public health and hygiene control, military service, and state education was designed for the regulation of society.

In this period, associational activities expanded further. This was largely in response to adverse material conditions both at home and at work: *conventillos* and *talleres* (workshops) were the main areas where solidarity developed. But this expansion was also a response to state penetration into the interstices of everyday life: to the ethnic societies and mutual aid societies that had emerged in previous decades, new resistance associations, popular libraries, musical and theatrical groups, clubs, and the fi st *gremios* (trade unions) were added (Romero 1995). As is still the case nowadays, these associations had manifold and overlapping goals as well as highly informal but effective organizational structures. The most important characteristics of these grassroots organizations were their spontaneous origins and the experience of direct participation and management they provided to their members (Gutiérrez and Romero 1995). Socialist and anarchist activists played crucial but differing roles in promoting and expanding these associations. The Socialist Party was more intellectual and favored inclusion in the political system. It promoted popular libraries and cultural groups and an ideology that placed a high value on a well-educated citizenry. In contrast, the anarchists were against political inclusion and the naturalization of immigrants (PEHESA 1982, 1983). Their ideology proclaimed a new world order without states. The anarchist discourse drew on the immediate material problems of the popular sectors. During this period, labor struggles were linked to political struggles. A novel form of participation emerged: the *luchas gremiales*. The *gremios* gained momentum because they dealt with day-to-day problems affecting most workers.[9] Between 1900 and 1910 a series of general strikes, led by anarchist leaders, unified for the fi st time the lower-class population in the city of Buenos Aires. In 1901 the fi st Central Union was formed by socialists and anarchists, and in the midst of a cycle of mobilization the fi st general strike took place in 1902. Socialists and anarchists split into two different organizations because of disagreements over strategy. Socialists gathered in the UGT (Unión General de Trabajadores) and proposed negotiation with the state and social and political reform via Congress. Anarchists created the FOA (Federación Obrera Argentina), which advocated direct action and refused to negotiate with the state. At the same time, a very incipient ideology started to emerge, *sindicalismo,* which was proreform and declared itself politically nonpartisan.

Violence and direct mobilization in the streets usually accompanied general strikes. Confl cts were not only over workplace issues but also over housing conditions. The general strike of tenants of 1906 was the most important event of this kind (Suriano 1984). These confrontations with the state left a mark on the political culture of the popular sectors. While the *criollo* sectors were incorporated through clientelistic networks, anarchism helped to shape a contentious culture and repertoire of collective action based on class solidarity.[10] These cultural traditions born out of confrontations with the state would soon compete with a new tradition, reformist and socially integrative, born out of the process of upward social mobility and the emergence of modern political parties, especially the Radical Party (Unión Cívica Radical, UCR), which, after attempting a "revolution" in 1905 to demand free and fair elections, gradually became a mass party. Indeed, the general strikes and the violent episodes that regularly accompanied them were abandoned as a main strategy after 1910. That year, with the celebrations of the centenary (the hundred-year anniversary of the May Revolution), a general strike was called. The state responded by issuing the Social Defense Law, the last in a series of highly repressive anti-immigration laws, aimed at destroying the leadership of the anarchist movement, which was composed almost entirely of foreign nationals (Panettieri 1967; Gutiérrez 1983).[11] These state actions promoted the expansion of *sindicalismo,* to the detriment of anarchists within the labor movement (Godio, Palomino, and Wachendorfer 1988).

Organization and Negotiation (1912–30)

The Sáenz Peña Law, passed in 1912, established universal, secret, and compulsory voting for all Argentine men. Like the Social Defense and Residence laws, the Sáenz Peña Law was an elite response to a series of contentious episodes coming from different sectors of society—the general strikes, a *chacareros'* (small farmers') strike, and the Radicals' "revolution" of 1905—to regain legitimacy and restore order (Romero 1995). But the Sáenz Peña Law, born out of mobilization, promoted further mobilization and new areas of participation (Gutiérrez 1983). Mass party affiliation and increasing voter turnout throughout this period culminated in 1928 with the fi st massive election in Argentina's history. The opening of political opportunities by free and fair elections, the consolidation of mass parties, particularly the Radical Party, and the repression of anarchist leaders changed the predominant forms of contention and participation among the popular sectors. Parties and *sindicalismo,* each working separately, became the main channels of popular participation in the city. Parallel to the process of enfranchisement of the population, labor confl cts continued, but in general they had a less violent character; the goals of *sindicalismo* were more moderate and specific. *Sindicalismo* had a probargaining strategy with employers and the state. The further development of the capitalist agro-export economy and a slower pace of immigration helped to create a more structurally integrated society compared to the heterogeneity that had characterized the turn of the century. Unions became bigger and more bureaucratized. But this was not a fully peaceful period. In response to the postwar economic crisis and the opening of political opportunities by the new Radical government, a series of strikes in key sectors of the economy took place. The state ruled in favor of workers in most cases, but the events that culminated in the Semana Trágica (Tragic Week) in 1919 showed that repression was also a very important tool to preserve social order when things got out hand (Godio, Palomino, and Wachendorfer 1988). Indeed, the Semana Trágica was a regression to the old anarchist times, as unionist leaders lost control of the mobilization (Romero 1995).

Parties and unions took parallel roads. During this period, parties expanded dramatically, changing the forms of participation and contention. Neighborhood party committees aiming at recruiting members and promoting party ideology replaced and reabsorbed many of the small-scale organizations that had emerged at the turn of the century. The traditional functions of many mutual aid and cultural societies were taken over by party committees. The Socialist Party had a vertical organization and limited relations with unions, proposing social reform through Congress. It targeted skilled urban workers, and the leaders were professionals. It concentrated on educational and cultural activities (libraries, theater, technical training) to gain members even among the immigrants. The Radical Party had an open structure with many posts to fill. Relations with *gremios* were promoted but never incorporated as an institutionalized area within the party. The party's main avowed goal was free and fair elections and respect for the constitution. Radicals targeted *criollo* sectors or second-generation Argentines among the middle sectors and public employees. The local Radical Party committee was a typical machine ready to link its clientele to the state through the *puntero* (grassroots party activist). The *puntero* provided services, including access to a whole set of networks (police, employment, hospitals, etc.).

Demographic changes also affected the grassroots associations that were not absorbed by party expansion. More and more, ethnic and cultural associations were led by better-educated middle- and upper-class sectors. Their structure became more vertical and less spontaneous.

Changes in political participation were the result not only of changes in the economy and political opportunities but also of the urban development patterns that led to the emergence of new neighborhoods within the limits and in the near-periphery of Buenos Aires. The development of transportation and the availability of credit to buy land and build one's own house dispersed a heterogeneous mass of workers (Romero 1995). The resulting spatial split between residence and workplace, in addition to the reduction of the working day and the consequent availability of some free time, helped to forge a social identity centered more in the neighborhood, family, and leisure and less in the world of work. The popular sectors' identity became more "popular" and less class oriented (Gutiérrez and Romero 1995). This is illustrated by a new form of organization that began to emerge in the neighborhoods: the *sociedades de fomento* (hereafter SFs).[12] These were, and still are today, voluntary organizations aimed at improving the infrastructure of the respective neighborhoods and promoting cultural and leisure activities, including dances and festivals. At the neighborhood level, SFs were not the main locus of politics. The local party committees were, and they made extensive use of the available *puntero* and clientelistic practices. But even though these two kinds of neighborhood associations had conflcts around election time (as still happens in Buenos Aires), they had close ties. The SFs were an embryonic form of democratic participation: one could elect and be elected, voices were raised about the problems of the neighborhood, and relations with the municipal government were learned (PEHESA 1982, 1983; Gutiérrez and Romero 1995; Cavarozzi and Palermo 1995). In their early development, these organizations were ethnically and ideologically homogeneous. They also shared in the culture of mobilization: in 1920 they organized and led a large-scale rally to the Municipal Legislature to protest irregularities in the distribution of municipal housing units (García Delgado and Silva 1985).

Because of changes in associational activities brought about by changes in the legal and political system as well as in the economy and in urban development, the popular sectors turned to differing sources of solidarity under different circumstances (PEHESA 1982). For bargaining over labor conditions they trusted and supported *sindicalismo,* for open confrontation with the state they supported the anarchists, and when election day came along they voted for the Radical or Socialist Party. Finally, through the SFs they helped build up Buenos Aires as a city and in large part themselves as citizens (PEHESA 1982; Gutiérrez 1983; Gutiérrez and Romero 1995; Cavarozzi and Palermo 1995).

Neighborhood Trenches (1930–45)

In the 1930s, amid the world economic crisis, a civic-military coup ushered in more than a decade of authoritarian rule based on electoral fraud. The networks of neighborhood party committees practically disappeared, since the lack of official resources prevented them from providing services, and many of the associations of the previous periods either vanished or became bureaucratized. But new associations emerged along with the territorial expansion of Buenos Aires (García Delgado and Silva 1985). With the closing of political opportunities at the national level, these associations provided the popular sectors a space for social and political participation. SFs, sport clubs, and popular libraries flourished during this period, thanks to the efforts of many activists (PEHESA 1982). The negligible intervention of the state regarding infrastructure in popular neighborhoods gave the SFs a multiclass character: organizing around neighborhood demands, they became socially and ideologically heterogeneous (García Delgado and Silva 1985). One important issue is that the SFs continued their contacts with city officials even after the coup of 1930. It was for this reason that they became centers of city management and mediation with local authorities. Their legitimacy derived from this management capacity. SFs' ideology emphasized that society could be progressively improved. To accomplish this, they called upon solidarity among neighbors, but with the conviction that ultimately the state had the responsibility, with the SFs' support, to implement changes (García Delgado and Silva 1985). Dialogue with the state within the given legal framework was the underlying principle of these organizations. By petitioning to transform the urban space into public goods (parks, paved streets, lights, etc.), SFs helped to turn neighbors into citizens (Gutiérrez and Romero 1995).

Indeed, life in the neighborhoods changed the view of a society radically divided between the haves and have-nots into one in which solidarity and collaboration were possible. The concept of "social" justice began to take shape, well before Peronism came to power (Gutiérrez and Romero 1995).

Print and radio had a tremendous impact in popular culture during this period. Most SFs had a popular library and organized lectures. These had a ritualistic appeal: good clothes and clean appearance were a must, setting an example of personal improvement and "higher culture." In addition, liberals and socialists, the Catholic Church and the nationalist Right published affordable books to propagate their ideologies. Books and magazines such as *Crítica* and *Claridad* helped disseminate ideas of progress, reform, and justice (Zimmermann 1995; Gutiérrez and Romero 1995). A shared hope of a more equitable but not radically different society permeated the culture of the popular sectors. The spread of this cultural trend was possible thanks to improving economic conditions: better access to housing for most of the population (affordable houses built by the municipal government and the Socialist Party and a great fund-raising campaign by the Catholic Church in 1919), changes in labor regulation (an eight-hour workday, Sunday rest, and pension funds), and health policies initiated during the Radical governments of the previous years helped in transforming popular culture. This culture became less contentious, more distanced from work

and production issues and more concerned with issues of social reproduction such as housing and infrastructure.

Along with neighborhood associations, unions expanded their activities at the shop-floor level. Industrial diversification led to new
unions. In this context, socialists and communists saw in the Confederación General del Trabajo (CGT) a tool to advance their political
projects. Furthermore, Buenos Aires became a real metropolis: commerce spread throughout the city, grassroots organizations formed federations (García Delgado and Silva 1985), and their interlocutors became not just friendly with the municipality but also with legislators, the
mayor, and other authorities (Gutiérrez and Romero 1995).

Yet before the advent of Peronism, participation and organization
had entered a declining phase because some basic goals had been obtained and, more importantly, because local leaders had become con-
solidated and now dominated most grassroots organizations in a bureaucratic fashion. The consequent decline of grassroots associations
explains in great part the quasi-demobilization that preceded the emergence of Peronism.

In sum, for the popular sectors, citizenship was contained and defi ed not only by the right to vote but also, and more importantly, by
a network of local institutions that processed demands and provided
some accountability between residents of the city, the state, and other
interests. Early developments (still limited) with regard to social rights
in the areas of housing and health policies reinforced the view that social justice via reform was indeed possible.[13]

Struggles for Symbolic Space: The Expansion
of Democracy (1943–55)

Toward the end of the World War II, the popular sectors in Buenos
Aires again became highly mobilized. The city was once more a contentious space for confl cting political and cultural hegemonic projects. A
complex set of economic, political, and cultural factors contributed to
the mobilization of the popular sectors. With the expansion of light
industry, massive migrations from the countryside, and the consolidation of Buenos Aires' near-periphery came the revitalization of popular

participation in unions and (to a lesser degree) in local party committees. But above all, a series of laws creating social rights, enacted by Juan
Domingo Perón during his tenure as secretary of labor during the government of General Farrell (1944–45), further mobilized the poor and
legitimized Perón as the natural leader of the working classes. The
massive street demonstration of October 17, 1945, in support of Perón
(who had been imprisoned) was afterwards commemorated annually as
a ritualistic and enduring form of participation among the popular sectors. A new style of mobilization in the city, the *movilización callejera*
(massive street demonstration), and the sense of each participant's personal direct relation with a charismatic leader, appeared as new elements in the culture of the popular sectors (Romero 1995; Plotkin 2003)
and has been inscribed ever since in the repertoire of popular contention. While street mobilizations had a spontaneous component, their
effectiveness derived ultimately from union leadership coordination
and a low threat of police repression. As the fi st democratically elected
president since the demise of Radical president Yrigoyen in 1930, Perón
promoted a vertical and direct relationship with the masses for which a
set of ritualistic procedures was implemented, the most important one
being, as already noted, the reenactment, every year, of the massive mobilization of October 17, 1945, in the Plaza de Mayo (May Square) just
across from Casa Rosada (Pink House, the Presidential House).

The state expanded significantly for the organization of Peronista
support. State-promoted participation included the unionization not
only of workers but also of the lower middle classes, public and private
sector employees. The preexisting Labor Party was dissolved and the
Peronist Party was created for the 1946 election; this was a vertical
machine structured to channel the leader's message. A network of *unidades básicas* (Peronist Party local headquarters, hereafter UBs) spread
throughout the neighborhoods and competed for membership with
the Radical and Socialist parties (Romero 1995). The UBs provided the
same kinds of services as other party committees: they became decentralized agencies through which needy citizens received goods in kind,
such as sewing machines, bicycles, jobs, and Christmas cakes. The UBs
also were centers for the dissemination of the Peronist ideology, but
unlike earlier grassroots organizations they did not encourage debate;

rather, they promoted top-down communication to those who were not part of union organizations. All in all, UBs were not arenas of real participation but an institutionalized top-down channel between state and society. Along with unions and UBs, the media played a very important role in diffusing Peronist ideology and organizing pro-Peronista support.

Peronism enacted a broad agenda of social and political rights. But all the more progressive leaders of the CGT were displaced, including most of the leaders who had organized the mobilization of October 17, 1945. The CGT was brought under Perón's control and lost a great deal of its independence. But while this was true at the top level of union organizations, at the shop-floor level there was a great expansion of union activism that questioned the authority of capitalists. The government allowed a series of strikes in 1946 but afterwards abolished the right to strike. The expansion of participation at the workplace and the use of mobilization as an expression of contention have to be understood in the context of a populist regime in which depoliticization and plebiscitarianism were the rule (PEHESA 1982; Romero 1995). As noted, voting was an important part of the repertoire of participation available to people but was not the only one. Although street mobilizations were often organized at the national level, the symbolic foci were the workers of Greater Buenos Aires and the downtown Plaza de Mayo, where Perón addressed the masses. The mobilizations soon lost their spontaneous features and organization, and manipulation by the government became predominant (Gutiérrez and Romero 1995; Romero 1995). A system of negative sanctions was informally enforced against those who did not participate in the events or were not members of the Peronist Party. The party's membership card was useful for gaining access to resources. In many places no affiliation to the union or to the party meant no job. Furthermore, it is well documented that unions and state agencies together organized mass demonstrations, providing transportation and other incentives. Mobilization dates were known well in advance and were attached to various kinds of celebrations. For the popular sectors, a day in the Plaza was a political as well as a recreational activity. For the government, it was a form of plebiscitarian legitimation against the pluralist discourses of the opposition (Romero

1995). Street demonstrations helped constitute (and reinforce) the identity of the participants; they were a privileged space where, through a series of discursive interpellations, the opposition between "the people as the disadvantaged" and "the oligarchy and foreign interests" was invented (Laclau 1979, 2005). In this context, spontaneous organizations tended to be co-opted or dissolved.

Many public libraries, theatrical groups, and socialist centers disappeared during this period. In particular, the SFs that survived became another channel of controlled participation. The state created the *juntas comunales* (community councils) to deal at the local level with municipal issues. The consequent overlap with SFs and UBs created tensions (García Delgado and Silva 1985). Nonetheless, the idea of upward mobility and social integration was reinforced, as well as a belief in the state's central role in the achievement of social justice. Peronism reinforced a nonclass culture more akin to middle-class than to workers' values. Participation was to be channeled within certain predefi ed parameters and direct action discarded.

But even though participation was controlled, the emergence of Peronism entailed the democratization by contention of public space in the city. Above all, mobilizations during Peronism meant an assault by the popular classes on the patrician city, a struggle for the democratization of space in Buenos Aires. The horror of the middle and upper classes who witnessed the poor "invading" the city center has been widely documented. Podalsky (2004) recounts the multiple anxieties that Peronism in the city, that is, Peronism as a force reclaiming urban space for the popular sectors, produced among Buenos Aires' middle and upper classes. Indeed, after the fall of Peronism, sustained efforts were made to erase the popular presence from Buenos Aires. These included several transformations of the built environment (e.g., the building of new skyscrapers) and the reallocation of city expenditures to favor the north side of the city as opposed to the popular south.

Resistance (1955–66)

In 1955, a military coup ended the Peronist regime and inaugurated a new cycle of military and weak civil governments. Peronism was banned from electoral competition, a move that in fact helped deepen the

Peronist identity of the popular sectors. Although from exile Perón indicated for whom his followers should vote, it was through unions that
the popular sectors expressed most of their demands. The CGT and all
union activity at the national level were forbidden; leaders raised their
demands at the base, in the factories. Peronism became a true workers'
movement focused on immediate demands concerning wages and employment issues. The threat of physical repression was always present.
During the fi st years after the coup, known as the years of "Peronist
resistance," union leaders led a series of violent strikes. These strikes
coincided with civil-military confl cts during the Frondizi government
(1958–61). Protesters were violently repressed while some union leaders were co-opted. Street demonstrations were banned. Graffiti, popular
music, and soccer fans' songs became channels of popular resistance.
Neighborhood associations were hit hard: the *juntas comunales* were
dissolved, and no channel of communication with the municipal government was left open. The state refused to grant legal recognition to
any SFs whose bylaws would not explicitly prohibit political activities of
any kind. The chance to be heard was left to the willingness of whoever
incidentally was in office. This was also true during the government of
Radical president Illia (1963–66), even though this government promoted what García Delgado and Silva (1985) have referred to as *vecinalismo de petición,* or grassroots participation by petition. The presenta-
tion of petitions was no guarantee that authorities would respond with
an appropriate course of action. In this period, with the support of the
Communist Party, a federation of shantytowns and precarious neighborhoods of Buenos Aires was formed, but it would not become significantly active until well into the 1970s.

Political Mobilization and Violent Contestation: (1966–76)

The military coup of 1966 inaugurated what O'Donnell (1972) has defi ed as bureaucratic-authoritarianism. The military attempted to implement a corporatist model of society. After an early period of resistance and repression, unions became quite moderate in their demands
and bargaining strategies. The governments of the so-called Revolución Argentina (1966–73) aimed at incorporating neighborhood associations into a political system with no parties. These associations

would be the main channels and support of the new state. Community councils would be formed as the only participatory spaces allowed for the popular sectors. During these years, the SFs gained political influence and a wider institutional structure: new and old leaders supported and promoted by the military regime joined in the formation of federations and confederations of SFs aimed at dealing with problems in municipalities throughout the country and in neighborhoods of Buenos Aires City (García Delgado and Silva 1985). However, the "normalization of society" (O'Donnell 1988) that the regime tried to implement ended suddenly with the Cordobazo. This social protest started in the city of Córdoba, four hundred miles away from Buenos Aires City, and unleashed a confl ct in which were condensed the many contradictions of bureaucratic-authoritarianism. It was a massive and violent event initiated by workers and joined by students. Social protest reemerged with the Cordobazo and rapidly spread to other cities, triggering the reinvigoration of shantytown dwellers' organizations, tenants' associations, religious groups, and cultural groups. By 1971, political parties and unions regained space after the military government called them to take part in a *salida pactada* (pacted transition). But guerrilla movements had already appeared on the scene, with a message of radical change and violence.

The return of democracy in 1972 and of Perón from exile in 1973 led to the burgeoning of many new and old organizations: at the factories workers joined *comisiones de base* (workplace committees), and at home they formed grassroots organizations to struggle for better environmental and living conditions. The street demonstrations of earlier periods regained center stage. Widespread violence accompanied these events. Perón's arrival at Ezeiza Airport in Buenos Aires resulted in urban warfare unleashed between groups of the Far Right and the Far Left. Violence became an accepted part of the repertoire of contention. *Montoneros,* the leading guerrilla movement, attempted to co-opt all organizations, with some success at fi st. But within the popular sectors the old traditions of social progress by reform clashed with the guerrillas' conception of politics as war (PEHESA 1982; Romero 1995). The third Peronist government (1973–76) did not promote relationships between SFs and the municipal governments, and even though in 1974 the SFs formed a confederation (COENFO), they did not receive any support or official recognition (García Delgado and Silva 1985). Furthermore, in the most comprehensive study of Argentina shantytowns so far published, Ziccardi (1983, 1984) reports that Peronism in this period had at best an ambivalent attitude toward shantytown associations, ranging from conditional support to threats of eviction.

A New City, a New Social Order (1976–83)

The military dictatorship that took power in 1976, the Proceso de Reorganización Nacional (PRN), was an attempt to radically transform politics, economy, culture, and society. Buenos Aires became a primary target of this transformation. A plebeian culture fed by popular governments and tolerated by previous military regimes had to be defi itively destroyed. The PRN not only stopped the wave of popular mobilization that the democratic opening and the guerrilla movement had generated but also sought to change the whole texture of society (O'Donnell 1988). In contrast to other military coups, the PRN's tried to eliminate all forms of contentious politics and with them their alleged causes: Peronism, the welfare state, and a plebeian popular culture permeated with the idea of social justice. "Order" and "normalization" were to be extended to all spheres of life: not only politics but also factories, schools, the workplace, the street, and even the family. The popular sectors were repressed and excluded from most spaces. The PRN designed a series of policies to expel them from the city or at least make them invisible. First, although employment rates remained at their historical average, industrial reconversion left many people with precarious jobs. Industrial reconversion also entailed relocation of industries and their workers far away from Buenos Aires. If Peronism and its plebeian culture were to be defeated, industrial workers had to be also. Unions were severely repressed. Shantytown leaders and dwellers were persecuted and their housing destroyed by brutal eradication policies (Bellardi and De Paula 1986; Oszlak 1991). Highway construction helped to further expel the popular sectors from the city and to fragment neighborhoods. No channel of participation remained intact. Unions and SFs were taken over by military *delegados,* and federations and confederations were prohibited, as well as any horizontal relationships among neighborhood associations.

After several years of harsh repression, little by little civil society began to rebuild networks and spaces of participation. Human rights organizations were the fi st to challenge the dictatorship and introduce new forms of contention. Mothers of the disappeared used the Plaza de Mayo for their silent rounds every Thursday in the center of Buenos Aires. The core of Argentina's urban public space would become the black hole of the military and upper-class hegemonic project.

Compared to human rights organizations, neighborhood associations look rather traditional and less confrontational. Indeed, the government of General Viola (1980–81, the second one since the coup of 1976) initiated contacts with SFs to form closer ties with them before the return to the restricted democracy that he envisioned. His purpose was to co-opt local leaders, creating a new political leadership that would replace party activists. These people were going to be community leaders who would link civil society to the municipal governments. After a period of systematic repression, the military mayors of the municipalities in Greater Buenos Aires approached clubs, schools, and hospital cooperatives, professional associations, commerce bureaus, and SFs in the hope of legitimizing their policies. In contrast to Onganía in 1966, Viola, by promoting local identities, sought to create, not to a fully vertically controlled system of participation, but rather an official political party for a restricted type of semidemocracy. The SFs would be the contractors of public services, while the municipalities would supervise the works. The emerging sense that articulated demands would not necessarily be met by repression gave some impulse to popular organization. We must also keep in mind that after the initial repressive phase of the PRN, cleavages among various levels of the state appeared, not only because the decentralization of services (including education and health) created confl cts between mayors and governors regarding responsibilities and resources, but also because the three branches of the armed forces had diverging views about whether and what kind of democracy, if any, should ever return. These contradictions within the regime created a less hostile political environment for some forms of popular organization. Middle-class sectoral associations (professional and commercial associations) welcomed the military initiative to remove former local activists and leaders, while popular organizations, representing workers, small merchants, community and religious groups, and SFs, were more cautious in their approval of Viola's initiatives. Other associations were born out of some specific demands: groups that built their own houses, consumer unions, housekeepers, tenants, and so forth. Independent union activities began cautiously as *ateneos* (cultural centers). These organizations substituted for the roles that parties and unions could not assume.

The Resurrection of Civil Society (1982–89)

Argentina's defeat by Great Britain in the Falklands War in 1982 dramatically accelerated the collapse of the PRN and triggered the transition to democracy. While popular mobilization did not provoke the transition, it pushed it forward by weakening any remaining legitimacy and bargaining power of the PRN.

Right after the end of the Falklands War, massive demonstrations in various municipalities in the near-periphery of Buenos Aires against rising taxes, the so-called *vecinazos,* rapidly spread. Under the leadership of SFs, a myriad of popular organizations (neighborhood committees, housekeepers' associations, elderly centers, local commerce bureaus, etc.) joined in the *vecinazos*. The protests included gatherings in the municipalities' main squares, closures of all shops and offices, and nonpayment of taxes. The *vecinazos* spread throughout the southern and western counties of the near-periphery of Buenos Aires, the poorest areas of the metropolis. When the confl ct seemed to be spiraling out of control, the governor of the province of Buenos Aires began negotiations with the federation of SFs. The so-called Lanuzaso (the mobilization in the municipality of Lanús) exemplifies how the *vecinazos* started and developed.[14] The organization of the mobilization shows a popular expertise acquired through many years of struggle. One group of neighbors called for a public meeting to be held in one of the SFs of Lanús. This SF in turn called on all the other grassroots organizations of the municipality, thus scaling up the protest. Pamphlets had a very important role in this mobilization, the municipal workers' unions providing the printing materials. Neighborhood committees were crucial: they organized streetcorner meetings to keep inhabitants informed. The result was a demonstration in front of Lanús City Hall. The young, the elderly, and women who had never participated did it this time. A feeling of antimilitarism permeated the mobilization. People started throwing stones, and the mayor was forced to give audience to some of the organizers. After this peak of mobilization, the Multipartidaria (the multiparty coalition formed to negotiate the transition with the military) promised that whichever candidate became governor of the province of Buenos Aires would resolve the rising tax problem. The *vecinazos* had multiple effects, one of which affected the traditional SFs leadership: massive mobilization and civil disobedience challenged the legitimacy of many "overly cautious" SFs leaders (García Delgado and Silva 1985).

At the same time in this period, organized land invasions became a new form of popular contention. Lack of housing and the availability of public land in the near-periphery of Buenos Aires in a context of low repression led to these invasions. The seizures were carefully planned to prevent the resulting neighborhoods from looking like shantytowns (Cravino 2001). However, after years of evictions by the military government, shantytowns in Buenos Aires increased in number and population. Popular self-organization revitalized in parallel.

No doubt, the dark years of the PRN changed the political culture and the repertoire of contention of the popular sectors in crucial ways. Years of severe repression and human rights violations delegitimated violence and guerrilla tactics as a strategy of resistance. In turn, with the rebirth of democracy in 1983 various gestures of civil disobedience (including refusal to pay taxes, hunger strikes, blockade of national highways, artistic happenings, and silent mobilizations) became the main legitimate forms of contention. The new strategies of contention and participation were intended not to defy the law but to make the rule of law effective. The military regime left as a legacy of its atrocities a revalorization of civil liberties, peace, and personal security as well as the rejection of violent action (García Delgado 1984). While unions and political parties became the main actors of Argentina's new democratic national politics, grassroots activities expanded significantly. Many wanted to participate somehow and somewhere.

Within the neighborhood associations, a new *vecinalismo* also developed during these years: from the *fomentismo* of the traditional SFs concerned only with urban infrastructure and contacts with the municipal authorities, a broader and more participatory movement emerged. Street demonstrations took a new form. They were no longer the prerogative of Peronism; the Radicals also used them to call on their followers as well as citizens. Mobilizations were no longer a festive day out at the Plaza de Mayo. Other places gained importance: the Cabildo, the Congress, the Concejo Deliberante (City Council), the courts. If violence had ever permeated the culture of the popular sectors, after the PRN it lost its appeal and its value.

*   *   *

In this brief historical account I have examined more than a century of popular contention. As I have shown, the strategies of participation and organization of the Argentine urban poor are complex and varied. Changes in state building, in political regime, and in patterns of capitalist development have interacted with the strategies people create to defend their interests and claim their rights. The modern and modular repertoire of contention among the urban poor in Argentina is primarily based upon collective mobilization and petitioning to authorities. The two decades that preceded Peronism (1925–45) were crucial for the separation, in the consciousness of the urban poor, of the realms of *work* and *home*. While many innovations in strategies of contention came out of struggles in both realms, from that period on (1925–45) demands over production and social reproduction took divergent roads. Urban demands, understood here in a broad sense as demands for better environmental and living conditions, became disentangled from work-related demands. This split was reinforced by the labor movement's historically very weak ties to grassroots urban organizations and the tendency of political parties to compete rather than to collaborate with them (García Delgado and Silva 1985).

This split between the realms of residence and work is not peculiar to Buenos Aires. As I mentioned before, in his study of New York City

Katznelson (1981) portrays a similar process: workers assumed a worker identity at work, but once at home they felt they belonged to their neighborhood or area, which often determined their principal social and eventually political identity. The historical account above also shows that grassroots urban organization in Buenos Aires is highly fragmented and lacks, except for very short periods, extensive linkages with other organizations, especially those organized at the national level, such as unions or political parties. This, as I hope to show in the following chapters, adversely affects the collective action capabilities of the urban poor to improve their living conditions and, at the same time, to democratize urban space.

CHAPTER 3

___

Buenos Aires

A Divided City

Buenos Aires is as *divided* a city as it is contentious. In many ways the landscape of Buenos Aires mirrors the successes and failures of Argentina's political, social, and economic development. As discussed in chapter 2, Buenos Aires has been the battlefield of distinctive and opposing sociopolitical projects. Its current sociospatial structuration may be seen as the crystallization of the ideological and social changes that accompanied those struggles.

Social divisions in Buenos Aires are spatially structured as a result of distinctive urban development and state housing policies. Popular contention has not produced a reasonably equal and democratic city.[1] Indeed, the appropriation of urban space by the popular sectors in Buenos Aires has been geographically bounded to the southern part of the city (south of Avenida Rivadavia). As we saw in the preceding chapter, only during brief and exceptional times did the popular sectors gain symbolic and physical access to the rich enclaves of the north. The idea of Buenos Aires as a homogeneous physical and social landscape is one of the nation's myths. Historically, there are three important eras in the sociospatial structuration of Buenos Aires. Pedro Pírez (2005) has summarized them as (1) the formation of the Great City (1880–1930); (2) popular suburbanization (1930–75); and (3) metropolitan polarization (1976 to the present).[2]

In the early years of the formation of the "Great City" (1880–1930), two distinctive geographical axes emerged in Buenos Aires: north-south and center-periphery. Both axes are still predominant. The north-south axis divides the population by socioeconomic status, with the upper classes in the north and the popular sectors in the south. The center-periphery axis separates the city's commercial-fi ancial center from the small properties in the proximal outskirts of the city owned mostly by second-generation immigrants. The development of the latter area was a function of the expansion of transportation (city railways, underground, and buses) and infrastructure, especially drinkable water (Pírez 2005).

In the last two decades, like other Latin American cities, Buenos Aires has suffered the consequences of neoliberal economic reform. As Portes and Roberts (2005) report, significant changes have occurred in urban systems and urban life during this period. Urban segregation, poverty, inequality, and precarious labor conditions have increased in most cities of the region. To this should be added rising crime and, partially as a consequence, the decline of primate cities as economic dynamic centers. While in 1970 Buenos Aires contained half of Argentina's urban population, this proportion declined to 37 percent in 2002 (Portes and Roberts 2005: 51). Graph 3.1 shows the trends in population growth for Buenos Aires since 1740; while from the late 1940s through the 1980s population growth stagnated, from the 1990s onward population has steadily declined.

DIMENSIONS OF SOCIO-SPATIAL INEQUALITY

Buenos Aires' high score on the Human Development Index (0.836 in 2004, the highest in the country) seems an exception to the socioeconomic reality of most Latin American cities (PNUD-Argentina 2006).[3] However, a more detailed analysis of official statistics reveals that living conditions in Buenos Aires have indeed deteriorated in the last three decades. Crime rates have been rising consistently in the city since the early 1990s (graph 3.2). In 1992, 102.7 crimes were committed in Buenos Aires per ten thousand inhabitants; by 1998, this fi ure had risen to 565.9 crimes per ten thousand inhabitants.

GRAPH 3.1. Population trends in Buenos Aires, 1740–2005 (number of persons).

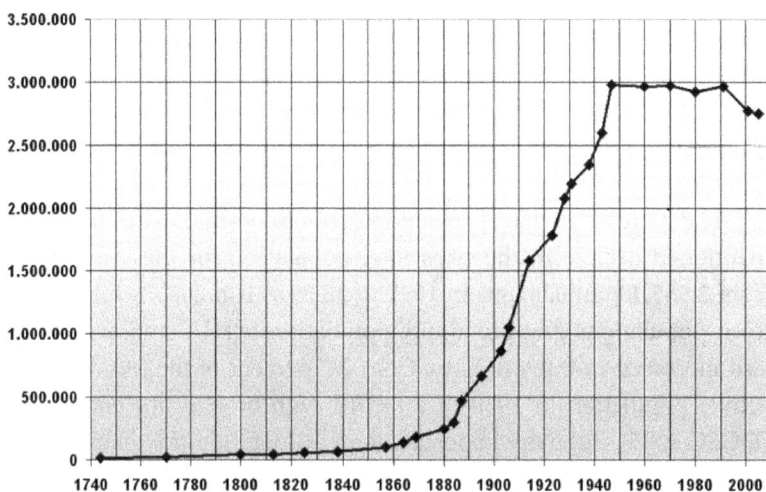

Source: DGEC (2005).

GRAPH 3.2. Crime rates, city of Buenos Aires (per ten thousand inhabitants), 1991–98.

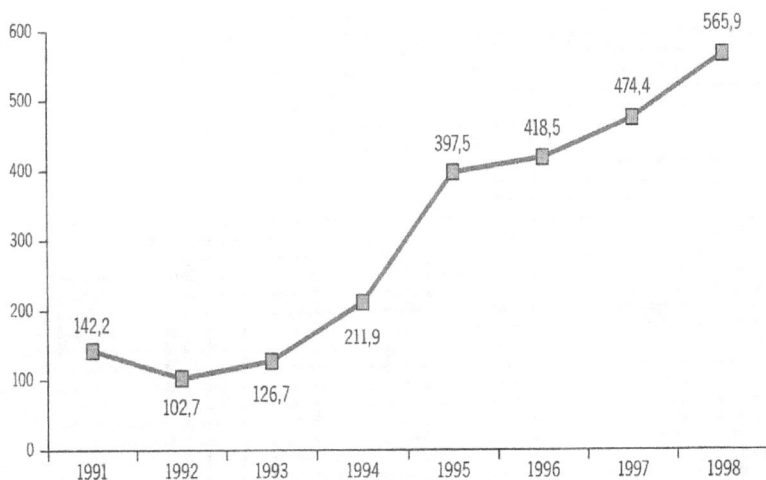

Source: CPE (2000).

While poverty measured by the UBN (Unsatisfied Basic Needs) Index has remained stable at around 7 percent of the total city population since the 1980s (INDEC 1984, 1990; DGEC 2005), housing conditions have worsened.[4] Between 1991 and 2001, the total population living in shantytowns doubled, from 50,945 to 108,056 (see graph 3.3).[5] Note also that in 1983 only 12,593 of Buenos Aires inhabitants lived in shantytowns.

The increase in shantytown populations contrasts with the already mentioned decline in the city's total population for the same period from 2,965,403 inhabitants in 1991 to 2,759,971 in 2001; while shantytown populations grew, total city population fell. Unemployment has also increased in Buenos Aires, from 2.3 percent of the (economically active) population in 1980 to a record high of 11.4 percent in 2003 (DGEC 2005). But more important than the deterioration of living conditions in the city as a whole is the fact that Buenos Aires has become more than ever a sociospatially divided city.[6] Most "precarious" housing is located in the south of the city.

Precarious housing includes all insecure forms of housing in which inhabitants are subject to forced eviction, such as family hotels, *conventillos* (collectively inhabited houses), shantytowns, and slums, as well as

GRAPH 3.3. Shantytown population growth, city of Buenos Aires, 2001.

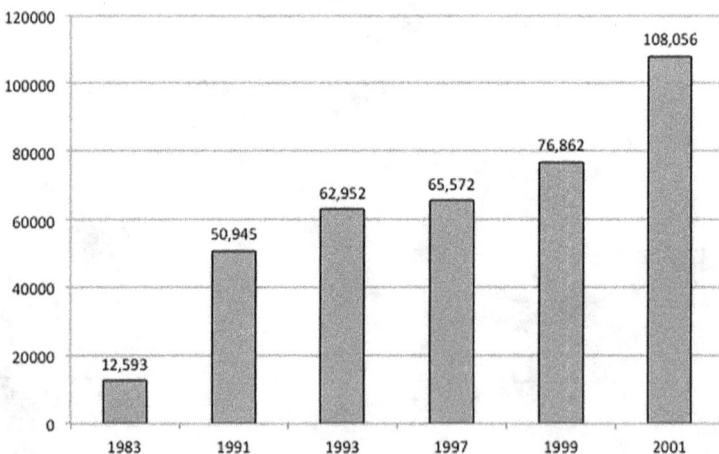

Source: Coordinación del Plan Estratégico (2001).

illegally occupied homes or *casas tomadas*. Most precarious housing and specifically most shantytowns are located in the south of the city (map 3.1), so that about 95,000 of the 108,056 total shantytown inhabitants live in the south.

Furthermore, analysis of the 1991 and 2001 census data (by *Centro de gestión y participación*, CGP) regarding unsatisfied basic needs clearly shows that the south of the city concentrates most of the urban poor (map 3.2).[7] Poverty differentials measured by the UBN Index range from 5 percent in the north to about 20 percent in the south of the city.

MAP 3.1. Buenos Aires shantytowns by neighborhood, 2003. Shantytowns in Buenos Aires are named by number.

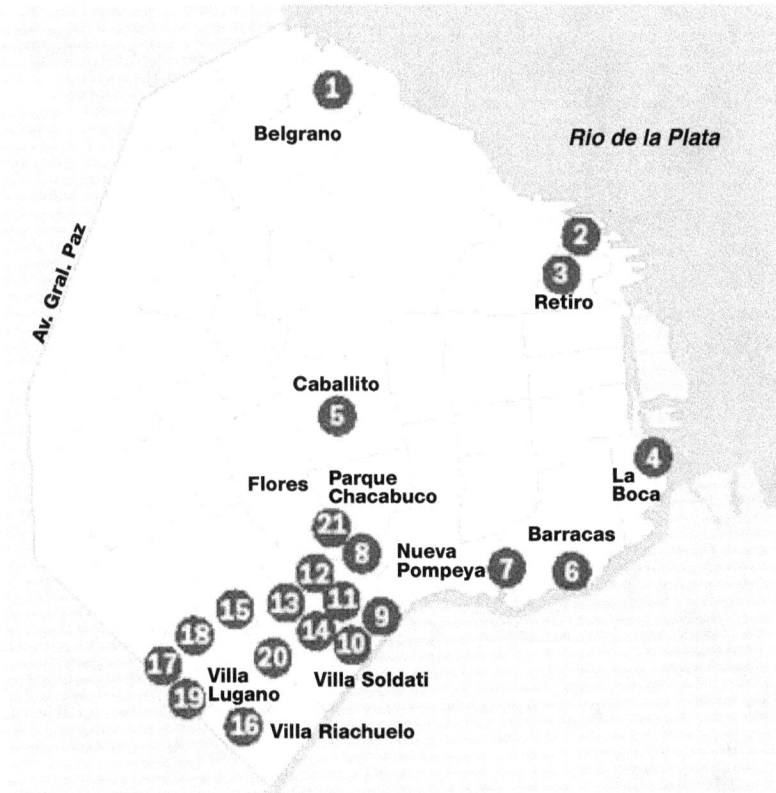

Source: Based on data from Centro de Estudios para el Desarrollo Económico Metropolitano, Ciudad de Buenos Aires (CEDEM).

MAP 3.2. Percentage of population in households with unsatisfied basic needs by numbered CGP, Buenos Aires, 2001.

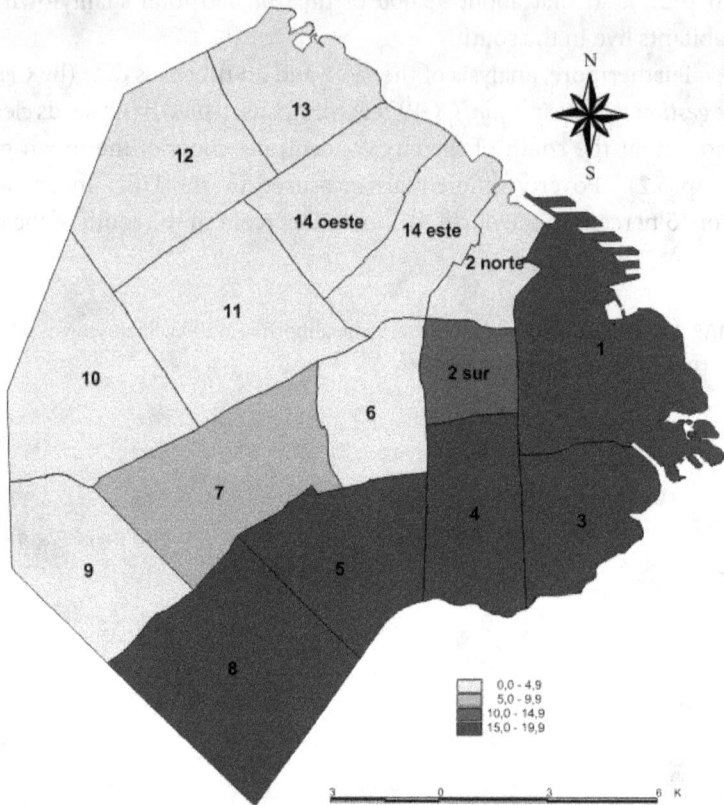

Source: DGEC (2005).

In relation to education, Buenos Aires is also a sociospatially divided city. The north concentrates the highest proportion of college graduates. In the south, the maximum average level of educational attainment is primary school or incomplete high school (DGEC 2005). Furthermore, the percentage of those aged five to seventeen years who are attending school is much lower in the south (map 3.3); in the north the rate nears 100 percent.

MAP 3.3. Percent of those aged five to seventeen attending school, by numbered CGP, Buenos Aires, 2004.

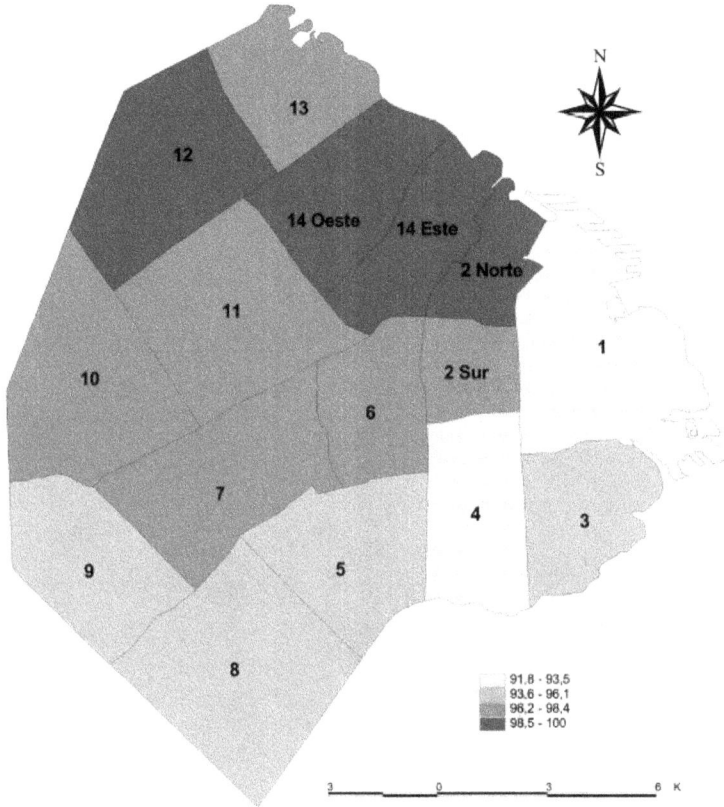

	91.8 - 93.5
	93.6 - 96.1
	96.2 - 98.4
	98.5 - 100

Source: DGEC (2005).

The unequal distribution of education in the city parallels significantly higher fertility (map 3.4) and infant mortality (map 3.5) rates in the south. While in the north the fertility rates can be as high as thirteen births per thousand inhabitants, in the south they climb to eighteen births. Likewise, infant mortality rates are much higher in the south: while in the northern sectors of the city there are up to eight deaths per thousand births, in the southern sectors there are up to seventeen deaths per thousand births.

MAP 3.4. Fertility rate (per thousand inhabitants) by numbered CGP, Buenos Aires, averaged for the years 2002–4.

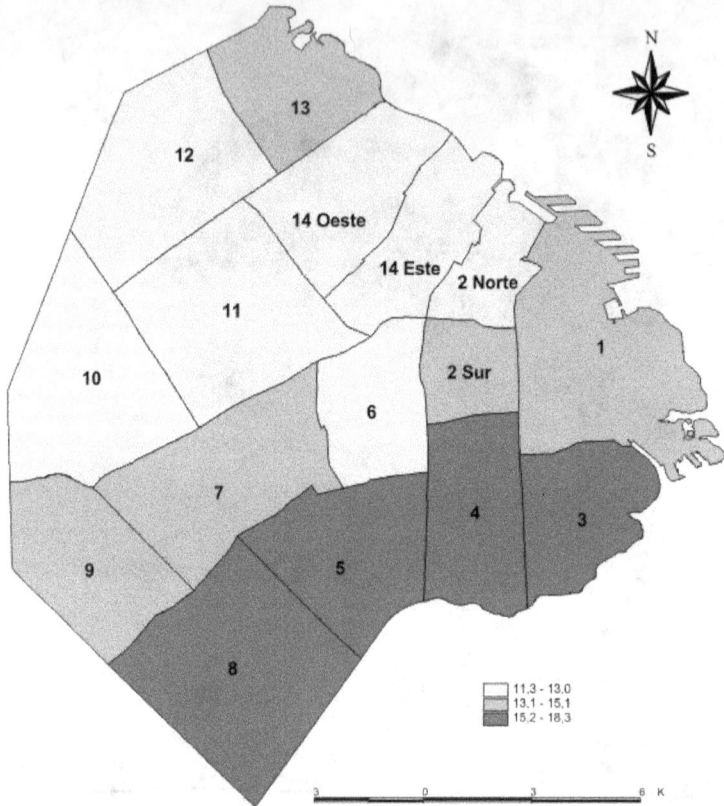

Source: DGEC (2005).

These patterns of inequality in Buenos Aires have been present since its early days and have been reinforced in the last decades in spite of the political democratization of the city.[8] They are the social landscape or context in which popular contention unfolds. As a context this landscape performs as a given: it creates opportunities for action while at the same time it sets limits to what is possible. Popular contention in Villa Lugano, as I will show, has aimed at transforming the city's unjust social landscape.

MAP 3.5. Infant mortality rate (per thousand births) by numbered CGP, Buenos Aires, averaged for the years 2002–4.

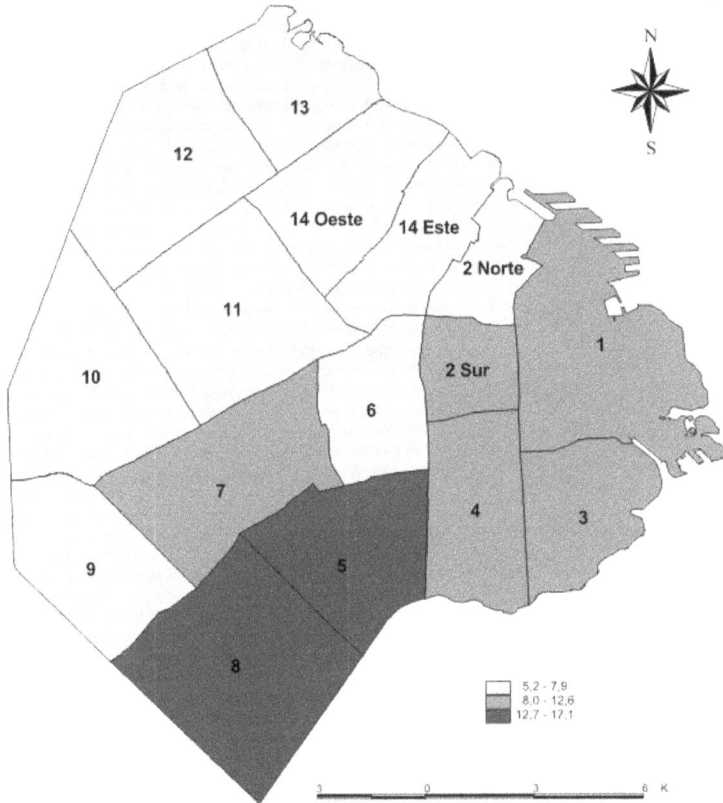

Source: DGEC (2005).

VILLA LUGANO: A FRAGMENTED NEIGHBORHOOD

On October 18, 1908, Francisco Soldati, an immigrant from Switzerland, acquired some land in the southern part of Buenos Aires and decided to inaugurate a new neighborhood, which he named Villa Lugano. A poster from that time (fi ure 3.1) reads: "Villa Lugano. Seven hundred lots in eighty monthly payments, no interest rates, with immediate title and possession, Sunday, November 7, 2:00 p.m."

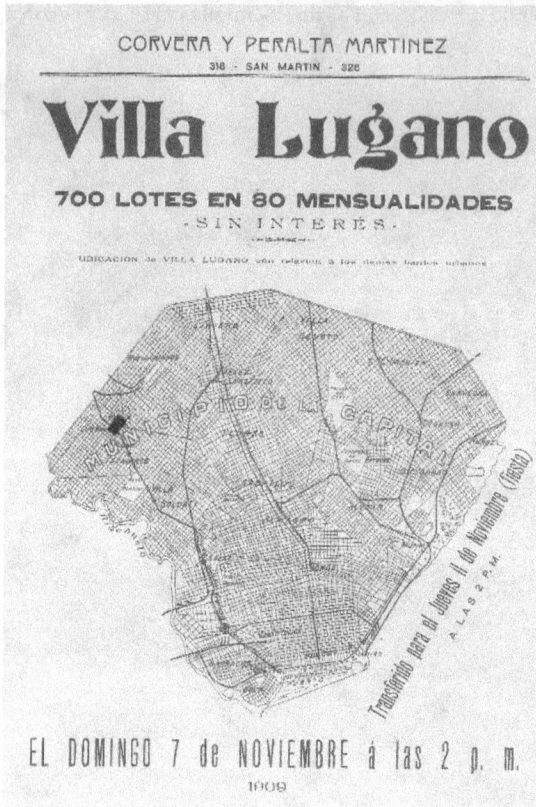

FIGURE 3.1.
Poster for Villa Lugano real estate sale, 1909. *Source:* Instituto Histórico (1979).

Little by little, immigrants with European background, especially from Italy and Spain, began to buy Soldati's lots and build their houses. Two clearly differentiated areas soon developed: the higher-elevation areas with rather expensive houses following the architectural European model of International Style or protorationalism, and the lowland areas with a very basic type of housing (wood construction, one room, with a small kitchen and a bathroom detached from the main structure).[9] At the same time, infrastructure was being put up by Soldati himself, with no intervention from the state. The subsequent history of Villa Lugano reflects the political, economic, and social changes undergone by Buenos Aires and its people during the twentieth century.

Nowadays Villa Lugano is (along with Mataderos, Villa Soldati, and Barracas) one of the neighborhoods in Buenos Aires where popular sectors mostly predominate. Map 3.6 below shows Buenos Aires' neighborhoods and their corresponding administrative units, the CGPs. Villa Lugano's CGP is #8.

Indeed, Villa Lugano can be conceived as a heterogeneous conglomerate of popular neighborhoods located in the southern and poor corridor of Buenos Aires City. I decided to focus my research on this

MAP 3.6. Neighborhoods and CGP subdivisions, Buenos Aires. Villa Lugano is part of CGP no. 8.

Source: DGEC (2005).

neighborhood because it combines exceptional economic, demographic, and political features. This is the area of Buenos Aires that has the highest proportion of urban poor. Seven percent of the 107,322 inhabitants of Villa Lugano live in conditions of extreme poverty. In 1983, 14 percent lived in shantytowns (*villas miserias*); today almost 38 percent do so (Alvarez de Celis 2003; DGEC 2005). Pockets of poverty where 46 percent of households have unmet basic needs coexist with areas of better, but still very modest, living conditions.[10] Between the 1970s and the 1990s, Villa Lugano experienced a population growth of 25 percent, with a concomitant deterioration of infrastructure and public services. This population explosion contrasts with the declining population of the city as a whole. Table 3.1 shows Villa Lugano's population characteristics in comparative perspective for the period 1990–2001. Villa Lugano's population trends for shantytown dwellers parallel those of Buenos Aires as a whole: they almost doubled from 1991 to 2001. Of the total shantytown population of the city, 88.5 percent live in the southern neighborhoods. Villa Lugano concentrates 37.5 percent of the total shantytown population of Buenos Aires. Furthermore, while northern Buenos Aires registers shantytown percentages even lower than those of developed regions of the world (less than 1 percent), in Villa Lugano shantytown percentages approximate those of developing regions such as Latin America as a whole—above 30 percent.

Electorally, Villa Lugano is one of the most important districts of Buenos Aires, with 92,703 registered voters. This was the only neighborhood in Buenos Aires in which Peronism had never been defeated until the national election of October 1999 (won by the center-left Alianza). Traditionally, the Radical Party has won the elections in Buenos Aires; but not even in the 1983 election, the fi st after the transition to democracy that elected Radical president Raúl Alfonsín, could the Radicals beat Peronism in Villa Lugano. This area was at the time of my research also the place of residence of several important Peronist union leaders. Graphs 3.4 and 3.5 show the patterns of voting for Peronism and Radicalism in Villa Lugano from the transition to democracy in 1983 until 1996. The graphs compare Villa Lugano's voting patterns to those of upper-class (Socorro and Pilar in the north), middle-class (Flores and San Carlos Norte in the center), and other lower-class (Cristo Obrero in the south) electoral districts.

TABLE 3.1. Villa Lugano's Population in Comparative Perspective, 1990–2001

	Year	Urban Population	Slum/ Shantytown Population	% Population in Slums/ Shantytowns
World				
	1990	2,285,693*	714,972*	31.3
	2001	2,923,184*	912,918*	31.2
Developed Regions				
	1990	694,260*	41,750*	6.0
	2001	753,909*	45,191*	6.0
Latin America/Caribbean				
	1990	312,995*	110,837*	35.4
	2001	399,322*	127,566*	31.9
Argentina				
	1990	28,141*	8,597*	30.5
	2001	33,119*	10,964*	33.1
Buenos Aires City				
	1991	2,965,403	50,945	1.7
	2001	2,768,772	108,056	3.9
Buenos Aires City (Northern neighborhoods)				
	1991	1,861,970	5,672	0.3
	2001	1,695,904	12,456	0.7
Buenos Aires City (Southern neighborhoods)				
	1991	1,103,433	44,823	4.1
	2001	1,072,868	95,600	9.0
Villa Lugano				
	1991	100,866	22,546	22.4
	2001	107,322	40,213	37.5

Source: Data from Alvarez de Celis (2003), PNUD-Argentina (2006), and UN-Habitat (2006).
* (thousands).

GRAPH 3.4. Votes for Peronism, 1983–96 (per electoral district).

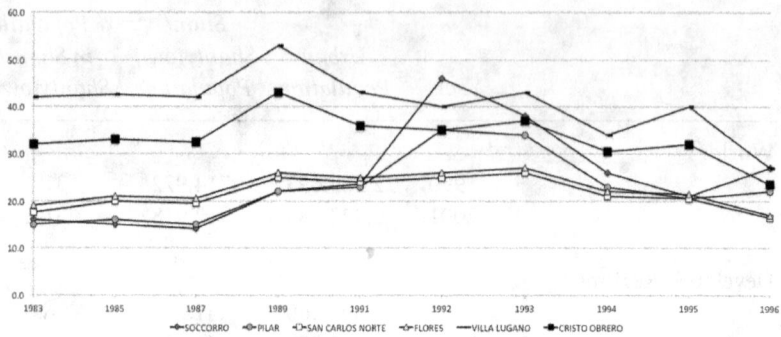

Source: Burdman (1998).

GRAPH 3.5. Votes for UCR, 1983–96 (per electoral district).

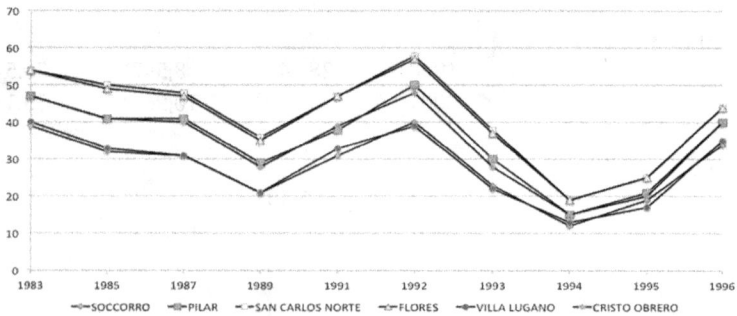

Source: Burdman (1998).

A striking feature of Villa Lugano is its spatial fragmentation. Five shantytowns, various state-built high-rise condominiums, and an old area of low-cost privately owned houses make up the neighborhood (fi ure 3.2).

Shantytown dwellers have increased in Buenos Aires by a factor of ten since 1980.[11] In Villa Lugano, they represent about one-third of the total population. Villa 20—the shantytown where I chose to conduct part of my research—is the biggest in Villa Lugano. From 1980 to 1991, its population grew 74 percent, more than any of the other four shanty-towns of the neighborhood. According to census data, 40 percent of

FIGURE 3.2. Panoramic view of Villa Lugano.

Source: Portal Barrial, VillaLugano.com.ar.

Villa 20's household heads are not regularly employed.[12] Figures 3.3 and 3.4 give a human face to Villa 20.

Villa Lugano also comprises ten state-built high-rise condominiums *(complejos habitacionales);* the condominium Barrio General Savio—the one I included in this study—typifies the main features of this type of habitat. Most of its residents are schoolteachers, low-level state employees, members of the police and noncommissioned military officers, and former shantytown dwellers benefited by public housing programs. Barrio General Savio was built to accommodate forty thousand people. The system of pedestrian circulation and the location of shops produce a distribution of space that is extremely adverse to social interaction among the dwellers (Caballero 1985). Figure 3.5 shows the daily reality of Barrio General Savio.

The Old Town neighborhood of Villa Lugano has a typical immigrant working-class character (see fi ures 3.6 and 3.7). Low-cost housing, sometimes prefabricated, usually on the land of the residents' parents, is the standard construction in this area. Skilled and semiskilled

FIGURE 3.3. Villa 20 shantytown.

Source: GoodAirs, www.goodairs.com. Photo courtesy of Ian Mount.

FIGURE 3.4. Villa 20 shantytown alleyways.

Source: GoodAirs, www.goodairs.com. Photo courtesy of Ian Mount.

FIGURE 3.5. Condominium Barrio General Savio.

Source: Portal Barrial, VillaLugano.com.ar.

workers, small business owners, and retired workers make up the social fabric of Old Town. Most of Barrio General Savio and Old Town residents belong to the so-called "new poor," the middle to lower classes that have moved downward as a result of enduring inequality and the repeated economic crises of the country.

Table 3.2 summarizes the main features of the three habitat zones of Villa Lugano, which are representative of the district's spatial fragmentation.

To the above description of Villa Lugano should be added the fragmentation caused by several highways that run through the neighborhood. The vagaries of public transportation add to the problem. As Katznelson argues (1981), the organization of social space is never random: "People, their homes and their workplaces are not just placed here and there by accident." Villa Lugano's spatial disorder discloses long-term trends of state intervention. Each housing area has had a particular relation with the state. Shantytown populations were established by illegal occupations and have been either threatened with eradication

FIGURE 3.6. Villa Lugano's Old Town train station.

Source: Portal Barrial, VillaLugano.com.ar.

FIGURE 3.7. Typical housing in Villa Lugano's Old Town.

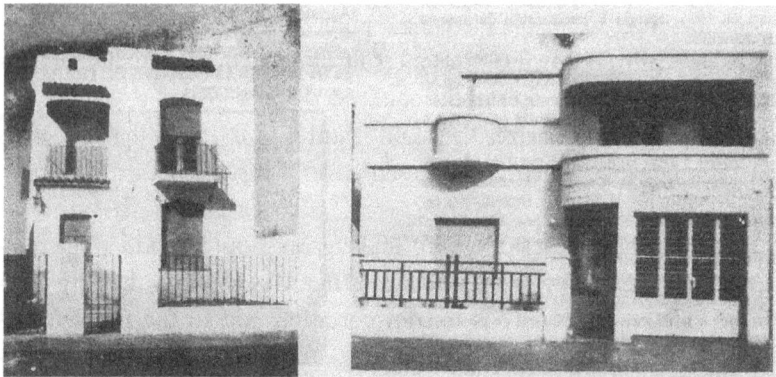

Source: Instituto Histórico (1979).

TABLE 3.2. Villa Lugano's Zones (Included in the Survey)

	Villa 20	Barrio General Savio	Old Town
Type of housing	Shantytown	State-built high-rise	Low-cost houses
Access to housing	Illegal occupation	Govt. program	Market
Population (2001)[a]	16,348	25,000	30,000
% of Villa Lugano total population	15.23	23.29	27.95

Source: Elaborated from Alvarez de Celis (2003) and DGEC (2005).

[a] Estimates. Official census data by neighborhood fraction are available only for Villa 2

or co-opted with the promise of land titles. High-rise housing has been assigned by state agencies mostly in a clientelistic way, while those who live in Old Town have purchased their houses through the market.

State social policies are systems not only for the correction of inequality but also, and equally importantly, for social structuration and the ordering of social relations. Social policies help defi e relevant boundaries of collective identities because, especially for the very poor, they constitute a crucial component of their livelihood. Thus the way social policies are organized and delivered by the state comes to delineate social identities, status communities, and solidarities (Esping-Andersen 1985). In the case of housing policy, the ordering of social relations and the delineation of solidarities are inextricably intertwined with the constitution of material and symbolic space. Housing policy in Argentina has been the weakest component of the welfare state. It has been highly fragmented and clientelistic in its organization and delivery of services and has relied more on targeting than on universalistic programs (Lo Vuolo 1995). This has hindered the emergence of solidarity among lower-class *porteños* for demanding better housing and living conditions at the neighborhood level.

In this social and political landscape the Comisión de Vecinos de Villa Lugano emerged. This is the topic of the next chapter.

* * *

Buenos Aires is a socioeconomically divided city. Moreover, its social divide is spatially structured. Since early times, the northern part of Buenos Aires has outpaced the quality of life in the south. Aggregate or average statistics do not help us much to uncover the divided nature of Buenos Aires. The city as a whole is highly developed and has the highest rate of human development of all regions in the country. Indeed, Buenos Aires' Human Development Index ranks the city among the most livable in the world. However, disaggregated data brings to the fore the heterogeneity of social conditions in the city. We should reject the idea of Buenos Aires as a homogeneous, progressive, and democratic urban space.

Within the southern, poor corridor of the city, Villa Lugano, the neighborhood where I conducted my research, exemplifies to the extreme the sociospatial structuration of inequality. In various ways, it embodies the reality of many of the southern neighborhoods of Buenos Aires as well as of those further south of the city borders in the *conurbano bonaerense* (Greater Buenos Aires). But social divisions are complex and multiple. Villa Lugano itself is a fragmented social space, in which areas of modest living conditions coexist with others lacking even the most basic infrastructure. In this diverse social landscape, resulting from long-term trends of state intervention, collective action among the urban poor takes place.

With this in mind, in the next chapter I discuss the dilemmas and opportunities that Villa Lugano's residents encountered when they tried to act collectively to improve the living conditions of their neighborhood. A complex set of factors enmeshed in the social landscape just described helps explain the successes and failures of popular contention.

PART III

Dynamics of Contention

CHAPTER 4

An Analytic Narrative
of Popular Contention

SHIFTING POLITICAL OPPORTUNITIES

The surrender of Argentine troops in the Falklands War on June 14, 1982, precipitated the collapse of the PRN, the highly repressive military dictatorship that had ruled Argentina since 1976. In the following months, while intense negotiations were under way between political leaders and the military to hold elections and restore democracy, a wave of urban popular collective action and grassroots organization emerged in several neighborhoods of Greater Buenos Aires and soon spread out to other parts of the city. Under the incentive of potentially lower levels of state repression, a myriad of grassroots organizations—*sociedades de fomento, juntas vecinales, comisiones vecinales,* and sport clubs—joined forces and mounted one of the most contentious forms of opposition the military had to face during the transition process (González Bombal 1985).

From a narrow perspective, this wave of contention can be depicted as an immediate response by long-aggrieved popular sectors in a context of increasing urban crisis deepened by the military regime's decentralization policies.[1] But from a broader perspective, it may also be seen as the response of a renewed *movimiento vecinalista* (neighborhood movement) or of urban *basismo* to the attempts carried out by the military regime to drastically transform the social and political contours of local civil society (García Delgado and Silva 1985; Cavarozzi and Palermo 1995).[2] As the transition unfolded, urban *basismo* expanded to other neighborhoods of Buenos Aires and began to include (besides lower property taxes) other demands. Even though this wave of popular contention was nonlinear and fragmentary—while in some neighborhoods it receded, in others emerged anew—*basismo* became a relevant factor during and in the aftermath of the transition.

In what follows I present an analytic narrative of the emergence in the 1980s and the eventual decline throughout the 1990s up to the present of the Comisión de Vecinos de Villa Lugano (Villa Lugano Neighborhood Committee, hereafter CVL), a network-type organization that effectively mobilized residents and grassroots associations for improving environmental and living conditions in the neighborhood. A complex set of factors explain the dynamics of the CVL. While old urban grievances were at the core of Villa Lugano residents' motivation to act collectively, changes in the political opportunity structure brought about by the transition created the initial incentives for the expansion of grassroots organization by lowering the costs of participation. Furthermore, the inauguration of democracy and, more importantly, the triumph of Radicalism in the 1983 national elections significantly expanded these initial incentives: in a context of intense local partisan competition and shifting political alignments, the new city government promoted an "open-door" policy toward popular participation. Yet as we shall see, the relationship between political democratization and the expansion of urban popular movements is complex; democratic politics created incentives for participation but also posed a series of at times insurmountable obstacles for neighborhood movements.

Whereas shifting political opportunities created the initial incentives for popular contention in Villa Lugano, factors such as organization, leadership, and discursive practices must be brought to the fore to explain its cyclical nature. These factors, as I hope the following analytic narrative reveals, are in turn intertwined with the physical and symbolic space (or landscape) of contention.

RECLAIMING URBAN SPACE: THE CVL

Hard Times

In 1982, according to the national register of roads *(catastro)*, Villa Lugano was the neighborhood with the highest proportion of dirt roads in the city of Buenos Aires: of the 440 dirt roads in the city, 117 were located in Villa Lugano. The lack of *pavimento* (paved roads) in most of the neighborhood came along with a significant number of other problems: absence of sewage, proliferation of rodents, regular flooding, muddy roads, and garbage accumulation. The lack of *pavimento* became a disorganizing experience for Villa Lugano residents. For years, neighborhood residents prayed for rain to stop so as to avoid flooding and its repercussions: piling up furniture, walking through water up to their knees when going to or returning from school and work, and enduring the unbearable humidity and rotten smell that remained for days. Meanwhile, housing prices kept falling. At the same time, the lack of *pavimento* became an organizing symbol: neighbors gathered to help one another (mostly the elderly and the disabled) when the water rose. From time to time, they also gathered to write and sign petitions to demand the paving of the roads. In a neighborhood built by Italian and Spanish immigrants, grassroots organization and petitioning to improve infrastructure were part of Villa Lugano's political and cultural traditions.[3] At least from the 1960s onward, grassroots organizations, primarily SFs, had petitioned the authorities for paving, though with little success and many times at the risk of being severely repressed.[4] The "resurrection of civil society" that accompanied the democratic transition gave renewed impulse to old and newly formed grassroots organizations, local leaders, and neighbors to join forces and demand, once more, better environmental conditions, above all the paving and drainage of all dirt roads. During 1983, throughout Villa Lugano activists and some neighbors began to gather signatures and to call for street-corner assemblies to mobilize other neighbors to petition for paving.

In spite of these early mobilization attempts, it was not until December 1983, right after President Raúl Alfonsín assumed power, that a group of committed left- ing activists (especially from the Communist

Party and the Partido Intransigente) and some Villa Lugano residents with no party affiliation decided to call for a general neighborhood assembly and launch an umbrella association, the Comisión de Vecinos de Villa Lugano, which would combine the until then dispersed individual and organizational efforts to demand paving.[5] Betty, a forty-nine-year-old former industrial worker, became one of the core activists of the CVL. She describes her participation there as follows.

> I came to CVL because of Juancito. He showed up one night and knocked at my door. He told my husband that he had joined other neighbors in organizing a committee for the paving and also to improve the neighborhood infrastructure in general. I did want the *pavimento* so badly! When my father was still alive, people collected signatures, and signatures, and more signatures. With just two drops of rain, the whole neighborhood flooded. It was like living in the colonial period. When Juancito showed up, many of my close neighbors began to attend the meetings. The idea was to get together, to unite and improve Villa Lugano. Victorio, Amalia, and Omar were already present, they were the leaders. This was under the Alfonsín government. At that time, I was no longer scared to participate precisely because of democracy. There were a lot of people participating! We went from home to home; we "walked" the neighborhood a lot. Even children helped deliver flyers and put up posters in the streets announcing the CVL meetings.

Eduardo is a fi y-four-year-old white-collar employee who also became one of the core activists of the CVL.

> I do not know how the rumors began, but some neighbors got together and started attending the CVL meetings. One neighbor gave impulse to another neighbor, and that is how it all happened. The individual needs and the neighborhood problems led us to organize. I wanted to go to the meetings above all for our common needs.

Eduardo's wife, Isabel, is a fi y-two-year-old housewife who also became a core activist of CVL. Her account of her decision to participate reveals the placed-based networking process by which the CVL came into existence.

I honestly do not remember how I got involved. But it was Betty, yes, yes, it was she who came and knocked at my door [Betty lived just across the street]. She was the fi st one to be in touch with Victorio. I did want the paving so badly, that's why I started going to the meetings. For many years we gathered signatures to demand for the paving, but I had never participated in any organization before joining the CVL.

Another core activist, Hector, a fi y-seven-year-old skilled worker and sympathizer with the Radicals, similarly describes the beginning of his participation in the CVL. Like Betty's, his was a face-to-face recruitment carried out by the same person, Juancito (an activist with close ties to the Partido Intransigente), who was in charge of working on this particular area of Villa Lugano. Placed-base strategies of mobilization became from early on a landmark feature of the CVL.

Juancito came to see me. I did not know him. He told me there was a meeting in the Belgrano sports club for the paving if I wanted to go. I was interested in the issue and I began going to the meetings. I considered what was happening in Villa Lugano an injustice. I had never participated before for the paving. Victorio, Omar, and Amalia were already there when I fi st came to the meetings. In those early times, a lot of people came to the CVL's meetings and from all areas of the neighborhood.

The short time, at the end of 1983, in which the CVL came into existence shows that well-rooted grievances are necessary but not sufficient conditions to trigger urban popular collective action: the incentives provided by changes in political opportunities (lower costs of participation) and the presence of committed activists whose "threshold for participation" is comparatively lower (Granovetter 1978) are also necessary conditions.[6]

The fragments from the in-depth interviews with core activists transcribed above reveal the crucial role played by a few participants whom most interviewees called leaders: Victorio, Omar, and Amalia. Interviews with Victorio (a forty-seven-year-old architect with ties to the Partido Intransigente at the time) and with Amalia (a forty-three-year-old small printing fi m owner with ties to the Communist Party) suggest that Omar, a sixty-five-year-old construction worker and active member of the Communist Party, was the main initiator of the CVL. I asked Omar how the CVL had started.

> We got together with some neighbors, Leonardo, Joaquín, Balbo. They did not belong to the party as I did. It is true that I had a mandate from the party to work on social issues. But what happened is that with Joaquín we went to school together, with Emilio we used to played soccer . . . Balbo, I knew him from the streetcorner, and it was the same way with many others. The *pavimento* would be an improvement for everyone, not just for me. I called as many people as possible to participate. After all, they were all Peronists here!

As clearly described by Omar in the above fragment, the CVL emerged and initially expanded as one person after another crossed the participation threshold out of motives rooted in neighborhood ties.

Good Times: The Open-Door Policy

With the motto "Movilizados por la democracia, la pavimentación y desagües de todas las calles de tierra de Villa Lugano" (Mobilized for democracy, the paving and drainage of all dirt roads in Villa Lugano), the CVL called for a fi st general neighborhood assembly on January 4, 1984. This was held at the Yupanqui Club, an old and respected institution devoted to sports in Villa Lugano. The pamphlets announcing this meeting made strong use of a language of rights.[7]

> Neighbor, are you worried by the lack of pavement, traffic lights and streetlights, and emergency health services close to home? Like anybody else, you would like to be able to enjoy these public services. One crucial way for this to happen is by petitioning authorities. Petitioning is a right that also entails an obligation: you should participate and mobilize. Come to the CVL meeting and bring your ideas!

In this fi st meeting the CVL gathered over four hundred participants. This was a significant number when compared not only to past public meetings in Villa Lugano but also to other mobilizations in

Buenos Aires involving demands for better environmental and living conditions. The CVL had assembled not only all Villa Lugano residents, but also grassroots organizations leaders, the elected neighborhood advisers *(consejeros vecinales)* who made up Villa Lugano's Neighborhood Advisory Council (Consejo Vecinal), and both council members representing Villa Lugano in the City Council (the Concejo Deliberante, or legislature of Buenos Aires): Norberto "Beto" Larrosa of the Radical Party and Osvaldo Pérez of the Peronist Party.[8]

According to participants, from this very fi st public meeting both councilmen aimed at demobilizing the CVL, fi st by arguing that they had already submitted several projects to the City Council for the paving of all dirt roads and second by arguing that direct citizen participation was not the proper way to channel demands to the municipal government. Larrosa and Pérez predicted that the CVL would not fi d an audience in the new Radical Party city administration. In spite of these attempts at deflating this fi st assembly and discouraging future activities, the CVL insisted that both councilmen arrange a meeting with the newly appointed mayor of Buenos Aires, Julio César Saguier.[9] The CVL leadership was convinced that only by dealing with top officials would they make significant progress with their demand.

Omar describes the effort to gain access to Mayor Saguier and the tensions it generated with the councilmen, especially with Larrosa:

> We went with Leonardo [another core activist] to Beto Larrosa's home. We wanted him to take up the paving issue. His wife was there, she thought we wanted something related to the party. We said, no, no! This is not at all a party issue, this is a neighborhood issue. She just wanted us to become party members! We wanted Larrosa to help us set up a meeting with Saguier. We just wanted to talk with those with the real power, with those who pull the strings in city politics.

Saguier was a close collaborator of President Alfonsín and a member of Movimiento de Renovación y Cambio, the party faction led by Alfonsín and the crucial organizing force behind his triumph in the 1983 presidential elections. Under pressure from the CVL, Larrosa finally helped set up a meeting with the mayor.

As in the process that led to its emergence, face-to-face networking allowed the CVL to gather 2,500 signatures to support a petition demanding the paving of 117 dirt roads. The CVL was originally conceived by its leadership as a neighborhood movement rather than as a neighborhood organization. For this reason, and in contrast to other organizations such as SFs, the CVL had neither legal status granted by the state nor a formal internal structure. Furthermore, it did not have building facilities as most neighborhood organizations did, so weekly meetings and other events had to be held by invitation at other neighborhood organizations' facilities, generally sports clubs. The lack of legal status aimed at avoiding some of the legal restrictions imposed by the state on SFs, the most important being the prohibition to debate political issues or to have explicit links to political parties at the risk of losing legal status and, with it, eligibility for state fi ancial aid.[10] The fact that SFs, as well as sport clubs, are entitled to monetary subsidies from the state has in many instances diminished their autonomy to pursue demands and has promoted clientelistic ties with city officials and *punteros* (local party brokers). In addition, the activities of SFs are legally restricted to a specific territory or number of streets. The CVL's lack of legal status would allow it to represent the entire neighborhood of Villa Lugano and to demand the paving of all its dirt roads. Thus conceived as a movement, the CVL required a flexible internal structure to allow the participation not only of residents but also of leaders of other grassroots organizations (SFs, sport clubs, elderly associations), of local party leaders, and, if possible, of councilmen as well as elected neighborhood advisers. This institutional informality would also make possible for the CVL a combination of conventional (petitions and contacts with officials) and unconventional (streetcorner assemblies, face-to-face encounters with councilmen, disruption of city council meetings, etc.) forms of contention. Both strategies, as we saw in chapter 2, were inscribed under different and sometimes confl cting cultural traditions: the gathering of signatures was typical of *fomentismo*, the streetcorner assemblies of urban left ctivism.

On March 30, 1984, fi een members of the CVL attended the long-awaited meeting with Saguier in City Hall and, instead of presenting a signed petition, invited him to visit the neighborhood and receive the petition in a public gathering. The mayor accepted. A series of streetcorner assemblies strategically located in the most critical areas of Villa Lugano preceded the mayor's visit on April 11, 1984. The CVL encountered some initial resistance from neighbors who did not want paving, and its concomitant increase in traffic, to break the peacefulness of Villa Lugano. Shantytowns residents' attitudes toward the paving varied: those living on the border of Old Town did not oppose the demands for paving, but few participated in the early CVL meetings. When they did so it was to make sure that paving would not significantly alter the present design of the shantytowns; they were also interested in the paving of the main roads that bordered the shantytowns so as to have access to public transportation. But shantytown dwellers that lived in the most intricate alleyways of the shantytowns feared the worst, that the design of the new streets and sewage system would mean that once again, as under military rule, they would be evicted from their precarious housing. The CVL leadership guaranteed these neighbors that their demands and needs would be taken into consideration.

During his visit Saguier received a petition signed by 2,500 neighbors. This event left an imprint in the collective memory of Villa Lugano: those whom I interviewed mentioned that never before had a mayor visited the neighborhood and that the work of the CVL had made it possible. After walking on the muddy dirt roads, Saguier promised to pave within a year half of the 117 dirt roads demanded by CVL. Omar describes Saguier's visit to the neighborhood.

> It was all muddy, even though it was not raining. On every streetcorner there were people waiting for him, every two hundred meters people just challenged him [lo apretaban]. When he reached this part of the neighborhood he said, "I don't want to see anymore." Then Victorio gave him a drawing of the flooding's patterns, and that was it.

After Saguier's visit, the CVL's activities expanded significantly. Weekly streetcorner meetings, with an average of one hundred people present, were regularly held, and efforts at incorporating more participants and other neighborhood associations intensified. Less than a year after its emergence, the CVL had successfully mobilized Villa Lugano residents and was close to achieving a thirty-year-old demand. In December 1984, under intense neighborhood mobilization organized by the CVL, the city administration accelerated the public bid for the fi st paving plans, which included eighty streets. In February 1985, the fi st twelve streets began to be paved. According to CVL participants, this was a turning point that legitimized the CVL across all neighborhood sectors as a truly umbrella organization that many people and other smaller organizations called upon to receive direct or indirect help. According to the core activist Eduardo,

> The CVL mobilized people and put on the agenda the problems and needs of the neighborhood. Of course, we were not the only factor, but the CVL made a statement, "We, the neighbors are here and we want this." We became for public officials the fly on the horse's back, biting to make them move forward.

And the CVL leader Omar stated,

> I am convinced we have created something new with the CVL: an organization of neighbors without any written rules or official minutes. We had nothing, no budget or building, the only thing that we had was Article 14 of the 1853 Constitution, which guarantees among other things the right to free speech and autonomous association.

This story seemed to have a happy ending: the CVL had achieved a long-standing demand by claiming rights of citizenship and had established horizontal linkages with several grassroots organizations; the local government had been responsive to people's demands; and confl cts with local elected representatives seemed to work out in favor of Villa Lugano. But this was just the beginning of the story.

Complex Times: Holding the Government Accountable

Before the paving on the fi st twelve streets was fi ished, the work slowed down and eventually stopped. In protest, the CVL called for a march to the City Council in downtown Buenos Aires on September 19, 1985. One of the main strategies of the CVL was to repeatedly pressure the legislative branch so as to force councilmen to hold accountable the city executive for not enforcing ordinances approved either by the legislature itself or by city government decrees. This strategy of pressuring government branches (and within branches different key sectors such as secretaries or undersecretaries or different party blocs in the City Council) was a conscious and explicit attempt to make horizontal accountability work in city politics.[11] Smulovitz and Peruzzotti (2000) have conceptualized the pressure strategies undertaken by civil society to activate horizontal accountability mechanisms as "societal accountability."

The pamphlets used to convene the march reveal several discursive threads but are still expressed within the frame of the language of rights.

> This is why we mobilize: we say no more to living with rats, garbage, and mud. We are the ones who provide the resources for the city budget. We do not want to have only obligations, although we honor them. We want and fi ht for our rights. Where are our taxes going? We want them [to go] back into Villa Lugano because it is our money, we do not want it to go to Recoleta [the upper-class neighborhood par excellence].

> Come to the march and express yourself, as a neighbor and as a taxpayer. The participation of all is the guarantee to get the paving.

> The paving has to become a reality and not just be the expression of a wish, because we the neighbors of Villa Lugano have paid for the paving for years by paying our taxes, we have the right to it.

Two days before the march, on September 17, 1985, in an attempt to stop it, Saguier called for a last-minute meeting with the CVL. Negotiations failed. The organization of the march included the repertoire of contention the CVL managed better: a series of streetcorner meetings at critical areas of Villa Lugano not only provided a way of keeping the neighborhood active but also became an information network for those who were unable to attend meetings or take trips to City Hall or to the nearby City Council.[12] Because a shuttle service with five buses departed from four of the most critical areas and because many Villa Lugano residents worked downtown, the CVL was able to gather a significant number of participants, around three hundred, including leaders of several grassroots organizations (fi ure 4.1).[13]

FIGURE 4.1. CVL gathering at City Hall, September 19, 1985.

Source: Revista ¿Qué Pasa? September 20, 1985.

At the front door of the City Council, security personnel, allegedly following Larrosa's orders, threatened protesters with guns.[14] A nasty fi ht broke out. To avoid further confrontation, councilmen from other political parties intervened. Six members of the CVL were allowed to enter the council building to negotiate a future meeting with the undersecretary of Public Works, the construction company (CELIA S.A.) in charge of the paving, and one councilman from each political party represented in the legislature (a total of six).[15] The avowed goal of the meeting was to establish a feasible schedule to implement the paving plans.

The outbreak of this confl ct during a campaign to reelect national and city legislators prompted Saguier to accept a second invitation to visit Villa Lugano. He did so twenty-four days before elections were to be held, on October 6, 1985. CVL participants were aware of this fact, but their pragmatism led them to stress that "as long as elections are held, Villa Lugano will get paving as well as other infrastructure projects." CVL's activists repeated again and again that while "public officials, elected or otherwise, come and go, any infrastructure work done in Villa Lugano remains." This was their goal: improving the environmental and infrastructure conditions of the neighborhood, no matter who would get the political credit. The second visit to the neighborhood by Saguier gathered around 1,500 persons as well as members and authorities of several SFs and sports clubs, local party activists, one councilman for each party represented in the legislature, and several neighborhood advisers. Saguier promised that by November 1986 all the streets already tendered would be paved; otherwise, he encouraged people to "fill with rubbish" the front door of City Hall. The 1985 elections proved that in spite of the allocation of significant resources to Villa Lugano and the efforts of the Radicals, political identities still mattered: Peronism won once again in the neighborhood while the Radicals lost votes in favor of center-left arties.[16]

In May 1986, CELIA S.A. sued the city government. With the implementation of the national economic stabilization plan Austral, devaluation of and changes in currency generated several distortions in the fi al value of the already contracted paving plans, as well as delays in the city government's payments to the construction companies. CELIA S.A. was determined to go ahead with suing the city government and stopped work on the paving.

The CVL played a mediating role between the city government and the companies involved in paving. All companies that had bid on the paving had links with members of the city government (both the legislature and executive). Participants as well as city officials I interviewed suggested that both councilmen of Villa Lugano had business connections with the construction companies. CELIA S.A. had close links to Pérez, who had apparently agreed with Larrosa that the government would grant the fi st paving contract to this company while the Radicals would take the political "credit" for the work. Originally, the paving of all dirt roads had been a project presented to the City Council by Peronists. For these actions, Pérez was later sanctioned by the party and denied reelection.

With the support and presence of councilmen from the Radicals, the Peronists, the Intransigentes, and the center-right Partido Federal, the CVL held a meeting with CELIA S.A. and the city government. The CVL stressed that even though they wanted the paving done, they would support the city government if CELIA S.A. did not review its position of significantly increasing the price of the paving plan and suing the city government. After a four-hour-long negotiation, CELIA S.A. partially revised its position, and an agreement among all parties was reached to complete the work. Under the auspices of the Peronist, Intransigente, and Partido Federal councilmen (but not the Radicals), an agreement was signed, including the clause that it had been "signed under the pressure of the Villa Lugano neighbors." This was another important symbolic victory for the CVL, whose activists were extremely proud that for the fi st time ever an agreement of this kind included "the neighbors" as a relevant party.

The CVL had still another mediating role to play. The agreement had to be approved by the City Council within sixty days; otherwise it would expire. Larrosa contacted the CVL and informed them that the Radicals would not pass the agreement. Before the session during which the agreement had to be approved, the CVL visited every party commission president (other than the Radicals) in the City Council and secured their support in the voting. This pressured the Radicals to approve the agreement. In September of 1986 the paving work began again.

New Times: Health for the Poor, Health for All

After endless hours of meeting in City Hall with public authorities, or-ganizing assemblies, gathering signatures, and establishing a network of grassroots organizations, the foundational goal of the CVL—the paving of all dirt roads in Villa Lugano—seemed achieved. But perhaps more important than the near achievement of this goal, the struggle for the paving had left a mobilized neighborhood with significant social capital for collective action: hand in hand with their leaders, CVL participants gained knowledge on when and how to negotiate with authorities, how to deal with local and private interests, and what repertoire of conten-tion to use on what occasions.

Eduardo summarizes best how many CVL activists felt about learn-ing to participate:

> I learned many things participating in the CVL. For example, I learned [things] about *trámites legales* [legal petitions] that I had had no clue about, like sending a *carta documento* [a certified letter] to officials. I did not know you had the right to do so. I learned how to put forward a demand, how to ask, whom to see, whom to see fi st, etc. I learned that numbers matter, it is one thing for one person to visit an official, an-other for ten people to visit an official. I can go on and on.

This know-how, along with the near realization of the foundational goal, led the most active members of the CVL to elaborate a social agenda for Villa Lugano that encompassed other critical deficiencies affecting the neighborhood. The agenda now included issues of health, housing, transportation, and general infrastructure as well as oversight over the ongoing paving projects. It was published in the September 1986 issue of the *Revista Nueva Lugano* (see fi ure 4.2).

FIGURE 4.2.   The CVL's action program, 1986.

PROGRAMA COMISION VECINOS LUGANO

PUNTO 1.— PAVIMENTO:
Continuar activamente hasta lograr el pavimento de todas las calles de tierra de Lugano. Hemos propuesto a la Secratería de Obras y Servicios Públicos de la Municipalidad la elaboración de un plan de 24 ó 30 meses hasta concluir con las calles de tierra.

PUNTO 2.- SALUD
Reapertura del Centro de Salud de Chilavert y L. de la Torre (ex Tellier) Construcción de un Hospital, los Centros de Salud existentes son insuficientes para la actual población y menos aún para la futura. La demolición del Salaberry hace imprescindible su construcción para una prestación sanitaria preventiva adecuada al progreso de la ciencia actual.

PUNTO 3.- EDUCACION:
Participar en el Congreso Pedagógico, para contribuir a una educación progresista y moderna consustanciada con la revolución científica y técnica de la época actual. Luchar por una estructura de Gobierno de la Educación con la participación de los padres. Propiciar la construcción de Centros Materno-Infantiles, Jardines Infantiles y las Escuelas necesarias para nuestro barrio.

PUNTO 4.- VIVIENDA:
Cumplimiento de la Ordenanza Municipal No. 39.753 publicada en el B.M. No. 17.223 y su anexo publicado B.M. 17.227 (22-2-84).
Dicha Ordenanza establece las pautas programáticas para la radicación y solución integral en villas y núcleos habitacionales transitorios de la Ciudad de Buenos Aires.

PUNTO 5.- TRANSPORTES:
Alargue de recorridos de diversas líneas de colectivos y horarios nocturnos.
Apoyar e impulsar la construcción del Pre-Metro, frente a presiones de las empresas privadas.

PUNTO 6.- Cruces peatonales - Semáforos - Refugios - Escaleras de acceso. Puentes peatonales: tubulares provisorios:
4 sobre la Autopista, 3 existen, 1 más sobre Basualdo.

2 restantes sobre la Avda. Gral. Paz: 1 en el cruce sobre Chilavert - 2 en el cruce sobre Corrales.
Acuerdo ya establecido con el Sub Secretario, Ingeniero Dujobne.
Semáforos: Prioridad: Avda. Cruz y Larrazabal (Escuela Primaria No. 5 "Armada Argentina" e Industrial "Ing. Del Pini"). Castañares y Piedra Buena - Castañares y Murguiondo. Refugios paradas de colectivos: establecer prioridades en los lugares de mayor concentración de pasajeros, como puede ser sobre la Avda. Cruz y en los Barrios: "Savio", "Cdte. L. Piedra Buena", "Cardenal Coppello" etc.
Escaleras de Acceso: a la Autopista Dellepiane y Piedra Buena y a la Gral. Paz y Strangford.

PUNTO 7.- Puente Vehicular y peatonal, sobre vías "Gral. Belgrano": Lugano está cortado por las vías del ferrocarril, tiene 6 cruces en 30 cuadras, 4 de ellos con barreras, el puente puede ser construido sobre la Avda. Riestra a partir de la calle Larraya, está facilitado por los terraplenes existentes desembocando en la misma avenida y la Avda. Argentina, dotaría a una amplia zona del barrio de una infraestructura que actualmente lo aisla de las comunicaciones mínimas (trasnporte, comercio, urgencias, salud, seguridad, etc.)

PUNTO 8.- CULTURA:
Construcción de Anfiteatro, centro de actividades artísticas y culturales puede ser aprovechado el talud existente en Saladillo y Strangford y la Avda. Gral. Paz.

PUNTO 9.- Sede para la Comisión de Vecinos y Subsidio.

PUNTO 10.- CONGRESO INSTITUCIONAL:
Propiciar la realización de un Congreso Institucional (de LUGANO) para la elaboración de un Programa y Plan que contemple el desarrollo edilicio, socio-cultural, urbanístico, productivo y comercial, con la participación efectiva de todas las instituciones sociales, culturales, políticas y gubernamentales.

Source: Revista Nueva Lugano, September 1986.

The CVL aimed at using a repertoire of contention similar to the one that had proven so successful for the realization of paving: a combination of mobilization and direct contacts with public officials, and a flexible and loose-knit organizational structure. Most activists were convinced that theirs was the best strategy. The incorporation into the CVL agenda of old neighborhood demands—such as the reopening of several health centers that had been closed by the military regime, and the legal settlement of shantytown populations (i.e., the granting of land titles to residents and the provision of public funds for upgrading of housing)—aimed at expanding the CVL's activities and its influence by incorporating new participants, both individuals and organizations.

By the end of 1986, the CVL entered into a period of goal renewal. It continued focusing on the ongoing paving projects as an agency of societal accountability for the enforcement of both the paving contracts already signed and the city paving codes.[17] The incorporation of the health issue as a CVL goal brought new participants: representatives from Villa 20 as well as several SFs from the state-built housing projects and Old Town. These new participants became regulars in the CVL weekly meetings. The CVL designed a proposal to cover the emergency and primary health care needs of all sectors of Villa Lugano. Out of the seven health centers in the neighborhood, two were no longer operating: the mother-child center had been closed by the military regime and was being used as an office by the Municipal Housing Commission (Comisión Municipal de la Vivienda, CMV); and Health Center #27 was being used by the National Food Plan (Plan Alimentario Nacional, PAN) created by Alfonsín's government. The CVL's goal was to demand the reopening of all health centers and the extension of their emergency wards' working hours. One of the leaders of the CVL (Victorio, an architect with close ties to the Partido Intransigente) drew a triangle linking three health centers according to their location and accessibility. Geography was at the center of this proposal. Since Health Center #3, located in Barrio General Savio, already provided twenty-four hours of emergency care, the CVL included in its proposal the addition of one twenty-four-hour emergency health care center on the north side of Villa Lugano (Health Center #1) and another on the west side (either Health Center #7 or #5); both are in Piedrabuena, a state-built apartment complex similar to Barrio General Savio but smaller.

By November 1986, while the CVL was involved in the fi al design of the health proposal, Councilman Larrosa began his reelection campaign (elections for the City Council would be held in 1987) by promising the construction of a new hospital in Villa Lugano.[18] *Pintadas* (graffiti) throughout Villa Lugano read, "Beto Larrosa cumple, Pavimento, Hospital y Premetro para Lugano" (Beto Larrosa keeps his word, paving, hospital, and Metro [tram] for Lugano).

The construction of the future hospital generated a heated debate: If it was going to be built, why spend social energy and time on the health centers? The CVL decided to support Larrosa's project of a new hospital and to join forces with him and the city's undersecretary of health (who aspired to be national congressman for Buenos Aires). But from the outset CVL participants suspected that the construction of the hospital was an electoral balloon and a way for Larrosa to compete with (and deflate) the CVL health plan. The hospital was included in the municipal budget of that year and the place chosen was bordering Barrio General Savio. In any case, the CVL decided to try for both the health centers and the hospital and to keep on working on the paving.

Participate as Much as You Want!

At the same time, the city government launched in mid-1986 a participation program that would adversely affect the internal solidarity of the CVL. The program of *concejos de gestión democrática* (councils for democratic administration, CGDs) was created by an ordinance establishing in each of the forty-six neighborhoods of Buenos Aires councils for the participation of neighborhood grassroots organizations, which would make proposals to City Hall and discuss their needs. The idea was to establish a federation of grassroots organizations in Buenos Aires. The city government supported this participation structure by creating an undersecretariat of *gestión democrática* (democratic management); Dallochio, a Radical councilman with close ties to Renovación y Cambio, took up the post.

Some members of the CVL saw in the CGD another opportunity for channeling Villa Lugano demands, while others were suspicious of the new structure because, as in the case of SFs, party activity was legally prohibited. Even though participation in the CGD became a contested issue among the CVL leadership, most core members agreed to participate. One of the CVL leaders (with close ties to the Partido Intransigente, Victorio) became president of the CGD of Lugano and pushed through this new channel the health proposal designed by the CVL.[19]

Closing Doors

Further changes in the political environment in which the CVL operated were under way. In January 1987 Saguier died after a long illness and was replaced by the city councilman and president of the City Council Facundo Suárez Lastra, one of the youngest members of the Radicals' Junta Coordinadora Nacional faction (hereafter JCN), which had gained increasing influence within the national government.[20] The advances of JCN were made in a context of deepening economic crisis, labor unrest, intense struggle within Peronism, and threats of military upheavals. Suárez Lastra was committed to completing all the paving plans, but his administration was less keen about the previous administration's "open-door" policy with regard to grassroots organizations. While Saguier had been willing to accept and even promote the mobilization and redistribution of city resources to the poorest neighborhoods in the south, Suárez Lastra aimed at demobilizing activists, decentralizing services, and lowering public spending.

Victorio, one of the main leaders of the CVL, described the negative effects of Suárez Lastra's administration on the politics of participation in the city:

> Suárez Lastra did his part to oppose participation. For example, many neighbors decided to participate in the CGD and then suddenly he decided to end the whole project with a simple ordinance. He had a strategy to demobilize people. With him clientelism grew significantly; many politicians came to Villa Lugano to offer goodies, and people reasoned, Well, I can get to the councilmen and officials by myself and get what I want individually, why bother wasting my time participating?

Location, Location, Location

Rather soon it became evident that in contrast to the paving issue, the issue of how to organize the provision of health services for the whole neighborhood attracted no consensus among CVL activists. Disagreement emerged regarding which health centers should be open for longer hours and which ones needed more equipment. The two health centers proposed in the CVL project were very close to the two biggest shantytowns of the neighborhood, Villa 5 and Villa 20. Their location immediately brought to the fore a deep-rooted confl ct between conceptions of who the neighborhood's proper *demos* was, who its citizens were, and who had rights to what social services. There was consensus among CVL participants that as taxpayers Villa Lugano residents had the right to the same infrastructure as better-off neighborhoods. But with health and, as I will later show, housing issues, a whole set of diverse interpretations of democracy, the role of the state, and the defi i-tion of the citizen emerged.

The CVL had successfully articulated a cultural frame of mobilization that included the ideas of citizens as taxpayers, democracy as a tool for improving living conditions, and the state as a target and an ally. But when issues were raised that cut across different sectors among the poor ("different" because of their habitat or type of housing) who had differing organizational traditions at the local level, partisan affiliations, and political values, then social hostility emerged, preventing the CVL from creating a frame of meaning adequate for the articulation of a continuously successful urban movement.

The health centers issue drew new members to the weekly meetings of the CVL, primarily representatives of the shantytowns, who tended to be immigrants from neighboring countries (especially Chile and Bolivia, and to a lesser extent Paraguay). Neighbors from Old Town, who had been very active during the paving struggle and had no partisan affiliations, also participated often in these meetings, as well as in meetings with officials at City Hall and the legislature. Despite disagreements, the CVL was still acting as a united whole. But backstage discontent was growing.

After many failed attempts, on February 6, 1987, the CVL obtained a meeting with the secretary of health of Buenos Aires, Veronelli. During this meeting, the new city administration's different style of doing politics became evident. The secretary was hostile to the CVL's demands. He stressed that the health problem was not economic but organizational. He also suggested that the health centers in the shanties had security problems and that municipal personnel consequently avoided working there after 4 p.m. Some members of the CVL (those with close ties to the Communist Party) pushed for the reopening of the mother-child health center. After debating for more than two hours, Veronelli agreed to reopen it (though in the end this never happened) and insisted upon upgrading Health Center #3, located in Barrio General Savio. The CVL aimed at pursuing the same strategy that had been successful with the paving and extended an invitation to the secretary to come to Villa Lugano, which he reluctantly accepted.

Even among the leadership of the CVL there was now a sharp split on which health centers to include in the petition. Those with ties to the Communist Party insisted upon the mother-child health center, which was located close to one of the shanties. This was an old demand of the Communist Party in the neighborhood. Those with ties to the Intransigentes argued that Old Town and some of the smaller housing projects also had vulnerable populations and that geographically speaking it would make more sense to reopen one of the centers closer to these areas of Villa Lugano. To make things worse, the CVL proposal had to deal with the opposition of the director of Health Center #3 in Barrio General Savio, a Radical Party member who aspired to become the director of the future Lugano Hospital and sabotaged any project for the reorganization of the health centers.

Divide et Impera

The secretary of health fi ally visited Villa Lugano. The meeting on February 23, 1987, in Barrio General Savio, gathered an impressive number of associations, including SFs, shantytown juntas, the CVL, and local politicians (including Peronist candidates to neighborhood councils). In contrast to other events organized by the CVL, this meeting lacked a concerted strategy among the associations involved. Juan Cimenz, leader of the Villa 5 shantytown, dominated most of the meeting, emphasizing the social situation of Villa 5, not of Villa Lugano as a whole. In a similar vein, residents of the Piedrabuena housing project requested twenty-four hours of emergency service just for Health Center #7 (bordering Villa 5).

Despite internal divisions, during the meeting the CVL pushed for the reopening of the mother-child health center. Secretary Veronelli decided to extend the daily opening hours of the health center of Villa 5 but did not agree to extend services in Health Center #7, which was one of the centers included in the CVL health triangle project. Furthermore, he stated that the resources for the mother-child health center would be taken from Health Center #3 in Barrio General Savio. He argued that this was necessary because of Suárez Lastra's decision to cut down municipal personnel. This provoked a strong reaction from the shantytown leaders of Villa 20, whose population used Center #3 as their primary health care provider (it was practically across the street from them).

The CVL and the nonshantytown organizations were disappointed by the outcome of the meeting. However, on the positive side, as a result of the health issue many associations of Villa Lugano became involved in the activities of the CVL, as well as individuals from all sectors of the neighborhood. The CVL continued with its regular activities of ensuring accountability with regard to the paving projects (monitoring and pressing for completion), in which members of Villa 20 and other SFs now became involved as well.

After learning that Secretary Veronelli had planned another visit to Villa Lugano to assess the critical situation of Health Centers #5 and #7, the CVL tried to develop a united front on the health care issue with the CGD and its participating organizations. But soon a cleavage emerged: some grassroots leaders with party ties (mainly Peronists) who had been involved with the activities of the CGD and had worked closely with its president (the CVL leader who belonged to the Intransigentes) had insurmountable ideological differences with Communist activists who were very active in the CVL and had also joined, though reluctantly, the CGD. These differences were expressed in disagreements about the role and profile of grassroots organizations: *basismo* versus *fomentismo,* and mobilization versus co-optation. According to the CVL leader Victorio,

> Peronist activists did not want to participate at all in the CVL, precisely because of the presence of other participants with close ties to the Communist Party. But the neighbors did not care at all about that. As long as

the demands put forward were related to the needs of Villa Lugano, people did not care about which party anyone belonged to.

It should be added that, in an election year, the Communist Party activists reemphasized their confrontational strategy and proposed the CVL to go back to convening streetcorner assemblies and to oppose the "verso radical" (the humbug of the Radicals).

Communist and Peronist activists did cooperate, at least temporarily, agreeing that the new meeting with the secretary of health would be rather confrontational and that a common strategy—of demanding that all possible health centers be reopened—would be crucial. A group of grassroots organizations as well as neighbors from all areas of Villa Lugano went to meet Veronelli at Health Center #5. But he was warned about the large number of persons attending and declined to go to the meeting. Instead, the director of Health Center #5 received the participants and proposed the formation of yet another association to help improve Health Center #5! The health issue became stalled. It had catalyzed a series of cleavages between different sectors of the neighborhood and within the leadership of the CVL. It had also negatively affected the participation of neighbors who had neither party nor SF membership and whose main concern was improving Villa Lugano.

Back to Square One

Delays in one of the paving plans suddenly brought many neighbors back to the CVL weekly meetings. Problems with the state-owned water company Obras Sanitarias de la Nación provoked flooding in one of the areas undergoing paving work. The CVL pressed for a meeting with Suárez Lastra, hoping to repeat the strategy that had been so successful with Saguier. But by the end of March 1987, after many attempts, the CVL had obtained only a meeting with the private secretary of the mayor. He requested the CVL (and members of the CGD who had also gone to the meeting) to submit a detailed report on Villa Lugano's needs, arguing that the mayor and his staff had "just arrived" at City Hall and had no knowledge of local issues. During this meeting, another cleavage reemerged: SFs versus *juntas vecinales* (such as the CVL). These were very different associations in terms of organizational culture (formal vs. informal), repertoire of contention (written petition vs. mobilization), territoriality (legally fi ed vs. loose), and relationship with the state (legally recognized and materially supported vs. no state recognition or resources). The CVL leader and Communist Party activist emphasized to the secretary of Suárez Lastra that the CVL was not a *fomentista* organization because "we do not like just to file petitions." This pushed things over the edge, and representatives from various SFs attending the meeting stopped participating in the CVL, although they kept on participating, at least formally, in the CGD.

The Suárez Lastra administration decided to reform the Secretariat of Public Works, which was in charge of the paving plans. Infrastructure would now be under a new undersecretariat of Works and Programs. When the CVL received this information, they immediately decided to meet the new officials. They were received by the new undersecretary, who was informed by the CVL about the paving projects. This fi st meeting went well: Undersecretary Kwitel committed some resources for traffic lights and accepted a monthly meeting with the CVL at City Hall to keep track of the paving projects. Kwitel, in an attitude already manifested by other officials, suggested that the CVL had to pressure the Economy Secretariat of the city government, "where all programs get stalled." Thus, despite the new municipal "closed door" policy, the CVL aimed to stay in contact with City Hall, since "If we fi ht with the officials, whom are we going to talk to?"

On April 4, 1987, the CVL called for a streetcorner meeting to discuss new delays in the paving projects. During this meeting, the CVL reintroduced the debate on Villa Lugano's agenda, and participants emphatically supported the preparation of a *carta documento* to be sent to City Hall. At this meeting, all participants recognized the CGD as a legitimate channel for Villa Lugano demands, a move that seemed to put an end to the confl cts this issue had raised within the CVL leadership. The feeling was of a new start for the CVL. National elections were very close, and CVL and CGD participants with party membership became highly involved in the electoral campaign. The two main leaders of the CVL became the candidates of their respective political parties (Communists and Intransigentes) for the Neighborhood Advisory Council.

Cancellation of meetings with several officials, Suárez Lastra's failure to respond to requests for a meeting, and a renewed threat by CELIA S.A. to stop all work because the city government's payments were supposedly overdue led the CVL to call for still another public meeting, this time with the participation of local representatives, including both local councilmen. During this meeting, Peronist councilman Pérez supported the demands of the CVL. Larrosa stressed that the problem was the executive branch and not the City Council. But more importantly, the councilman had information that CELIA S.A. had lied to the CVL and that payments were not overdue as they claimed. Accusations by the councilmen that the CVL was "playing politics" and that most of its members "belonged to the Communist Party" and were "Communist insects" led many people to leave the meeting. This meeting, along with CVL leaders' failure to notify some core members about it and the controversy over misleading information about overdue payments to CELIA S.A, deepened divisions within the CVL and between the CVL leadership and elected representatives. In addition, the meeting focused primarily on just one of the paving plans, which covered an area of Villa Lugano where Communist Party activists exerted a strong influence. The organization of this last meeting demanded much time and effort, and the focus on the paving problems of just one area of Old Town generated resentment among other participants.

Housing and the Decline of the CVL

Amid these confl cts, the former undersecretary of public works under the Saguier administration, the architect Dujovne who was then director of the Comisión Municipal de la Vivienda (Municipal Commission for Housing, CMV), contacted the CVL to discuss a pilot program for the settlement of Villa Zildañe (referred to also as Villa 6), a shantytown in Villa Lugano. Dujovne was one of the most important City Hall officials and had worked closely with the CVL regarding the paving. The new CMV director needed support from other sectors of Villa Lugano and saw the CVL as a good means to obtain this. If successful, this pilot project was to be extended to the other shantytowns of Villa Lugano. As might have been expected, the CVL's meetings began to attract the presence of several of the shantytowns' leaders and residents. Being face to face with shantytown residents and giving them equal space in the ensuing discussions was an awkward experience for some CVL participants, especially when those residents were not Argentine nationals but immigrants from neighboring countries. Furthermore, during these meetings CVL members viewed the confl cts between shantytown leaders and elected representatives very negatively.

At the same time, a big meeting was held in Villa 5 with the participation of the CVL and SFs from Barrio General Savio and Old Town. The meeting aimed at coordinating sectors of Villa Lugano to act on common interests, especially housing in light of the upcoming CMV pilot project. The president of the CGD (also a CVL leader) did not attend this meeting. CVL activists with ties to the Communist Party took the opportunity to criticize the CGD for the very limited opportunities for political participation that it offered. The CVL leaders then began to take different paths. As the 1987 national elections approached, members of the CVL who were party militants became absorbed by the electoral campaign. The CVL meetings were often canceled for lack of participation (at this point I was one of the regulars, and sometimes I was asked to stay to keep the meetings going). At the same time, with no explanation Suárez Lastra dissolved the CGD that had generated so much debate in the CVL, in Villa Lugano, and in other city neighborhoods.

The 1987 elections were a total defeat not only for the Radicals but also for the until then steadily growing Intransigentes. Like other left wing parties, the Intransigentes had assumed that grassroots work would yield political credit. The CVL leader and Intransigente candidate lost the election for neighborhood adviser by a slight margin. Instead, a candidate for the center-right Unión del Centro Democrático (UCD), Patricia Siracusano, who had never resided in Villa Lugano, won a slot in the Neighborhood Advisory Council. This was a catastrophic defeat for the Intransigentes candidate, who decided to quit participation of any kind and exit the CVL.

Right after these elections, some Communist activists began to participate in the CVL. To balance this participation and avoid the cooptation of the CVL by the Communist Party, Intransigente militants began also to show up in the meetings. This increased participation of party activists became a tipping point in the life cycle of the CVL. The original core activist group, made up mostly of individuals with no party ties, felt that the CVL had become an appendage of the Communist Party and decided to exit the CVL. However, they continued controlling the paving project without creating a new association, using the contacts they had built with City Hall (a total of 220 dirt roads were paved by 1989).

At the same time, City Hall (under Mayor Suárez Lastra, 1987–89) closed its doors to grassroots organizations. This happened as electoral competition among and within parties intensified, drawing many grassroots leaders and activists away from local and nonpartisan organizations. After almost three years of internal paralysis, Peronism regained political space under the new leadership of the Renovadores. In Villa Lugano, Peronism maintained its electoral base, the Radical Party and center-left parties declined, and center-right parties gained support. The instability of political alignments after the transition intensified competition at the local neighborhood level, and amid a severe economic crisis the use of clientelistic incentives became more pronounced. In a context of deepening economic crisis, the dissolution of political institutions or their closure to popular participation, increasing instability of political alignments, intensified local electoral competition, and overlapping participation channels, the health and housing issues created insurmountable cleavages within the CVL.

Soon after the exit of its core activist group, the CVL ceased meeting regularly and then eventually dissolved. On a dark rainy day in May 1988, Suárez Lastra fi ally visited Villa Lugano and signed the last plan for paving. At this meeting all local authorities were present, but the largest group absent, contrary to previous times in Villa Lugano, were the residents—fewer than forty attended this gathering. The excitement of citizen participation that the CVL had generated was gone.

LONG-TERM POLITICAL OPPORTUNITIES AND CONTENTION

Formal Institutions

As discussed in chapter 1, while short-term changes in political opportunities help trigger episodes of collective action, other more structural features of the political system create opportunities and constraints for people's mobilization. Formal institutions (in this case state structure) are one of them. Until the constitutional reform of 1994, the mayor of Buenos Aires was appointed by the president of the republic. In 1882, Law 1260 established the government structure for the city. The government comprised two branches, executive and legislative. The Concejo Deliberante (City Council) was elected by city taxpayers,[21] but the mayor was appointed by the president of the republic. The mayor had the power to call the council into session, issue decrees, propose legislation, prepare the annual budget, and appoint all municipal employees. He also had the responsibility to implement and the power to veto measures enacted by the council. In turn, the council could reverse the mayor's vetoes with two-thirds of the votes, hold secretaries accountable, and impeach the mayor. In 1918, Congress passed the Reform of the Organic Municipal Law of the Federal Capital (Law 10240); by extending the national eligibility provision to the city, this reform removed several restrictions on voting and candidacy (Walter 1993).[22] Even though this institutional hybrid (an appointed mayor and an elected council) seemed to work rather well for the expansion of Buenos Aires in the twentieth century, it created different and confl cting incentive structures for the behavior of the executive and legislative branches of the city government.

Within this institutional structure, Buenos Aires City Hall policies should be analyzed in connection with the agenda of both the federal government and the party in office (Del Brutto 1989). At the national level, the government of Alfonsín sought to create a "Third Historical Movement" (Tercer Movimiento Histórico) similar to the ones promoted by former presidents Hipólito Yrigoyen in the 1910s and Juan Domingo Perón in the 1940s. To do so, Radicalism planned to implement public policies that would extend its political and cultural influence to sectors traditionally dominated by Peronism, such as grassroots organizations, urban clientelistic networks, and unions. Within this plan, City Hall had two programmatic goals: the expansion of citizen participation in all municipal programs and the implementation of a series of decentralization policies for the delivery of public services. The decentralization of services was originally conceived as a means of promoting participation at the local level rather than balancing the city

budget. By increasing participation, the Radical Party aimed at improving its electoral performance in the city. During the presidency of
Alfonsín, Saguier's administration (1983–86) emphasized participation
policies, while Suárez Lastra's (1986–89) emphasized decentralization
(Del Brutto 1989).

In contrast to locally elected officials—councilmen and neighborhood advisers—the executive branch of the city's Radical administration was initially open to grassroots organizations and demands and
was committed to the redistribution of resources to the poor southern
neighborhoods. There was a further incentive to be responsive to grassroots demands in Villa Lugano: while there were many Radical voters
(around 30 percent), this was the only neighborhood of Buenos Aires
City in which the Radical Party had been unable to defeat Peronism,
even in the 1983 national election. Furthermore, Villa Lugano had special appeal because it was the hometown of the well-known metalwork-
ers' union leader Lorenzo Miguel and was one of the last trenches of
significant support for orthodox Peronism. For these reasons Villa
Lugano was a symbolic space to be conquered by the Radicals. But City
Hall policies to increase participation and consolidate the Tercer Movimiento Histórico encountered resistance among local elected representatives, who perceived grassroots mobilization as a threat to their power
and legitimacy. National politics clashed with "the local."

Informal Institutions

A permanent feature of the political system that adversely affects collective action is the informal institution of clientelism.[23] Clientelistic practices constrain contentious collective action by, fi st, creating incentives
for competition among popular organizations in a context of scarce resources and, second, by generating *mistrust* among poor citizens due
to the perceived inequality in the distribution of clientelistic rewards
(some get anything, others nothing). Noncooperation among organizations and noncooperation among individuals reinforce each other
and hinder collective action.

Because of the hybrid structure of the city government, Saguier's
goal of promoting participation clashed with the interests of council-

men, including the Radical Party's own. Most councilmen saw in grassroots mobilization and participation a potential impediment to their ultimate goal of remaining in office. In contrast to city officials, councilmen had to win elections. This created a particular incentive structure for their behavior. First, to become a candidate one had to win intraparty elections. This was done primarily by creating a loyal constituency among party members in the neighborhoods by means that included the distribution of clientelistic rewards. Not only do machine politics operate by the exchange of services for votes in general elections, but, more importantly perhaps, the constituencies that they attract give candidates the leverage to avoid intraparty competition and to get more resources from their party. In this scheme, acquiescent neighborhood associations (like SFs and sports clubs) played a very important role, not only as recipients but also as components of a distributing network of clientelistic rewards. Furthermore, even though the electoral performance of local candidates depended upon the overall performance of their party in the elections because of the systemic effects of the closed electoral list (which in turn depended on the profile of the candidates that headed the list and on the performance of the government in general), if individual performance was below the party average, the party had the capacity to prevent nominations and hence reelections. In this context, any expansion of autonomous participation at the local level that might threaten the viability of a candidate was perceived as a situation that would hurt the chances of local politicians to become candidates. The paradox was that while at the national level elections tended to reinforce the legitimacy of democracy as a political regime, at the local level they could unleash antidemocratic and clientelistic practices that adversely affected the autonomy and organizational capacities of the urban poor.[24] Palermo (1986) has referred to this style of machine politics as *clientelismo de guante blanco* (white-glove clientelism). This is a type of clientelism that does not create captive clients for national elections but produces support from neighborhood associations by avoiding criticisms and mobilizations. It is exactly what the CVL stood up against.

Despite ideological differences, Villa Lugano's elected representatives shared a mistrust of the CVL, a loose organization that stressed its autonomy vis-à-vis parties and the state, seemed difficult to co-opt because of its informal institutional profile, and emphasized the effectiveness of vertical and horizontal accountability. Especially Larrosa perceived the CVL as a competitor for capitalizing the political benefits of public policy implementation (mainly paving) and as a disruption of his well-tailored clientelistic network. Larrosa also feared that the CVL would become a source of citizenship accountability and affect his less-than-transparent businesses in the neighborhood.[25] As has been documented, several councilmen, including Larrosa, had received bribes from companies that won bids for public works (Carnota and Talpone 1995). Paving was a business with high returns, and the CVL, by demanding accountability in the process of designing and implementing a public policy, became an unwelcome participant.

Confl cts with the Peronist councilman Pérez would be less harsh, primarily because Peronism was engaged in a heated internal dispute after its defeat in the 1983 national elections (Palermo 1986). The presence within the CVL of activists with close ties to left and center-left parties led both councilmen to perceive the CVL as a competitor for grassroots political capital. This was accentuated by a strong ideological cleavage between CVL activists of those parties and traditional Peronists in Villa Lugano, for whom it was almost unthinkable to work with the former. These facts created the incentives for a convergence of actions, in spite of their ideological differences, between councilmen Larrosa and Pérez to demobilize and discredit the CVL as a mere tool of the Communist Party. Despite these attempts, the CVL was able to take advantage of and expand the political opportunities provided for grassroots participation, fi st by the transition and then by the Saguier administration. However, as I discuss in more detail in chapter 7, clientelism and political manipulation by the city government created (dis) incentives for collective action by deepening place-based social hostility, a trap from which the CVL ultimately could not escape.

STRATEGIES OF MOBILIZATION

While political opportunities trigger collective action episodes and shape their development, movements sustain their activities through mobilizing strategies and cultural frames of meaning. In what follows, I describe two aspects of the strategies of mobilization used by the CVL: leadership roles and movement organization.

Leadership Roles

As discussed in chapter 1, most scholars of contentious politics agree on leaders' crucial role in initiating protest. This was the case for the CVL. As many of the fragments presented above reveal, two clearly defi ed leaders (Omar and Victorio) directed the CVL's actions. Without their presence, activities lacked focus and scope. Both leaders belonged ideologically to the left of the political continuum. Both had formal party ties. One was a Communist Party militant with thirty years of political activism. He had been imprisoned several times. He described his participation in the CVL as follows:

> In the 1983 elections, I was the Communist Party candidate for councilman, and social issues were my political and party goal. But here in the neighborhood the most important issue was paving and drainage. So I got together with some people; most of them did not belong to the party, but I had known them since childhood. It was not easy to get together, we were coming from the dark years of the dictatorship. I was imprisoned seven times before Alfonsín arrived. That's why I do not have my papers or documents filed from those early times of the CVL —we did not know for how long freedom would last.

Even though he employed a radical discourse that frequently was not well received by all members of the neighborhood, Omar maintained a pragmatic and flexible style with the authorities and during public meetings. He was one of the leading generators of projects and the main author of the CVL agenda. Although his identification with the Communist Party generated mistrust, the most stable group of members of CVL saw his role as crucial because of his ability to negotiate with public authorities. As Hector, one core activist, told me,

> Honestly, Omar was the soul of the CVL. His ideology had nothing to do with it. He talked with such conviction and self-confidence that if we

joined forces we would get the paving. He convinced me, and that is why I decided to participate.

Victorio similarly commented,

> The people that we assembled did not care who the CVL leaders were. Most of the people knew that Omar was a Communist Party activist, but people respected him deeply because he worked so much for the neighborhood, he walked the neighborhood a lot.

And Amalia, another core CVL member who at the time was also a Communist Party activist, stated,

> Omar asked me to participate in the CVL. He is very well known regarding neighborhood work, and he never took any personal advantage from this, no material benefits at all. He is so creative and has so much knowledge about Villa Lugano.

Omar invented the CVL motto "Movilizados por la democracia, la pavimentación y desagües de todas las calles de tierra de Villa Lugano" (Mobilized for democracy, the paving and drainage of all dirt roads in Villa Lugano) as well as the CVL's main discursive lines, which included the injustice of the north-south divide of Buenos Aires and the equal rights of Villa Lugano residents to city services as tax-paying citizens. These topics repeatedly emerged during meetings and in CVL pamphlets.

The other leader, Victorio, an Intransigente activist, became the president of the CGD. He recalls his participation in the CVL as follows, emphasizing the political opportunities triggered by the transition:

> With the transition everybody wanted to participate, it was just wonderful. Neighbors from different zones of Villa Lugano began to gather signatures to petition for the paving, we met and that's how everything started.

Victorio's style was more moderate than Omar's but was equally creative. According to Mainwaring and Viola's (1984) categorization, he was more an *animator* than a *dirigente,* and consequently he elicited broad consensus among the neighbors who did not have party identification or loyalty.

Even though both leaders belonged to the Left or Center Left, their trajectories prior to their incorporation in the CVL differed sharply. The Communist Party activist was part of the party machine and was several times nominated for the post of councilman and neighborhood adviser. His behavior was influenced by the strategy of his party in Villa Lugano. The Intransigente activist began participating almost simultaneously in the CVL and the party. He recognized as his only previous experience his militancy in the Movimiento Juventud Peronista Universitaria (Peronist University Youth Movement).

The local Intransigente Party committee chose him as a candidate for the Neighborhood Advisory Council in the 1987 elections. Probably his lack of previous experience led him to underestimate the resilience of traditional politics. Though he was well known for his work in the CVL and the CGD, the *trabajo vecinal* (work in the neighborhood) was not a good platform for electoral politics. As I mentioned before, defeat in the 1987 elections, and the hardening of the Communist Party strategy and discourse within the CVL, persuaded Victorio to abandon the movement and to take with him a good part of the stable core of activists. Personal frustration, due largely to the internal crisis of the Intransigentes, led him to exit the party too.

In spite of their differences, the CVL leaders privileged open communication with the entire neighborhood and the utilization of all possible institutional instances. Their behavior always aimed at adding new members and working toward a unified Villa Lugano.

Multiple ties of activist leaders created more problems than advantages or resources for the CVL. Up to March of 1987, double membership—in the CVL and in a political party—provoked tension between the two main leaders, but it did not generate serious confl cts. However, the presence of several communist activists eliminated the possibility of cooperation with the Peronists and increased fears that the CVL would be co-opted. This was clearly reflected within the CGD of Villa Lugano, where members sympathizing with Peronism explicitly rejected the possibility of cooperation with communist activists.

Movement Organization

Social Networking and Geography

While there is no general model of the effects of organization on contentious events, most scholars agree that in principle organization does increase the potential for success. The most salient feature of the CVL in this respect was its emphasis on face-to-face networking—indeed, as we saw, most initial recruiting was done by knocking at people's doors. Another relevant feature was an emphasis on geography. The CVL divided Villa Lugano into critical zones and conducted assemblies in the areas of Old Town where reforms were most needed—for example, where rain had the most negative effects. Geography was also at the center of the CVL's strategy to bring new issues to the fore, such as health and housing.

Main Orientations

Organizational Development

From its foundation, the CVL lacked legal recognition by city or national authorities. The group had no formal roles or appointments. This lack of formal organization contrasted with the tradition of SFs as well as with shantytown *juntas*. The legitimacy of the CVL came from its activities and its power to mobilize, as demonstrated by a series of events, crucially the informal recognition granted by Mayor Saguier when he visited Villa Lugano at the CVL's invitation. The main leaders made informality part of their strategies so that other organizations could be included within the CVL. However, while this flexible and informal organization could be successful in periods of high mobilization, it could jeopardize the survival of the organization at times when political opportunities were adverse and mobilization was low.

Functional Differentiation and Decision Processes

There was no voting process within the CVL, under the assumption that voting was a divisive strategy for local organizations and that consensus should be unanimous. This was a constant theme in the discourse of leaders and participants of CVL. They believed that voting should be used only to elect or punish local and national politicians. Functional differentiation was very low: for example, the task of writing the minutes for the weekly meetings and other events rotated among members. Monetary resources were not important to the CVL, in contrast to other neighborhood organizations. Money was collected only for very specific goals, such as fl ers for meetings.

Linkages with Similar Organizations
From its foundation onward, the CVL aimed at being an umbrella organization and gathering all neighborhood and political associations of Villa Lugano. Contacts were frequent, but in the end political and ideological cleavages and differences in institutional structure and culture kept the CVL from becoming a full neighborhood movement.

Institutional Culture
The CVL's members defi ed the organization as politically nonpartisan. Its main goal was to challenge the state to make effective their rights as taxpayers and to end urban segregation between the northern and southern parts of the city. As its basic motto indicated, members believed that the organization's existence depended upon democracy. Consequently, beyond any material demand the defense of the "democratic system" was a priority: without democracy, they insisted over and over, "we could not even petition for street paving." Most CVL participants rejected the *fomentista* mode of sheer petitioning, which they saw as limited to "bureaucratic management." This created splits with participants belonging to *fomentista* organizations. The CVL strongly believed that mobilization was the only way to move the municipal bureaucracy forward. While their repertoire included assemblies and direct participation of neighbors, they also demanded constant meetings with and accountability of municipal officials to implement policies and redistribute resources. On the other hand, leaders with Communist Party ties were especially likely to advance the idea that, in response to the local bipartisan and clientelistic machines (Radicals and Peronists), CVL could emerge from the local urban space as an alternative, a new form of neighborhood association with the goal of making a politics of residents' "own interests." This is why the CVL valued and

emphasized local power and demanded the replacement of all neighborhood advisers and councilmen by others who would "truly belong" to Villa Lugano.

*   *   *

We have seen that shifting political opportunities at the national and local level, formal and informal institutions, and leadership and organization all converged to help explain the CVL life cycle as the successive crossing of participation thresholds. From highly committed leaders to core activists, occasional participants, and simple bystanders, the CVL became a true umbrella organization demanding environmental and infrastructure equality for all. In doing so, it significantly advanced the democratization of urban space in Villa Lugano and the city of Buenos Aires. However, the new goals of health and housing, while initially seeming to renew and expand participation, initiated the collapse of the CVL by revealing and reinforcing deep social and cultural cleavages present in Villa Lugano. As we saw, changes in political opportunities at the national and local levels adversely affected the organizational capabilities of the CVL and contributed to its fi al collapse. The CVL was unable to cross the last threshold of participation to become a true neighborhood movement: it was unable to reach out to areas of Villa Lugano other than Old Town. Indeed, changes in political opportunities, especially at the local level (a new closed-door policy at City Hall, the intensification of local partisan competition, and the strengthening of clientelism), were to blame for the CVL's failure. But as the next two chapters will show, deep sociopolitical and cultural cleavages rooted in the geography of Villa Lugano were also crucial factors for explaining the CVL's fate. To further uncover the causes of this unfortunate turn of events, in the next chapter I explore popular political culture and its connections with the discursive practices (or frame of meaning) put forward by the CVL. This exploration will help explain why, in the end, the CVL failed to articulate a frame of meaning with high resonance for all residents of Villa Lugano and to overcome adverse political developments.

PART IV

The Politics of Signification

CHAPTER 5

———————

Framing Collective Action

As discussed in chapter 1, while changes in political opportunities help trigger episodes of collective action, their sustainability depends upon (besides organization) the formation of cognitive frames of meaning. In the frames perspective, movements are signifying agents: through their framing activities they give meaning and interpretation to different situations, and this, in turn, may mobilize potential followers. Recall that Snow and Benford (1992) identify three aspects of a movement's framing activities that affect both consensus formation and action mobilization. The fi st is *diagnostic framing*: movements have to identify the problem of concern and attribute it to a cause. Blame on the problem at hand can be placed on technological, political, economic, or moral causes. The second is *prognostic framing*: movements should also propose solutions, strategies, tactics, and specific targets. And the third is *motivational framing*: movements need to provide a "vocabulary of motives" for participation, a moral justification for people to engage in collective action.

The mobilizing potential of movements' framing depends on the resonance of the frame. Building upon George Rudé's assertion (1980) that the mobilizing potential of beliefs and ideas depends upon their interconnection with popular culture, Snow and Benford (1992) contend that the closer the frame is to the everyday life of the people called upon, the greater the chance of high resonance. Accordingly, if a frame has empirical validity (its diagnosis, prognosis, and motives seem plausible), experiential commensurability (it reflects a common problem and people agree on strategies), and narrative fidelity (the frame resonates with existing cultural traditions), then frame resonance will be high. As most students of cognitive frames of meaning have noticed, leaders and organizers do not construct from scratch the symbols needed to mobilize people. This chapter looks into popular political culture, traditions of participation, and social identities as the foundation that provides leaders with a reservoir of symbols (and constraints) to construct collective action frames. Delving into popular political orientations (i.e., the cognitive and evaluative positioning of individuals toward political actors and the political system as a whole) and social identities (i.e., the way "actors perceive their interests, role in society, and relationship to other groups and institutions"; Mainwaring 1987: 143) is crucial for explaining the dilemmas the CVL faced in framing and sustaining collective action in Villa Lugano.

Knowledge of popular political culture is not just the study of opinion polls. It requires the use of multidisciplinary resources. In what follows I explore popular political orientations and social identities by combining survey and ethnographic data and by bringing into focus the historical fi dings on traditions of popular participation (or the repertoire of contention) discussed in chapter 3.

THE STUDY OF POPULAR POLITICAL CULTURE IN ARGENTINA

In the early 1950s, Gino Germani—the founding father of the social sciences in Argentina—portrayed the political culture of the Latin American poor as a set of changing and contradictory orientations, values, and attitudes brought about by the clash of traditional society with the forces of political democratization and economic modernization. More than five decades after Germani's *Estructura social de la Argentina* (1955) was published, we still do not know much about the political orientations and social identities of the urban popular sectors and how these may affect their capabilities for collective action and the legitimacy of democracy at the local and national level.

This neglect is largely due to the fact that most scholarly work on democratization has emphasized the role of elites and institutions and has paid little attention to popular political culture and its connections with mobilization. This is at odds with the contemporary history of Latin America. As in other countries of the region, in Argentina the political activation of the urban popular sectors was perceived by other actors as a worrisome factor that induced their support for authoritarian adventures. Indeed, for the middle and upper classes bureaucratic-authoritarianism was deemed the solution to the economic crisis produced (in their perception) by the popular sectors' "excessive" political protests and economic demands (O'Donnell 1988).

Political behavior cannot be directly derived from orientations or dispositions, but as James Scott has argued, "The realm of consciousness gives us a kind of privileged access to lines of action that may—just may—become plausible at some future date" (1985: 38). In this sense, the urban popular sectors' perceptions and evaluations of democracy and their orientations toward the political system are critical components in the processes that may or may not lead to the consolidation and expansion of democracy. Indeed, the democratization of political institutions is only one aspect of democratization (O'Donnell 2004). This process, if limited to the macropolitical level, may be too feeble to win allegiance from vast sectors of the population.

There are exceptions to this neglect. Some scholars have studied changes in popular social identities as a by-product of changes in the socioeconomic structure and, especially, the labor market (Svampa 2000; Kessler 2000; Lvovich 2000; Merklen 2000). Indeed, as I mentioned in the Introduction, since the transition in 1983 Argentina has experienced cycles of hyperinflation, neoliberal economic restructuring, and state disintegration that have led to the increasing structural heterogeneity of the popular sectors and to the impoverishment of important parts of the middle class (Katzman 1989; Smith 1991; Golbert and Tenti Fanfani 1994). Although Argentina is still among the countries with the lowest levels of poverty in Latin America, in the last three decades poverty there has grown more than in any other country of the region (Feres and León 1990; Altimir, Beccaria, and González Rosada 2002). Most striking is that in Argentina poverty has increased faster since the transition to democracy began in the early 1980s. In the 1970s, 8 percent of all households lived below the poverty line and only 1 percent below the indigence line.[1] Between 1970 and 1980, the number of households living below the poverty line increased to 9 percent and the households below the indigence line to 2 percent. But between 1980 and 1986, households below the poverty line increased to 13 percent of the total, and the number of households below the indigence line doubled to 4 percent. Furthermore, data for the period 1986–91 indicate another increase of 6 percentage points in urban poverty at the national level (Altimir 1993). Throughout the continent, the increase in poverty has mainly affected urban areas. Argentina is no exception: in 1970 only 5 percent of the urban households lived below the poverty line, in 1986 12 percent did, and in 2000, 21 percent did (Altimir, Beccaria, and González Rosada 2002). In addition to the marginalization of already poor households, the process of sustained impoverishment in Argentina has brought about the expansion of a new social sector, the *pauperizados* or the "new poor": wage earners of the public sector, semiskilled employees and workers, educated youths with semiskilled employment, and senior citizens who previously met their basic needs of health and housing but whose income has now fallen below the poverty line (Bustelo and Minujín 1991). In the 1980s, this new sector represented 4 percent of the poor households of Greater Buenos Aires. In the 1990s, it mounted to 18 percent, a growth of 338 percent in proportional terms (Minujín 1992: 24). This increasing impoverishment has been reinforced by deep changes in the labor market, growing rates of unemployment and underemployment, and the rapid development of *cuentapropismo* (the informal sector). By the mid-1990s, more than 13 percent of the urban labor force was engaged in informal activities such as small businesses and personal services (Golbert and Tenti Fanfani 1994). Impoverishment and informal employment have led to the same outcome: the amorphousness of the class structure and the decline of organized labor (Portes 1989; Portes and Roberts 2005).

While the above-mentioned studies are important, they do not address issues of political culture—popular perceptions of democratic institutions, conceptions of citizenship, and the state. My research on movements' framing activities emphasizes the crucial relevance of attitudes toward democracy and the emergence of a specific language of citizenship for the construction of high-resonance cognitive frames of meaning. As Bendix (1961) has persuasively argued, the inauguration of democracy may radically change the forms of popular contention and participation precisely by inscribing into public discourse the ideas of citizenship and equal rights. While my aim is primarily to explore popular political culture as a reservoir of symbols (and constraints) for the framing of participation, I am convinced that this topic is also relevant per se and in relation to the legitimacy of democracy.

In a similar vein, post-transition studies on voting behavior have reassessed the debate on the presumed authoritarian character of the urban poor (Godio 1995; Adrogué 1999; Seligson 2001). The election in poor regions of Argentina of some former members of the armed forces suspected of gross human rights violations and of high-ranking police officers who support zero-tolerance policies on crime or *mano dura* suggests that Germani's observation of the confl cting coexistence of "authoritarian" and "democratic" orientations, values, and attitudes within the urban popular sectors deserves renewed attention.[2] However, empirical evidence seems to confi m that in Argentina as well as in Latin America the lower classes are not less democratic than other sectors of society (Booth and Seligson 1984; Tiano 1986; Seligson 2001). Furthermore, democracy seems to be for them the most desirable political regime (Ranis 1992; Moisés 1993; Seligson 2001). Although these are important contributions, I argue that they give only a partial account of popular political orientations and that the simplistic dichotomy between authoritarian and democratic attitudes is misguided. Important questions remain unexplored: What is the meaning of democracy for the urban popular sectors? What type of democracy are the lower classes willing to support? What do they expect from a democratic regime? How do they evaluate the workings of democratic institutions? How do they evaluate clientelistic practices? How do they perceive their fellow citizens? These are important questions because although the short-term stability of democracy may not depend on popular support, its quality and extension do. Moreover, these queries may help us to explore the social roots of what O'Donnell (1994) has theorized as delegative democracy: a political regime characterized by apparently omnipotent presidents, quasi-plebiscitarian elections, weak democratic institutions, clientelism, low participation, and low accountability.

In this chapter I argue that popular political culture in Argentina is far from being a system of homogeneous meanings, values, and dispositions. As E. P. Thompson (1993) has pointed out, *popular culture* is a loose and descriptive term that refers to a confl ctual and changing arena, historically and socially situated. In Argentina, the sociopolitical fragmentation of the urban poor has been largely overlooked.[3] The strong identification of the urban poor with Peronism led most students of Argentina to assume the homogeneity of their social identities and political orientations. Furthermore, the unionized working class has been the main object of research in studies of the popular sectors. The unions' close ties to Peronism have reinforced the conventional view of high homogeneity and internal solidarity of those sectors. As I hope to show, this view is empirically unwarranted.

In the next section, I explore whether potentially salient sociopolitical cleavages exist among the urban poor in Villa Lugano and how these may affect the formation of cognitive frames of meaning and thus their capabilities for collective action.

METHODOLOGY

The data presented in this chapter are based on thirty in-depth interviews and on a survey of neighborhood residents (N = 506) that I conducted in 1995. The survey sample was stratified by each of the housing areas of Villa Lugano described in chapter 3. For each housing area, I used a multistage random sampling strategy. The questionnaire consisted of two-thirds closed and one-third open questions. Its application lasted approximately an hour and fi een minutes. Confidentiality was assured. The survey was pretested (N = 157). Appendix A provides the demographics of the survey. The sample was evenly distributed in terms of gender. It followed the age categorization usually applied in surveys (89 percent of the interviewed were people of working age). Almost 90 percent were Argentine citizens. Type of employment was fairly evenly distributed among manual, nonmanual, and housewives, and only 10 percent of respondents were pensioners. It is worth mentioning that the category of "housewives" may include many unemployed or temporary domestic personnel (cleaning women). Of those who were employed at the time of the survey, 57 percent said they had a formal job. Forty-three percent had reached or completed primary school and 41 percent secondary school. University education was minimal. An overwhelming majority had attended public schools. More than half of the households had between four and nine members, and their heads were predominantly male. As in any survey, the question on household income was the most unreliable, but on the basis of both household and personal income, 64 percent of those included in the sample could be bracketed as middle to low income. Finally, in terms of class self-identification, 56 percent said they belonged to the "lower class," 19 percent identifi d as "middle-lower class," and 23 percent identifi d as "middle class."

The survey included questions on orientations toward and evaluations of the workings of democratic institutions (parties, Congress, the presidency, the judiciary, and local government); the role of the state (social policies—housing and health—and economic development); participatory experience in unions, political parties, and grassroots organizations; and personal economic situation and living conditions. In addition, the survey contained questions on residents' perceptions of others who lived in a different zone of the neighborhood, especially in the context of the growing numbers of illegal immigrants who were settling in the area (Appendix B). For comparative purposes, some of these questions were taken from surveys applied elsewhere in Latin America or in western or eastern Europe.[4]

DEMOCRACY: THE VIEW FROM BELOW

The majority of Villa Lugano residents (56 percent) felt that democracy should guarantee, before anything, decent living conditions to the whole population (table 5.1).[5] This suggests that without a minimal degree of social equality democracy would be likely to lose support among these respondents. The data also indicate a preference for social over political rights. However, 27 percent of the respondents agreed that democracy should guarantee, before anything, the condition of free and fair elections. Another 15 percent answered that free elections and decent living conditions should be equally guaranteed by democracy. Taking these two last groups of respondents together, it is clear that for a rather high proportion of Villa Lugano residents (42 percent) free elections were a fundamental component of democracy.

TABLE 5.1. Definitions of Democracy

Democracy Should Guarantee before Anything:	Female (%)	Male (%)	Total (%)
A decent level of living conditions to everybody	59	52	56
The freedom to choose th government in free elections	25	29	27
Both things should be equally guaranteed	14	17	15
DK/DA	2	2	2
Total	100 (n = 260)	100 (n = 246)	100 (N = 506)

The qualitative interviews help to contextualize and further inter-pret the survey data. For Villa Lugano residents, democracy encom-passed an array of meanings and expectations. Minimal defi itions of democracy and satisfaction with the actual workings of democratic in-stitutions coexisted with hopes of political and economic change. Here are some respondents' defi itions of democracy:

> To be respected and to respect, and to apply the principle that my rights end where the others' rights begin. (Female, housewife, forty years old, Barrio General Savio)

> Essentially, I believe democracy should protect the individual, it should give him more security. (Male, single, sixty-two years old, retired, Old Town)

For others, democracy meant frustration, broken promises, and elitism:

> You are asking me what democracy is for? I tell you, it is just for demonstrating how little the opinion of the people count for. This, what we are living, is not democracy. (Female, single, twenty-two years old, unemployed, Barrio General Savio)

Democracy and Authoritarianism

Despite this diversity of opinions, a theme that invariably appeared when I asked the question "What is democracy for?" was Argentina's violent past.[6] The experience of living under military rule had deeply marked the political orientations of these interviewees:

> I am totally satisfied with democracy. And do you know why? Because it has been more than ten years by now that we have a government chosen by the people. The only thing I wanted was the military out of politics. (Female, divorced, fi y-five years old, salesperson, Villa 20)

> Under the military dictatorship we could not leave our home without identification cards. The police took me twice because I did not have my ID. Without any doubt, I live better now. (Female, divorced, thirty-three years old, factory worker, Villa 20)

Although the contrast with the authoritarian experience had produced considerable satisfaction with democracy, lingering issues from the authoritarian period were also a source of dissatisfaction and frustration with it:

> With the inauguration of democracy I expected justice. I expected punishment for the authors of torture, kidnapping, and murder of many innocents. Democracy failed. This is why I am deeply dissatisfied. (Male, retired, married, seventy-one years old, Barrio General Savio)

It is clear from these fragments that one basic quality of democracy is to create the conditions for personal security (including the right to freely circulate in your own city without fear of arbitrary exercise of power). The following quotation shows how the images of military rule imprinted in popular consciousness gave, by opposition, meaning to democracy:

> Democracy gives us freedom of speech. The possibility to be on the street, at any time, without having a green Falcon [car often used by the military for kidnapping] after you; to have long hair without being a *guerrillero* [guerilla member]; to go to a public demonstration if you want. (Male, married, twenty-six years old, metalworker, Villa 20)

Democracy was also seen as having—in contrast to authoritarianism—a potentially equalizing effect. It allowed people to express their opinions and ideas, their complaints and demands. Susana was twenty-two years old and had been born in Villa 20. She was single and had a ten-month-old baby. She was tired of seeing so much poverty around. For her, the most important quality of democracy was to give voice to people like her before the rich and the powerful:

> Democracy helps us to be independent. It also allows us to speak freely, to speak the same ways as the ones who have money and power. (Female, single, twenty-two years old, Villa 20)

But civil liberties did not per se entail economic or social improvement. Even though democracy was perceived as a fundamental step to build up a peaceful and more solidaristic society, it did not bring necessarily better living conditions for the popular sectors. For some, democracy was about trust, not about economic development:

> Democracy is fundamental. Without it you cannot express your ideas, you get into situations in which you have to be careful *who you are talking to*, like during the military government. I did not expect that democracy would improve everything, freedom is one thing and economic problems another. (Female, housewife, fi y-five years old, Old Town)

> I feel freer with democracy, but this does not mean that we live in better economic conditions. I did not expect more than this. (Male, married, thirty-two years old, skilled textile worker, Villa 20)

Democracy as a Path for Economic Change

A cluster of respondents believed that democracy not only set the limits for tolerance and prevents violence but also provided chances to improve one's own economic situation. The civil and political rights guaranteed by democracy were perceived as conducive to these improvements. Probably this theme represents a deep change in the political orientations of part of the urban popular sectors in Argentina, since economic improvement has not been historically linked to the existence of civil and political rights.

Under democracy we can participate more if we want; with the military we could not speak. Now we can give our opinions and express our ideas without being repressed. There are more jobs and more possibilities to progress. (Male, married, thirty years old, informal textile worker, Villa 20)

Democracy allows us to live more peacefully than under military rule. The youth can go out without fear of repression. Also, living conditions can improve. (Female, married, thirty-nine years old, owner of a small food store, Villa 20)

Democracy as Panacea

Another cluster of respondents at fi st perceived democracy as a solution for everything. After decades of populist and authoritarian experiments, some individuals placed their expectations of economic and social change in political democracy. These were the respondents now most disenchanted with democracy.

I thought that with democracy everything would improve. But my own experience says that democracy is not useful at all. I am worse off under democracy. We had a better life under military rule, there was less drug trafficking and much more respect. We need more authority and respect. (Female, married, twenty-six years old, former textile worker, underemployed, Villa 20)

My family hoped that everything would change with democracy. I think that we should change some laws and that certain policies should have been made in a different way. (Female, single, twenty-eight years old, teacher, Villa 20)

I voted for Alfonsín, I was waiting for a solution for *everything*. During his presidency there was freedom, but he failed economically. (Married, thirty years old, self-employed textile worker, Villa 20)

Democracy as Political Regime

A third theme raised by the question "What is democracy for?" was the separation between democracy as a political regime and the economic performance of a given government. For some respondents support for democracy was bound not to policy outcomes but to the proper working of democratic institutions:

> Democracy is an act of freedom to choose and question the candidates. If the representatives do not accomplish their promises, democracy allows us to defeat them in free elections. (Female, married, forty-six years old, state employee, Old Town)

> The electoral campaign's promises and party platforms have not been realized. But it is not the fault of *democracy*, it is the fault of the politicians. (Male, married, retired, sixty-four years old, Barrio General Savio)

Democracy as a Way of Life

For some, not only the proper workings of political institutions but also everyday patterns of behavior among citizens defi ed a country as democratic. Democracy was incomplete if it worked only at the macro-political level; for a country to be truly democratic, the culture and values that permeate social relations had to be also democratic:

> I think we are approaching democracy. With this I mean we are learning as a country to be democratic. The change should be a cultural one; the people should become democratic. (Female, married, forty-four years old, municipal employee, Old Town)

> I feel I am a democrat, but until now we have demonstrated little of it. Argentineans are antidemocratic, I include myself. Democracy is useful to give people the chance to develop their intelligence as human beings. (Male, married, fi y-eight years old, retired, Old Town)

The qualitative data presented in this section sketch the diversity of opinions about democracy among the residents of Villa Lugano. The meaning of and the reasons for democracy were deeply enmeshed with the experience of authoritarianism. Many respondents perceived democracy as valuable per se, as a necessary condition for improving other spheres of life, and as a not-yet-fulfilled promise. Survey data also suggest that popular expectations toward democracy went beyond the guarantee of civil and political rights. For most Villa Lugano residents, long-term support of democracy seemed linked to its capacity to ameliorate social inequality and the hardships of poverty.

MODELS OF DEMOCRACY

As I mentioned in the previous section, O'Donnell (1994) has characterized several of the new democracies in Latin America as delegative. This type of democracy functions under the premise that presidents elected in free elections are enabled to govern the country as they see fit (59). Presidents see themselves as the embodiment of the nation and above political parties. Parties are seen not as representative channels of the citizenry but as "factions" that hinder the workings of the executive. Horizontal accountability (i.e., accountability to other democratic institutions such as the judiciary and the congress as well as various control agencies) is perceived as impeding "the full authority that the president has been delegated to exercise" (60). Were these orientations shared by the individuals I interviewed in Villa Lugano? Was there a broad acceptance of delegative practices among them, or were they divided regarding their preferences? How would this affect the formation of collective action frames? In this section, I present data that address the issue of delegative versus representative democracy.

The fi st dimension of delegative democracy is the supremacy of the executive power over political parties. I asked whether people agreed with the statement "Instead of political parties, Argentina needs an able and courageous man willing to achieve national unity."[7] Table 5.2 shows that in this matter the opinions among Villa Lugano residents were far from homogeneous: 59 percent of the respondents totally agreed with the statement, and 29 percent totally disagreed. Although these proportions suggest the existence of delegative tendencies among a majority of the interviewees, they also show some support for representative politics and distrust of omnipotent paternalist leaders.

I also asked Villa Lugano residents whether presidential power should decrease, increase, or stay the same.[8] Twenty-one percent responded that it should increase and 50 percent that it should stay the same (table 5.3). Only 16 percent responded that it should decrease. Note that by the time the survey was given, President Menem had already signed more decrees in his fi st government than all Argentine democratically elected presidents taken together. Menem also federally intervened in several provincial governments, including the government of the city of Buenos Aires.[9]

TABLE 5.2. Orientations toward Democracy

National Unity?	Female (%)	Male (%)	Total (%)
Totally agree	63	56	59
Partially agree	8	5	7
Depends	1	1	1
Partially disagree	3	4	3
Totally disagree	24	34	29
DK/DA	1	–	1
Total	100 (n = 260)	100 (n = 246)	100 (N = 506)

I complemented this question by asking if congressional power should increase, decrease, or stay the same. In a context of strong presidential supremacy, the answers make clear that most respondents preferred a Congress with less power. As table 5.4 shows, only 16 percent said the power of Congress should increase, 38 percent said it should stay the same, and 33 percent said it should decrease.

A typical argument against Congress in Argentina referred to its inefficiency, lack of technical know-how, and slowness in making decisions. This contrasted with the image of decisiveness that delegative leaders tried to convey.

> Congress takes a lot of time to make the important decisions. I think it should not interfere with the president. (Married, thirty years old, self-employed textile worker, Villa 20)

Even for those who favored a stronger Congress, these criticisms had some validity.

> If Congress doesn't work, the people applaud Menem when he signs a decree. I believe this is very bad. Why do we have senators and representatives then? (Male, married, sixty-eight years old, owner of a small business, Old Town)

TABLE 5.3. Power of the President

The Political Power of the President Should:	*Female (%)*	*Male (%)*	*Total (%)*
Increase	24	18	21
Stay the same	46	54	50
Decrease	15	17	16
DK/DA	15	11	13
Total	100 (n = 260)	100 (n = 246)	100 (N = 506)

TABLE 5.4. Power of Congress

The Political Power of Congress Should:	*Female (%)*	*Male (%)*	*Total (%)*
Increase	13	19	16
Stay the same	41	35	38
Decrease	31	35	33
DK/DA	15	11	13
Total	100 (n = 260)	100 (n = 246)	100 (N = 506)

A second dimension of delegative democracy referred to the division of powers and the respect of law. To address these issues I asked residents whether they agreed with the statement "If the president has to break the law to solve a serious national problem, it is better that he does it and solve the problem."[10] There was a significant split among Villa Lugano's respondents: 49 percent totally agreed with the statement, while 35 percent totally disagreed (table 5.5).

In general, these fi dings provide empirical grounds to suggest the existence of (1) a high proportion of Villa Lugano respondents with delegative propensities and (2) a rather sharp cleavage among these respondents regarding the acceptability of delegative practices.

TABLE 5.5. Orientations toward Democratic Institutions

Breaking of the Law by the President:	Female (%)	Male (%)	Total (%)
Totally agree	49	50	49
Partially agree	12	6	9
Depends	1	1	1
Partially disagree	3	4	4
Totally disagree	33	38	35
DK/DA	2	1	2
Total	100 (n = 260)	100 (n = 246)	100 (N = 506)

POLITICAL PARTIES' ROOTS IN SOCIETY

Political parties are an essential component of democracy. As Mainwaring and Scully (1995: 2) argue, parties not only shape the way democracies work but also provide information on how the political system functions; parties "are the main agents of political representation and are virtually the only actors with access to elected positions in democratic politics." The authors defi e four conditions of party system institutionalization: (1) the rules and nature of competition among parties are stable; (2) major parties have stable roots in society; (3) major political actors accord legitimacy to the electoral process and to parties; and (4) party organizations have reasonably stable rules and structures. In this section I deal with the second dimension of party institutionalization, parties' roots in society. What were the orientations toward political parties among Villa Lugano residents? Did residents perceive parties as truly representative institutions? Did they have party identifications? How did they evaluate parties' performance? Were parties perceived as legitimate actors in the political process? In what ways did popular orientations toward political parties affect democracy? Did negative orientations toward political parties and professional politicians reinforce predispositions for a delegative type of democracy?

Party Identification

Party preference is an important indicator of parties' roots in society. Table 5.6 shows that a high proportion of Villa Lugano residents—more than two-thirds—claimed to sympathize with a political party: 39 percent with Peronism, 26 percent with Radicalism, and 5 percent with other parties. Only 29 percent had no party preference.[11]

These results match the quite stable patterns of party competition in the neighborhood shown in table 5.7. From 1983 to the 2001–2 deep economic crisis that ended with the resignation of Alianza president Fernando de la Rúa, about 70 percent of the votes were received by the two main parties.

Ideological Self-Identification

Table 5.8 shows the survey results for a question on left- ight ideological self-identifi ation.[12] These data indicate that a high proportion

TABLE 5.6. Party Preferences

Political Party	Female (%)	Male (%)	Total (%)
Peronist (Partido Justicialista)	38	41	39
Radical (Unión Cívica Radical)	31	22	26
Left (Movimiento al Socialism and Partido Obrero)	–	1	1
Socialism	1	1	1
Liberals (Unión de Centro Democrático)	1	1	1
Right (Movimiento Modín)	–	3	2
None	29	30	29
DA/DK	–	1	1
Total	100 (n = 260)	100 (n = 246)	100 (N = 506)

TABLE 5.7. Voting Patterns in Villa Lugano, 1983–1999
(% of Total Vote Cast)

	1983[a]	1989[a]	1995[a]	1999[a]
UCR (Radicals)	45	24	10	
PJ (Peronists)	46	58	38	30
UCD (center-right)	1	6	4	
PI (Intransigentes)	5	4	–	
Modín (center-right, military based)	–	–	2	
FREPASO (center-left coalition	–	–	34	
Alianza (UCR-FREPASO coalition)	–	–	–	41
APR (Center-right coalition)				11

Source: Elaborated with data from Junta Nacional Electoral.

Note: UCR = Unión Cívica Radical; PJ = Partido Justicialista; UCD = Unión del Centro Democrático; PI = Partido Intransigente; FREPASO = Frente País Solidario; APR = Acción por la República; Modín = Movimiento por la Dignidad y la Independencia; Alianza = Alianza por el Trabajo, la Justicia y la Educación.

[a] Presidential elections.

of Villa Lugano residents (76 percent) could locate their ideological preferences along a left- ight continuum. Only 1 percent said they did not understand the question, and 7 percent did not know where to place themselves. The pattern of responses was concentrated on the center-right side of the continuum: 29 percent positioned themselves at the center, 25 on the center right, and 11 percent on the right. Only 11 percent declared themselves to be on either the left r the center left.

TABLE 5.8. Ideological Preferences

Political Position	Female (%)	Male (%)	Total (%)
Left	3	3	3
Center-left	4	12	8
Center	34	23	29
Center-right	19	31	25
Right	10	11	11
DU/DK/DA	30	20	24
Total	100 (n = 260)	100 (n = 246)	100 (N = 506)

If these survey data seem quite straightforward, the qualitative interviews reveal the complexities of ideological self-identifi ation for Villa Lugano residents. Although the results presented in table 5.8 seem to corroborate some of the literature on working-class ideological preferences, there are important caveats I should mention.[13] People may declare preference for the "center" to avoid being ideologically identifi d. Furthermore, the meaning of the political center in Argentina is equivocal. For some, this term is synonymous with liberalism and moderation; for others, it means the political Right. A good way to illustrate this is a quote from one of the qualitative interviews: "I am at the *center* [stressing the word to make sure I understood what he meant]; I am a conservative." Furthermore, the meaning of *right* and *left* is also equivocal. Some interviewees who defi ed themselves as *derechistas* (rightists) actually used the term to refer to being "in the right" or acting "by right" (*por derecha*) in the sense of obeying the law. To be *de derecha* was the opposite of acting "by the left" *(hacer cosas por izquierda),* a phrase synonymous with dishonesty and illegality. The identification of "right"— as acting according to the law—with *derechista* (rightist) is an example of the impact of authoritarian ideas on popular language. This should not be surprising after decades of authoritarian practices.

Although many respondents did locate their preferences along the left-ight continuum without much effort, they expressed skepticism regarding its ideological validity in Argentina's politics. Arguments against the validity of the continuum were based primarily on what respondents saw as the artificiality of the left-ight split. They denied the real existence of that split both among the people and among professional politicians. Furthermore, many of the respondents who declared sympathy with Peronism answered, "I am a Peronist," implying that this was enough to defi e somebody ideologically, or "Peronism is a movement *neither* of the Right *nor* of the Left," or "Peronism is a movement of the Right *and* the Left."

Showing deep skepticism concerning the fairness of the political game, a second cluster of respondents denied the existence of any ideological cleavage among politicians:

> Politicians are leftists and rightists at the same time. The differences among them are false. Their individual interests weigh an awful lot. Unfortunately, ideals do not exist any more. (Female, divorced, thirty-eight years old, Barrio General Savio)

> What can I tell you? Politicians are all the same; they fi ht among themselves only for the public show, but underneath they think and act in the same way, only to defend their own interests. (Female, housewife, formerly industrial worker, married to an industrial worker, forty-seven years old, Old Town)

The qualitative data presented here suggest that the issue of ideological preferences should be carefully contextualized and analyzed. In general, although the survey data show that a significant number of Argentine respondents felt they could identify themselves along the left right continuum, the qualitative interviews suggest that the left-ight continuum had multiple meanings and was not considered by many respondents to be the main dimension of politics. Nevertheless, this does not imply that in Argentina, as Mainwaring and Scully (1995: 39) argue, "Politics at the mass level is not highly ideological, and hence not deeply polarized." For example, to be a *gorila* (gorilla) means to be strongly anti-Peronist, a term as ideologically charged as *leftist* or *rightist* in other political environments. Below I present some data that portray divided urban popular sectors along cleavages that may or may not co-incide with the left- ight split. Issues such as the role of the state, demo-cratic institutions, and the evaluations of the process of economic restructuring will illustrate this.

Attitudes toward Political Parties

Pursuing the analysis of parties' roots in society, I asked Villa Lugano residents to agree or disagree with the statement "Political parties only divide the people."[14] This statement addresses the issue of whether parties produce confl ct instead of processing it. Table 5.9 shows that regarding this issue Villa Lugano respondents were sharply divided: 45 percent totally agreed with the statement, while 40 percent totally disagreed, and hardly any held nuanced opinions of the subject.

I also asked Lugano residents to agree or disagree with the statement "Basically, political parties are all the same."[15] The results indicate, again, a striking polarization among respondents (table 5.10). Sixty percent agreed with the statement, while 39 percent disagreed.

The question "Which is more important when you decide your vote, the candidate or the party to which the candidate belongs?" addresses the strength of party identification, and, in doing so, targets

TABLE 5.9. Opinions on Political Parties: Dividing the People

Divide the People	Female (%)	Male (%)	Total (%)
Totally agree	48	43	45
Partially agree	8	4	6
Depends	2	2	2
Partially disagree	4	8	6
Totally disagree	37	43	40
DK/DA	1	–	1
Total	100 (n = 260)	100 (n = 246)	100 (N = 506)

TABLE 5.10. Opinions on Political Parties: All the Same

Parties Are All the Same	Female (%)	Male (%)	Total (%)
Totally agree	55	46	51
Partially agree	7	12	9
Depends	–	–	–
Partially disagree	7	4	5
Totally disagree	29	38	34
DK/DA	2	–	1
Total	100 (n = 260)	100 (n = 246)	100 (N = 506)

another dimension of delegative democracy: personalistic leadership.[16] When deciding how to cast their votes, the majority of the interviewees (57 percent) focused on the candidate, and only 19 percent on the party to which the candidate belonged. Seventeen percent considered both things equally important (table 5.11 below). Although the results show a higher preference for individuals over political parties, it is important to note that one-third of the respondents considered the party an important part of their voting decision.

Attitudes toward Politicians

Orientations toward professional politicians were also diverse. I asked Villa Lugano residents to evaluate professional politicians' performance.[17] More than half of the respondents expressed a negative opinion: 42 percent said that politicians above all pursued their own interests and 17 percent that they only made the work of government more difficult. But 15 percent responded that it was hard to say because "there are good and bad politicians," and 25 percent believed that politicians did try to serve the country (table 5.12).

TABLE 5.11. Candidates versus Parties

Which Is More Important When You Decide Your Vote	Female (%)	Male (%)	Total (%)
The candidat	57	57	57
The party to which th candidate belongs	21	18	19
Both	17	17	17
Neither	2	2	2
Other answers	2	2	2
DK/DA	1	4	3
Total	100 (n = 260)	100 (n = 246)	100 (N = 506)

TABLE 5.12. Orientations toward Politicians

Politicians Are a Group of People:	Female (%)	Male (%)	Total (%)
Who seek their own interests	38	46	42
Who try to serve the country	27	24	25
Who make the work of the government more difficu	21	13	17
Hard to say	12	17	15
DK/DA	2	–	1
Total	100 (n = 260)	100 (n = 246)	100 (N = 506)

The preceding question refers to politicians at the national level. When I asked the same question regarding local politicians, an overwhelming majority of Villa Lugano residents (94 percent) expressed a negative and cynical view of them. Table 5.13 shows the responses to the question "What do you think about the neighborhood's politicians?"[18] Seventy-six percent responded spontaneously, "I don't know them." As confi med by the qualitative interviews, by this answer respondents implied that local politicians didn't do their job—which, according to respondents included, especially, the task of "walking the neighborhood's streets."

The qualitative interviews support these fi dings and anticipate an issue I discuss in later chapters: clientelism. For many, politicians were interested only in capturing people's votes to pursue their own interests.

> Politicians don't come very often, actually they do not show up at all. They become representatives only when they need the votes. They come, make a lot of promises, and leave. We vote for the party [the respondent is a Peronist], and then the candidates do whatever they want. If Perón and Evita were to come back from the dead, they would be horrified by this government [Menem's]. (Male, married, forty-two years old, textile worker, Villa 20)

TABLE 5.13. Orientations toward Local Politicians

	Female (%)	Male (%)	Total (%)
Positive	3	3	3
Negative	15	20	18
"I don't know them"	79	74	76
DK/DA	3	3	3
Total	100 (n = 260)	100 (n = 246)	100 (N = 506)

Politicians are bad, bad people. They are only interested in making money, in doing their "own business," not in representing the people. (Female, divorced, twenty-eight years old, municipal employee, Barrio General Savio)

Politicians promise a lot before the elections, and then who can fi d them! (Female, fi y-nine years old, small business owner, Old Town)

I only know Larrosa [UCR councilman], the perfect *atorrante* [mix of thief, pretender, and liar]. The rest of the local politicians never show up. (Male, married, retired, sixty-four years old, Old Town)

Others complained that local politicians neither represented nor channeled residents' demands.

I prefer a leader instead of political parties. We pay for the existence of parties and the salary of the *concejales* [city councilmen] and congressmen. Is it worthwhile? I do not think so. (Male, married, thirty years old, self-employed textile worker, Villa 20)

If we don't struggle, we get nothing. Politicians are very dirty, they are interested only in themselves; once they are appointed, *Chau!!* [they disappear]. (Female, married, cleaning lady, thirty-five years old, Villa 20)

Politicians do not work as they should. Having representatives in Congress, we had to organize ourselves because there was no response from above. (Male, married, civil servant, thirty-one years old, Villa 20)

Through politicians you do not get *anything*. When political parties participate in community organization, everything gets upside down. We vote for a list of candidates we do not know. The fi st one in the list is always well known, but the rest are all *truchos* [pretenders]. Politicians believe they know everything and that people know nothing. They do whatever they want without any control, we have no information about their actions. (Male, married, fi y-three years old, self-employed construction worker, Villa 20)

The perceived misbehavior of local politicians provoked distrust and skepticism toward their parties.

Political parties should be institutions representing the voice of the people. The problem is not the institution but the politicians who destroy everything. (Female, married, housewife, forty years old, Barrio General Savio)

Parties represent nothing and nobody. All of them are *prendidos* [engaged] in some kind of illegal business. (Male, married, sixty-eight years old, small business owner, Old Town)

Political parties are not helpful at all. We asked local politicians for support when we were fi hting to have our streets paved, and do you know what their response was? All they wanted was to get us to sign up for their parties. (Male, married, retired, seventy-one years old, Old Town)

In summary, the data presented here show that in Villa Lugano popular orientations toward parties were divided, party identifi ation was quite high, and national and (especially) local politicians were highly distrusted.

CONDITIONS FOR DEMOCRATIC RULE: THE JUDICIARY

Is equal treatment by the judiciary a condition for saying that a country is truly democratic?[19] For Villa Lugano residents it certainly was. An overwhelming majority—89 percent—believed that an independent and fair judiciary was an important feature for defi ing a regime as democratic (table 5.14). On the other hand, when I asked whether the law was equally applied to all in Argentina, 98 percent responded negatively (table 5.15).[20]

Another theme that reflected the gap between people's expectations about the legal system and its actual operation was the lack of individual security in the neighborhood. When I asked what were the most important problems of Villa Lugano, 40 percent of the residents responded, spontaneously, "lack of security." Lugano residents placed second the problem of infrastructure (37 percent), an issue that, as we saw, had deeply shaped the history of the neighborhood (table 5.16).

According to the interviewees, lack of security was not only the result of an increasing rate of criminality. Carlos, a thirty-year-old informal textile worker, had come from Salta—one of the poorest states in

TABLE 5.14. Justice as a Condition for Democracy

Is Equal Treatment by Justice an Important Condition for Saying That a Country Is Democratic?	Female (%)	Male (%)	Total (%)
Yes	92	87	89
No	6	11	9
DA/DK	2	2	2
Total	100 (n = 260)	100 (n = 246)	100 (N = 506)

TABLE 5.15. Opinions on the Rule of Law in Argentina

Is the Law Equally Applied to All Today in Argentina?	Female (%)	Male (%)	Total (%)
Yes	3	1	2
No	97	98	98
DK/DA	–	1	–
Total	100 (n = 260)	100 (n = 246)	100 (N = 506)

TABLE 5.16. Perceptions of Neighborhood Security

What Are the Most Important Problems of the Neighborhood?	Female (%)	Male (%)	Total (%)
Security	34	44	40
Infrastructure	46	28	37
Other issues	20	26	22
DK/DA	–	2	1
Total	100 (n = 260)	100 (n = 246)	100 (N = 506)

northwestern Argentina—ten years ago. He was married to Ana, who was from Bolivia and pregnant. They lived and worked in Villa 20. For him, lack of security was mainly due to the malfunctioning of the legal system.

> The most important problem today is security. This is because the judiciary works poorly. The courts have been granting impunity to the military and also to the robbers.

Josefi a had been living in Villa 20 for six years. Before that she had lived in the middle-class neighborhood of Flores until she lost her job as hotel manager. She now worked as a temporary cleaning lady. She also participated in the shantytown representative organization. For her, lack of security was related to another important institution of the legal system: the police.

> With democracy I expected everything. To be able to work. We have a lot of things to resolve yet. For example, I expected protection from the police, and it is exactly the contrary! We are in the situation of having to protect ourselves *from* them. We are in democracy to be protected! (Female, married, thirty-six years old)

Another resident of Villa 20 explained the lack of security as a function of the social organization of the shantytown.

> The problem of security is very complex. Here in Villa 20 we do know who the bandits are. They are very young, you know them and their families too. Are you going to report them [to the police]? I don't think so. (Female, married, thirty-seven years old, waitress)

THE STATE AND ECONOMIC RESTRUCTURING

Since the mid-1970s, Argentina has experienced the hardships of neoliberal economic restructuring. The assumption that privatization, financial opening, and budget reduction would lead to a small, lean, and efficient state proved mistaken. Even though neoliberal discourse seems to have permeated in various ways the whole society, it is highly contested within the popular sectors.

Table 5.17 shows that Villa Lugano residents were aware of the need to change the role of the state.[21] However, there was no consensus regarding the state's profile. A majority—53 percent—agreed that the state should improve the way it functioned, but without reducing its budget or its size. A significant 38 percent, however, believed the state should reduce its expenditures and the number of its employees.

More striking are the results shown in table 5.18. There was no consensus regarding state control over the economy.[22] Among Villa Lugano residents 44 percent agreed that the state should control only some activities of the economy, but 47 percent believed that the state should have a lot of control over the economy. Only 5 percent agreed with the most extreme version of neoliberalism, that the state should not intervene in the economy at all.

The state was perceived by many respondents as the main tool for defending popular interests (32 percent, table 5.19 below).[23] However,

TABLE 5.17. Orientations toward the State: State Size

The State Should:	Female (%)	Male (%)	Total (%)
Disappear	1	2	2
Continue as it is	6	4	5
Greatly reduce its expenditures and the number of its employees	35	41	38
Not reduce expenditures or employees, but improve the way it functions	54	52	53
Other	2	1	1
DK/DA	2	–	1
Total	100 (n = 260)	100 (n = 246)	100 (N = 506)

TABLE 5.18. Orientations toward the State: State Role in the Economy

To Solve Economic Problems, the State Should:	Female (%)	Male (%)	Total (%)
Have a lot of control over the economy	54	39	47
Intervene only in some activities of the economy	37	51	44
Not intervene in the economy	5	6	5
DK/DA	4	4	4
Total	100	100	100
	(n = 260)	(n = 246)	(N = 506)

about 60 percent had a negative view of the state: 35 percent agreed that it was a group of bureaucrats who defended only their own interests, while 23 percent perceived the state as a means for the rich to oppress the poor. The data presented in this section again show fragmented political orientations, far from the quite homogeneous picture one would expect from prevailing views about the Argentine popular sectors.

DEMOCRACY, DEVELOPMENT, AND CAPITALISM

Is democracy without economic development preferable to economic development under authoritarian rule? This was another contested issue among Villa Lugano respondents.[24] Thirty-nine percent valued democracy per se over economic development (table 5.20). But over one-third (36 percent) preferred economic development even at the price of not having democracy. Also a significant 25 percent believed that democracy and development were equally important and could be achieved at the same time. This is a response I would like to stress, since in the questionnaire the option of jointly having democracy and development was not included.

TABLE 5.19. Orientations toward the State: State Definitio

The Argentine State Is:	Female (%)	Male (%)	Total (%)
A group of bureaucrats who defend only their own interests	38	33	35
A means of oppressing the poor	21	25	23
The main guarantee for defendin popular interests	32	32	32
Hard to say	5	8	7
None	1	1	1
DK/DA	3	1	2
Total	100 (n = 260)	100 (n = 246)	100 (N = 506)

TABLE 5.20. Development and Democracy

With What Sentence Do You Agree the Most?	Female (%)	Male (%)	Total (%)
The most important thing i economic development, even if without democracy	38	33	36
The most important thing i democracy, even if with little economic development	37	40	39
Both things are equally important[a]	24	27	25
DA/DK	1	–	–
Total	100 (n = 260)	100 (n = 246)	100 (N = 506)

[a] Not a stimulated response.

Furthermore, the qualitative data suggest that residents perceived democracy not only as compatible with economic development but also as the best way to achieve it.

> I believe in democracy with economic development. The military had all the power to fix the economy, and they failed. Now we have to give the chance to democracy. (Married, thirty years old, informal textile worker, Villa 20)

> I think democracy is a tool to improve everything. We still have a long way to go. Argentina has many problems to resolve, but I am convinced that with *freedom* the economy will improve. (Married, fi y-five years old, employee in a private fi m, Old Town)

Although it is generally agreed that the popular sectors in Argentina have supported a capitalist model of economic development (e.g., Di Tella 1965), my qualitative and survey data indicate that capitalists themselves were highly distrusted by Villa Lugano residents and were not perceived as the driving force of national development (table 5.21).[25] More than two-thirds (79 percent) of the lower-class residents interviewed said that capitalists sought benefits only for themselves; 12 percent believed that, in doing so, capitalists also contributed to the development of the country; and only a tiny fraction (9 percent) saw capitalists as the main contributors to the development of the country.

TABLE 5.21. Perceptions of Capitalists

Capitalists:	Female (%)	Male (%)	Total (%)
Attempt to contribute to national development	7	10	9
Only want to obtain personal benefit	82	77	79
Both	11	13	12
DK/DA	–	–	–
Total	100 (n = 260)	100 (n = 246)	100 (N = 506)

Data from the qualitative interviews corroborate these results. José lived in Barrio General Savio. Like many of his neighbors, he was a municipal employee. For him, capitalists were

> all thieves, they are the powerful. They can drive the country to wherever they want. (Male, married, forty-six years old)

For other residents, things were more complex:

> It is relative, it depends on the type of business. Capitalists take care, fi st of all, of their *bolsillo* [pockets]. A good example is the multinational corporations: they leave the country whenever being here is not good business anymore. For me that's fi e. (Male, married, thirty years old, informal textile worker, Villa 20)

> It depends: if capitalists are national capitalists, I think they contribute to national development. But if they are foreign monopolies, they work for their own country. (Male, married, fi y-five years old, employed in a private company, Old Town)

ATTITUDES TOWARD UNIONS

Villa Lugano residents distrusted not only professional politicians and capitalists but also unions and their leaders.[26] Sixty-four percent of respondents had a negative opinion of unions; of these 20 percent spontaneously added that unions should not exist as institutions. Only 12 percent had a positive opinion, and 13 percent discriminated between "good and bad" unions (table 5.22).

To complement this picture, 46 percent of the interviewees believed that unions' political power should decrease, and 30 percent that it should stay the same (table 5.23).[27] These results are rather striking, since unions had been severely weakened not only by changes in the socioeconomic structure but also by the military and Menem governments' labor policies.

Corruption, collusive bargaining with employers, and lack of support during strikes were the reasons most often mentioned for distrusting unions and their leaders.

TABLE 5.22. Orientations toward Unions

What Is Your Opinion about Unions?	Female (%)	Male (%)	Total (%)
Positive	14	11	12
Negative	59	69	64
Good and bad unions	16	10	13
DK/DA	11	10	11
Total	100 (n = 260)	100 (n = 246)	100 (N = 506)

TABLE 5.23. Opinions on Unions' Power

The Political Power of the Unions Should:	Female (%)	Male (%)	Total (%)
Increase	12	11	11
Stay the same	31	29	30
Decrease	42	51	46
DK/DA	15	9	13
Total	100 (n = 260)	100 (n = 246)	100 (N = 506)

I belonged to the union because it was compulsory. I only wasted my time. Unions are not useful at all. The *delegados* [workplace representatives] asked us to go on strike and then . . . the *patrón* [employer] did not pay us the lost days. (Male, married, thirty years old, self-employed textile worker, Villa 20)

Unions are not useful at all. The leaders sell themselves for a *choripán* [a sausage sandwich]. They manipulate the rank and file. Before, unions did not exist and the workers still survived. (Male, married, twenty-six years old, formal metalworker, Villa 20)

For some, unions simply should not exist.

> The unions never listen to the workers. The leaders work for themselves, and nothing more. The *delegados* show up only before the elections and then, see you later, much later! I think unions are not necessary, they compulsorily retain part of your salary, and then we have to discuss alone with the *patrón* because they are too busy to defend us. (Male, married, forty-two years old, textile worker, Villa 20)

> Today unions are not useful at all. There is a lot of politics, and personal interests among the leaders. (Female, married, forty-five years old, salesperson, Barrio General Savio)

> The union leaders are too "married" to business. That's why they don't defend the workers anymore. (Male, single, twenty-four years old, employee, Barrio General Savio)

Although respondents recognize the failures of leadership, a few of them still perceive unions as the only tool available for improving the workers' situation.

> I think unions should exist. When I was a member, they helped the workers. Now nobody supports the workers, not even the unions. (Male, widower, sixty-two years old, self-employed construction worker, Villa 20)

> The situation is terrible. We have to change old minds: the present top union leaders are the Italian "Mafia." They have forgotten the workers, they work only for their personal benefit. I feel betrayed as a member of the workers' movement. (Male, married, fi y-five years old, self-employed cook, retired, ex-metalworker, Barrio General Savio)

> It is a shame, not the union as an institution, but the leaders. My union doesn't exist anymore. Since Menem was elected president, unions have been no more than another branch of the government. (Male, married, forty-six years old, municipal employee, Barrio General Savio)

> Sometimes the unions help you, sometimes they do business with the *patrón*. But I believe unions are necessary; otherwise, what are we workers going to do alone? (Female, divorced, thirty-three years old, factory worker, Villa 20)

ATTITUDES TOWARD POLITICAL PARTICIPATION

One important characteristic of delegative democracy is delegation. In a broad sense, delegation points to a narrow conception of citizenship participation. The role of citizens is just to participate in elections, after which officials should rule with little or no interference, either from other institutions or from citizens. I asked Villa Lugano residents if they agreed with the statement "Citizens have the opportunity to participate in politics by voting in elections. Then it is up to the president to rule the country the way she/he judges best."[28] As table 5.24 shows, 40 percent of the interviewees totally agreed with the statement, while 37 percent totally disagreed.

In contrast, an overwhelming majority believed that people should get together and act collectively on issues at the local level. Almost three-quarters (74 percent) of respondents agreed that neighbors should get together to solve neighborhood problems, and only 17 percent said the authorities should be left in harge of the solutions (table 5.25).[29]

TABLE 5.24. Orientations toward Citizen Participation

Citizens Participate by Voting in Elections, the Rest Up to President	Female (%)	Male (%)	Total (%)
Totally agree	40	41	40
Partially agree	16	11	14
Depends	–	2	1
Partially disagree	6	6	6
Totally disagree	35	38	37
DK/DA	3	2	2
Total	100 (n = 260)	100 (n = 246)	100 (N = 506)

While people agreed on the need to act collectively on local issues, they were divided on strategy. When asked what would be the best strategy, 43 percent cited demonstrations, 24 percent cited written petitions to authorities through an organization, and 18 percent cited personal contacts (table 5.26).[30]

These differences became more evident when I asked if neighborhood organizations should have close relationships with political parties

TABLE 5.25. Orientations toward Citizen Participation in the Neighborhood

Should Citizens Meet to Solve Neighborhood Problems?	*Female (%)*	*Male (%)*	*Total (%)*
Neighbors should meet	77	70	74
Leave the problem to authorities	16	17	17
Not worth the effor	1	1	1
Other	6	11	7
DK/DA	–	1	1
Total	100 (n = 260)	100 (n = 246)	100 (N = 506)

TABLE 5.26. Best Neighborhood Participation Strategy

Best Participation Strategy?	*Female (%)*	*Male (%)*	*Total (%)*
Mobilization	46	40	43
Petition	22	25	24
Personal contacts	18	18	18
Other	11	16	13
DK/DA	3	1	2
Total	100 (n = 260)	100 (n = 246)	100 (N = 506)

and/or the government to be more successful.[31] Half of the interviewees said popular organizations should have either limited or no relations at all with political parties (table 5.27). Again, responses were significantly divided. A similar division can be observed in the case of popular organizations' relationships with the government: 44 percent of interviewees said these should be limited or nonexistent (table 5.28).[32]

TABLE 5.27. Relations between Neighborhood Organizations and Political Parties

Relations between Neighborhood Organizations and Political Parties	Female (%)	Male (%)	Total (%)
Close	48	46	47
Limited	32	27	30
No relations	17	25	21
DK/DA	3	2	2
Total	100 (n = 260)	100 (n = 246)	100 (N = 506)

TABLE 5.28. Relations between Neighborhood Organizations and Government

Relations between Neighborhood Organizations and the Government	Female (%)	Male (%)	Total (%)
Close	52	54	53
Limited	27	22	24
No relations	18	22	20
DK/DA	3	2	3
Total	100 (n = 260)	100 (n = 246)	100 (N = 506)

*   *   *

The data presented in this chapter show that, regarding democratic institutions, political participation (national and local), and the role of the state, the political orientations of the urban popular sectors in Villa Lugano were deeply fragmented. Although there was rather widespread support for democracy and representative politics, there was also broad acceptance of delegative political views and practices. Issues such as economic restructuring and the role of the state further illustrate diverging political orientations among the respondents. Perhaps more importantly, the combination of survey and qualitative interview data suggests that, while the former are fundamental for gaining an overall view of opinion distribution, the latter provide contextualizing cues without which the multiple—and often ambiguous—meanings of democracy cannot be grasped. Hence, we should reject the assumption that the political culture of the urban poor is homogeneous, and we should ask how its heterogeneity may affect framing capabilities for mobilization at the grassroots.

To answer this question in the next chapter I delve further into popular political culture and ask what cleavages regarding participation and representation existed in Villa Lugano, what factors accounted for them, and how they may have hindered the CVL in putting forward a high-resonance frame of meaning.

CHAPTER 6

Discursive Dilemmas

In the previous chapter, I discussed the political orientations of Villa Lugano's residents. The data showed that these orientations are far from homogeneous. Indeed, opinions on issues such as strategies of local participation, political parties, the model of democracy, economic development, and the role of the state are significantly divided. The presence of contested issues within the realm of popular political culture is challenging for the framing activities of grassroots and social movements. This is even more so when movements' claim-making activities involve not just one but several public goods, some of which cut across the diversity of poverty, as was the case for the CVL in Villa Lugano. A high-resonance frame of meaning is crucial for the success of any social movement, but the probability of achieving it largely depends upon how fi mly movements' discourses are grounded in popular culture. When salient political cleavages are present in popular culture, those in charge of movements' framing activities face what I refer to as a *discursive dilemma*. By this I mean that if central aspects of popular culture are contested (as evidence from Villa Lugano suggests), decisions on what themes to include or exclude from a movement's discourse involve important trade-offs that may affect the chances of achieving a high-resonance frame and, ultimately, the movement's success. In its most general form a dilemma is an argument presenting at least two equally conclusive alternatives. In practice it usually implies a choice between at least two alternatives equally undesirable: $A \supset C$, $B \supset C$, $A \vee B$, therefore C, where ⊃ "if . . . then," and ∨ "either . . . or." A caveat is in order before proceeding with this line of argument. The heterogeneity of popular political opinions is not per se an obstacle to building a high-resonance discourse.[1] Indeed, heterogeneity of political opinions can be a valuable resource in the formation of broader discourses with strong appeal. But in general sharply divided political opinions make the framing activities of popular movements very challenging. Furthermore, in a context of adverse political opportunities and organizational weakness, these difficulties may prove fatal for a popular movement's survival.

In this chapter I discuss these issues by exploring some of the most salient and contested political cleavages in popular culture in Villa Lugano: strategies of local participation, the meaning of democracy, political (mis)trust, and the role of the state. I also look into the factors that may account for these cleavages, especially the effects of Villa Lugano's peculiar geography and how this, in turn, posed a discursive dilemma for the CVL. The question I am most interested in is whether social and political cleavages among the poor in Villa Lugano are placed based and, more specifically, if they are rooted in local territorial traditions. As we saw in chapter 3, Villa Lugano's geography reflects three distinctive settlement patterns, crystallized in well-defi ed neighborhood zones. These patterns entail a settlement history (how people gained access to their homes) and a particular view of territory, of land ownership, and, above all, of who has the right to live in the vicinity and, ultimately, in the city. Are cleavages in popular political culture place based? Does settlement in a particular zone of Villa Lugano affect residents' political views? If each zone of Villa Lugano has a distinctive political subculture, how does this affect the framing capabilities of popular movements and their eventual success in this and similar neighborhoods? In sum, if political cleavages are largely place based, what lessons can be drawn about how this might affect the sustainability and the scaling up of popular collective action in an urban setting?[2] As we saw, the CVL emerged out of one zone of Villa Lugano, Old Town, with a high-resonance frame of meaning centered on citizenship rights—more precisely, on the citizens-as-taxpayers' "right to the city." But after its emergence the CVL attempted to reach all zones of the neighborhood. Exploring the CVL's discursive dilemmas involved in scaling up claim making to other zones of Villa Lugano may shed light on the challenges for urban popular organization and networking throughout the city of Buenos Aires, a city that, despite its contentiousness, has not fulfilled its potential as a progressive urban space. It may also shed light on the crucial and often neglected effects of geography and territory on contentious politics.

To answer these questions I proceed sequentially. First, I further explore the political and social cleavages in popular culture in Villa Lugano described in chapter 5 by reducing the dimensionality of the survey data into a few components representing the main dimensions of variation in popular political culture (the dependent variables). To do so, I use optimal scaling (hereafter OS), a set of procedures designed for categorical data analysis and commonly referred to as the Gifi system of descriptive multivariate analysis (Gifi 1990; Van de Geer 1993a, 1993b; Michailidis and de Leeuw 1998).[3] Second, I model the determinants (the independent variables) of these dimensions using regression analysis (OLS, binary logistic and ordinal logit). In a third and fi al step, I discuss the statistical fi dings on political and social cleavages in popular culture in relation to the CVL's framing activities and the discursive dilemmas it faced.

IN SEARCH OF POPULAR POLITICAL CLEAVAGES

The relevant cleavages in popular political culture are many, and no study can completely and exhaustively address all of them. Decisions on what dimensions to explore depend as much on the research questions as on the political and social milieu in which they are enmeshed. The dimensions or cleavages I explore below derive from my direct participant observation of the activities of the CVL in Villa Lugano and the survey fi dings already presented; they provide a window to look into the realm of popular culture, one that in my view explains in large part the nature of grassroots participation in the city of Buenos Aires.

Strategies of Local Participation

In chapter 5, survey data showed that while an overwhelming majority of Villa Lugano residents believe people should get together to act collectively on local issues, they are significantly divided on which strategy is best to follow (tables 5.25 and 5.26). Strategies of participation are a crucial resource for mounting and sustaining contentious collective action. Disagreements over strategies can lead to the demise of grassroots organizations and social movements, even if goals are clear and widely accepted by most members and followers. The statistical analysis of the survey data yields two main dimensions of variation (or summary variables) on local strategies of participation (see chapter appendix, table 6A.1). I refer to the fi st dimension as *autonomous participation*. It summarizes the attitudinal survey items on whether neighborhood organizations should have close relationships and cooperate with political parties as well as with the government to be successful. The more procooperation the attitude, the lower the score obtained on the autonomous participation variable.

The second dimension of variation I refer to as *mobilization versus clientelism*. It summarizes attitudinal survey items on whether people think they should get together and act collectively to solve neighborhood problems or think they should just make personal contacts either with government officials or politicians. The more promobilization the attitude, the higher the score obtained on this dimension (see chapter appendix, table 6A.1).

On Democracy

We saw also in chapter 5 that on the meaning of democracy Villa Lugano residents hold rather diverse and sometimes confl cting opinions. This is especially true with regard to delegative democratic practices. To explore these opinions and make sense of them conceptually, I combined survey items designed to address delegative democratic practices with more conventional questions about basic democratic attributes. The statistical analysis yields two main dimensions of variation (see chapter appendix, table 6A.2). There is a clear distinction between a model of liberal representative democracy and a model of delegative democracy. The liberal model includes free and fair elections plus some basic conditions for the existence of a democratic regime qua regime, or what O'Donnell (2004) has referred to as the "surrounding freedoms" of a democratic regime, such as the existence of two or more political parties, freedom of association, freedom of speech, and so on.

The delegative model appeals to national unity and condones the executive's breaking of the law if "necessary" and/or overruling of decisions by Congress or the courts.

Political Mistrust

Another aspect within the realm of popular culture that I explore is political mistrust. As I mentioned previously, since the publication of Robert Putnam's *Making Democracy Work* (1993) the effect of political trust/mistrust on the quality of democracy has been much debated. Putnam's thesis that trust in others and trust in government are related and that, in turn, they constitute the grounding of a healthy democracy can be traced back to the "civic culture" tradition in U.S. political science (Almond and Verba 1963).

More recently this tradition, as reinvented in Putnam's thesis, has come under attack. Drawing on classic political liberalism, several scholars have forcefully argued (Hardin 1999, 2002; Cook, Hardin, and Levi 2005) that well-functioning democracies are based more upon *mistrust* than trust in government. They argue that trust in others or interpersonal trust is at best weakly related to the quality of democracy. I will return to this topic in the next chapter, but in brief, the issue of how much trust or mistrust is necessary to make democracy work is a matter of thresholds: once mistrust (social or political) becomes hostility (social or political), collective action and the quality of democracy are severely hindered.

By way of statistical analysis I arrive at three dimensions of political mistrust (see chapter appendix, table 6A.3). The fi st dimension of variation I refer to as *political (mis)trust* proper. It summarizes opinions on political parties, the state, and satisfaction with democracy. A second dimension of variation relates only to the issue of the coercive eviction of shantytowns from the city. Throughout the political history of Buenos Aires, there have been many attempts (mainly but not only by military governments) to "clean up" the city by expelling shantytown dwellers to its periphery under the argument that they are people of low moral standard, if not criminals. I use this dimension as a proxy for social hostility toward shantytowns and refer to it as *social (mis)trust*. A third dimension concerns views on local politicians; I refer to it as *local political (mis)trust*.

On the State

The fi al aspect of popular culture I want to explore in terms of potential effects on the CVL's framing activities is the meaning and role of the state. Scholars of collective action and social movements give a central role to perceptions of the state in the dynamics of mobilization. These perceptions create a series of (dis)incentives to act collectively. The survey items I employ for statistical analysis cover opinions on the state's social functions, role in the economy, and size. Recall from chapter 5 that most respondents (53 percent) agreed with the option that the state "should not reduce its size but improve the way it works," followed by the option that the state "should greatly reduce its expenditures and the number of its employees" (38 percent). The options "The state should continue as it is" and "The state should disappear" were chosen by only small percentages.

On the measure asking, "What is the Argentine state?" a proxy for the state's role in society, a significant number of respondents (32 percent) chose the option that the state was "the main guarantee for defending popular interests," but most respondents had a negative view, responding either that "the state is a group of bureaucrats who defend only their own interests" (35 percent) or that "the state is a means of oppressing the poor" (23 percent).

Finally, on the role of the state in the economy, 47 percent of respondents stated that the state should have "a lot of control on the economy." However, a significant number of respondents (44 percent) responded that the state "should intervene only in some activities of the economy." A marginal number responded that the state "should not intervene in the economy." These survey items constitute three clear-cut dimensions: state role in society, state role in the economy, and state size (see chapter appendix). The three dimensions refer to an ordinal pro-/antistate cleavage among Villa Lugano residents.

Summary

The statistical analysis using optimal scaling reduced the dimensionality of the survey data in a meaningful way. I defi ed two dimensions of variation or summary variables that contained most of the relevant information on Villa Lugano residents' orientations on local strategies of participation: *autonomous participation* and *mobilization versus clientelism*. On national political issues, optimal scaling helped defi e two dimensions of variation on democracy: *liberal democracy* and *delegative democracy*. Regarding mistrust, I defi ed the variables *political mistrust, social mistrust,* and *local political mistrust*. Regarding the state, three dimensions are relevant: *state size, state role in society,* and *state role in the economy*.

In the next section I turn to statistical analysis for exploring the determinants of the dimensions of variation or cleavages in Villa Lugano's political culture. I test the effects of social structural covariates as well as of geographical space-as-location. Finally, I speculate on how political and social cleavages in popular culture affect the framing capabilities of grassroots movements and organizations.

MODELING POPULAR POLITICAL CULTURE

To explore the determinants of popular political culture I tested two alternative models for each of the dimensions discussed in the above section. I was mostly interested in testing the effects of neighborhood zone as a determinant of political and social cleavages in popular culture. Notice that *zone* is a proxy for what I have referred to previously as "settlement patterns," defi ed as the process by which Villa Lugano residents gained access to their homes in the neighborhood and how this, in turn, may have influenced their conceptions of territory, land, and, more broadly, citizenship rights. Recall from the discussion of chapter 3 that one of the most striking features of Villa Lugano is its spatial fragmentation. Five shantytowns, various state-built high-rise condominiums, and an older area (Old Town) of low-cost privately owned houses make up the neighborhood. I included in the survey sample Old Town (a low-cost housing neighborhood), Villa 20 (a shantytown), and Barrio General Savio (a state-built high-rise). Besides Old Town, which I sampled in its entirety in the survey, I decided to include Villa 20 and Barrio General Savio because of their physical proximity and their rather longtime presence in Villa Lugano (dating back to the late 1960s).

For all the dimensions of popular culture (or dependent summary variables), models 1 and 2 tested for the effects of gender (1 = female,

0 = male); type of employment (1 = manual, 0 = otherwise); labor relations (1 = informal work, 0 = otherwise); hostile view of neighbors (1 = hostile view of neighbors, 0 = no hostile view of neighbors); union exposure (1 = yes, 0 = no); neighborhood activism (1 = yes, 0 = no); immigrant (1 = yes, 0 = no); and education (1 = low, 2 = medium; 3 = high).[4] The zone variable originally included three categories (1 = Villa 20; 2 = Barrio General Savio; 3 = Old Town). It was recoded into a series of dummy variables: zone 1 (1 = Villa 20, 0 = otherwise); zone 2 (1 = Barrio General Savio, 0 = otherwise); and zone 3 (1 = Old Town, 0 = otherwise). The models exclude the dummy variable zone 3 (1 = Old Town, 0 = otherwise) to avoid perfect collinearity. Zone 3 performs then as the "reference category" against which comparisons across zones are made.

In addition, model 1 tests for the effects of "Peronist" party identification (1 = yes, 0 = otherwise) and model 2 for effects of "Radical" party identification (1 = yes, 0 = otherwise).

Strategies of Local Participation

Both models show the significance of zone as a predictor of autonomous participation (table 6.1). Furthermore, among all predictors zone is the most statistically significant in both models (being an activist and being a manual worker are also significant predictors, at $p < 0.05$). One aspect I was interested in testing was the comparative spatial distribution of opinions, especially how opinions in Old Town (zone 3) differed from those in Villa 20 (zone 1). The reason to test for these effects was that residents in these two zones were the ones most involved in the mobilization of the neighborhood. We see that compared to Old Town (zone 3), people living in Villa 20 (zone 1) had a more autonomous view of local participation: they were less prone to take as positive cooperation of popular organizations with parties and government officials. People in Barrio General Savio (zone 2) held similar opinions to those of the Old Town, so people in these zones (2 and 3) held a less autonomous view of local participation than people in Villa 20 (zone 1). This is an important part of the puzzle to explain the decline of CVL, since it reflects differing views of Villa 20 residents versus Old Town residents on the best strategies for acting collectively on local issues.[5]

TABLE 6.1. OLS Regression on Autonomous Participation (Local Politics)

Independent Variables	Model 1	Model 2
(Constant)	-.052	-.011
	(.291)	(.284)
Female	-.095	-.112
	(.095)	(.095)
Manual worker	-.279**	-.293**
	(.129)	(.129)
Informal worker	-.098	-.113
	(.127)	(.128)
Hostile	.125	.136
	(.099)	(.099)
Union exposure	-.057	-.064
	(.117)	(.116)
Activist	-.363**	-.357**
	(145)	(.144)
Immigrant	.060	.046
	(.140)	(.136)
Education	.016	-.018
	(.080)	(.080)
Peronist	-.024	
(PJ)	(.132)	
Radical		-.245
(UCR)		(.185)
Zone 1		
Shantytown	.544***	.547***
(Villa 20)	(.145)	(.144)
Zone 2		
Housing Project	.084	.083
(Barrio G. Savio)	(.112)	(.111)
No. of observations	473	473
R-square	.056	.059
F-change[a]		
(zones 1 and 2)	7.311***	7.504***

Note: Standard errors are between parentheses. Tolerance levels are above .558 for model 1 and .563 for model 2.

[a] The F-change statistic indicates the significance of the model after the dummy variables zone 1 and zone2 are entered in the analysis.

*p <.1; **p <. 05; ***p < .01.

While most residents of Villa Lugano, independently of the zone in which they lived, had a participatory view of local politics, the results of regression analysis for the mobilization versus clientelism variable shows again that zone was the most important predictor of differences in opinion on this matter. This happened in both models (table 6.2 below). Furthermore, people living in Villa 20 (zone 1) held promobilization opinions similar to those of their neighbors in the Old Town (zone 3), while residents of Barrio General Savio (zone 2) were the least likely to have promobilization opinions. So in this case, and in contrast to the fi dings on autonomous participation, the two most active zones of Villa Lugano, Villa 20 and Old Town (zones 1 and 3), agreed that mobilization was the most useful strategy to solve neighborhood problems. This is an interesting fi ding because shantytowns have been often portrayed as passive reservoirs of clientelism. The other predictor worth mentioning is union exposure, which had a positive significant effect on the strategy of mobilization versus clientelism in local politics (at the 0.05 level).

TABLE 6.2. OLS Regression on Mobilization versus Clientelism (Local Politics)

Independent Variables	Model 1	Model 2
(Constant)	-.165	-.159
	(.295)	(.287)
Female	.092	.098
	(.095)	(.096)
Manual worker	.085	.091
	(.130)	(.130)
Informal worker	.073	.078
	(.128)	(.129)
Hostile	-.071	-.076
	(.100)	(.100)
Union exposure	.281**	.289**
	(.118)	(.117)
Activist	.157	.160
	(146)	(.145)

TABLE 6.2. OLS Regression on Mobilization versus Clientelism
(Local Politics) *(cont.)*

Independent Variables	Model 1	Model 2
Immigrant	-.057	-.061
	(.141)	(.139)
Education	.096	.093
	(.081)	(.080)
Peronist	.051	
(PJ)	(.133)	
Radical		.098
(UCR)		(.187)
Zone 1		
Shantytown	.069	.073
(Villa 20)	(.146)	(.145)
Zone 2		
Housing Project	-.354***	-.355***
(Barrio G. Savio)	(.112)	(.112)
No. of observations	473	473
R-square	.048	.048
F-change		
(zones 1 and 2)	6.480***	6.624***

Note: Standard errors are between parentheses. Tolerance levels are above .558 for model 1
and .563 for model 2.

*p < .1; **p < .05; ***p < .01.

Zone, then, was a significant predictor for both strategies of participation in local politics, autonomous participation and mobilization.
Furthermore, the most significant cleavage for the purpose of my argument was the one between Villa 20 (zone 1) and Old Town (zone 3) over
the best strategy of participation: neighbors of Villa 20 (zone 1) scored
higher than those of Old Town (zone 3) on the autonomous participation variable. We can conclude that cooperation with political parties
and government officials—the preferred option in Old Town—was a
potentially divisive issue among zones in Villa Lugano. Notice that the
CVL was emphatic on the positive role of cooperation with all political
parties, government officials, and local representatives.

On Democracy

Liberal Democracy

An overwhelming majority of Villa Lugano residents agreed upon a model of democracy that included a basic set of freedoms as necessary conditions to defi e a political regime as "democratic." These basic conditions of liberal democracy as defi ed by the survey questionnaire were not a highly contested issue among Villa Lugano's neighbors.[6] Still, table 6.3 below shows that place-based effects were at work: zone was a significant predictor for this dimension of popular culture. Compared to Old Town (zone 3), both Villa 20 (zone 1) and Barrio General Savio (zone 2) residents scored lower; their conception of democracy was more limited and did not include the full range of freedoms presented to them by the survey. Other important predictors were gender, type of labor market participation, and union exposure. Being female, being informally employed, and having had some union exposure were all positively associated with a high score on the liberal democracy variable.

TABLE 6.3. OLS Regression on Liberal Democracy

Independent Variables	Model 1	Model 2
(Constant)	.398	.311
	(.272)	(.266)
Female	.243***	.262***
	(.088)	(.089)
Manual worker	-.073	-.060
	(.122)	(.122)
Informal worker	.308***	.325***
	(.119)	(.119)
Hostile	.009	-.002
	(.092)	(.092)
Union exposure	.357***	.357***
	(.108)	(.108)
Activist	-.331**	-.346**
	(.134)	(.133)

TABLE 6.3. OLS Regression on Liberal Democracy (*cont.*)

Independent Variables	Model 1	Model 2
Immigrant	.051	.081
	(.133)	(.130)
Education	-.129*	-.121
	(.076)	(.076)
Peronist	-.051	
(PJ)	(.120)	
Radical		.256
(UCR)		(.170)
Zone 1	-.237*	-.249*
Shantytown	(.134)	(.133)
(Villa 20)		
Zone 2	-.867***	-.869**
Housing project	(.103)	(.103)
(Barrio G. Savio)		
No. of observations	461	461
R-square	.209	.213
F-change		
(zones 1 and 2)	36.170***	36.374***

Note: Standard errors are between parentheses. Tolerance levels are above .563 for model 1 and .570 for model 2.

*p < .1; **p < .05; ***p < .01.

Delegative Democracy

We saw in the previous chapter that, taken individually, survey items related to delegative democracy had a quite polarized distribution. This same polarization was seen in the distribution of opinions of the delegative democracy summary variable.[7] But the polarization could not be explained in this case by place-based effects. Zone was not a significant predictor for the delegative democracy variable (table 6.4). In model 1, gender and education were significant predictors. Being female was positively associated with supporting delegative democracy,

Table 6.4. OLS Regression on Delegative Democracy

Independent Variables	Model 1	Model 2
(Constant)	-.497*	-.634**
	(.287)	(.280)
Female	-.290***	-.258***
	(.093)	(.093)
Manual worker	.005	.028
	(.129)	(.128)
Informal worker	-.030	-.001
	(.126)	(.126)
Hostile	-.177*	-.195**
	(.097)	(.097)
Union exposure	-.066	-.066
	(.115)	(.113)
Activist	.276*	.254*
	(.142)	(.140)
Immigrant	-.121	-.073
	(.141)	(.137)
Education	.405***	.418***
	(.081)	(.080)
Peronist	-.066	
(PJ)	(.127)	
Radical		.445**
(UCR)		(.179)
Zone 1	-.128	-.145
Shantytown	(.142)	(.140)
(Villa 20)		
Zone 2	-.064	-.066
Housing project	(.109)	(.108)
(Barrio G. Savio)		
No. of observations	461	461
R-square	.110	.122
F-change		
(zones 1 and 2)	.447	.570

Note: Standard errors are between parentheses. Tolerance levels are above .563 for model 1 and .570 for model 2.

*p < .1; **p < .05; ***p < .01.

while higher educational attainment (as one might intuitively expect) was negatively associated: the higher the level of education, the less support for a delegative kind of democracy. This was also true in model 2, with the additional fi ding that in this model party affiliation did matter: being a Radical Party sympathizer was negatively associated with supporting delegative democracy. I conclude, then, that even though delegative democracy is a contested issue within popular political culture, it is not a place-based cleavage and hence is not a potential obstacle for framing activities at the grassroots, as the three previous issues are.

Political Mistrust

As in the case of delegative democracy, we see that zone was not a significant predictor for the variable of political mistrust in either model (table 6.5). Education was the most significant covariate (at the 0.01 level): the higher the level of education, the lower the score on political mistrust. Being an immigrant was also positively associated (at the 0.05 level) with lower levels of political mistrust. Being informally employed and expressing hostility toward neighbors were positively associated with higher levels of political mistrust (at the 0.05 level).

Two fi al dimensions are worth mentioning before turning to the discussion on the state: *local political mistrust,* summarizing opinions of local politicians, and *social mistrust,* a proxy for social hostility that measures support for the settlement or the displacement of shantytown dwellers.

For the latter issue (settlement versus displacement of shantytown dwellers in the city of Buenos Aires), zone is indeed a significant predictor (table 6.6).[8] As one might expect, differences across zones show that compared to the Old Town (zone 3), those living in Villa 20 (zone 1) as well as in Barrio General Savio (zone 2) are more supportive of the settlement of shantytowns. I will deal with this issue further in the next chapter on social hostility, but notice that education is positively associated with settlement (the higher the level of education the greater the likelihood of being in favor of settlement), while union exposure is negatively associated.

TABLE 6.5. OLS Regression on Political Mistrust

Independent Variables	Model 1	Model 2
(Constant)	-.803***	-.668**
	(.292)	(.287)
Female	-.134	-.142
	(.094)	(.095)
Manual worker	.028	.028
	(.129)	(.130)
Informal worker	-.256**	-.265**
	(.128)	(.129)
Hostile	-.235**	-.231**
	(.099)	(.100)
Union exposure	.036	.058
	(.117)	(.117)
Activist	.030	.057
	(.144)	(.144)
Immigrant	.292**	.237*
	(.141)	(.139)
Education	.276***	.257***
	(.081)	(.081)
Peronist	.214	
(PJ)	(.132)	
Radical		-.089
(UCR)		(.186)
Zone1	.061	.088
Shantytown	(.144)	(.144)
(Villa 20)		
Zone 2	.093	.090
Housing project	(.112)	(.112)
(Barrio G. Savio)		
No. of observations	472	472
R-square	.062	.057
F-change		
(zones 1 and 2)	.354	.379

Note: Standard errors are between parentheses. Tolerance levels are above .561 for model 1 and .567 for model 2.

*p < .1; **p < .05; ***p < .01.

TABLE 6.6. OLS Regression on Social Mistrust (Settlement vs. Eviction)

Independent Variables	Model 1	Model 2
(Constant)	-.811***	-.843***
	(.291)	(.285)
Female	.010	.023
	(0.94)	(.094)
Manual worker	.051	.062
	(.128)	(.129)
Informal worker	-.018	-.006
	(.127)	(.127)
Hostile	-.047	-.055
	(.099)	(.099)
Union exposure	-.264**	-.258**
	(.117)	(.116)
Activist	-.016	-.020
	(.143)	(.142)
Immigrant	.194	.204
	(.140)	(.137)
Education	.170**	.171**
	(.081)	(.080)
Peronist	.020	
(PJ)	(.131)	
Radical		.195
(UCR)		(.184)
Zone 1	.385***	.384***
Shantytown	(.143)	(.142)
(Villa 20)		
Zone 2	.500***	.498***
Housing project	(.111)	(.111)
(Barrio G. Savio)		
No. of observations	472	472
R-square	.073	.075
F-change		
(zones 1 and 2)	10.755***	10.675***

Note: Standard errors are between parentheses. Tolerance levels are above .561 for model 1 and .567 for model 2.

*p < .1; **p < .05; ***p < .01.

On the other hand, table 6.7 shows that opinions about local politicians cannot be explained by the effects of zone. In model 1, being an activist and being an immigrant are positively associated with more favorable views of local politicians and less local political mistrust. Model 2 shows that self-identification as a supporter of the Radical Party is also associated with these views.

On the State

State Size

Zone is not a significant predictor on opinions about state size. Table 6.8 shows the ordered logit results for the state size variable. Union exposure is the most significant predictor (at the 0.01 level), along with, but to a lesser extent, hostility toward neighbors (at the 0.05 level) and level of education (at 0.1 level). Union exposure increases the probability of an answer in the higher categories of the dependent variable, in this case having pro-state preferences, as does level of education. In contrast, hostility toward neighbors decreases the probability of pro-state preferences.

Role of the State in Society

Regarding the defi ition of the state and its role in society (What is the Argentine state?), again zone is not a significant predictor (table 6.9). Being an immigrant increases the probability of a pro-state answer ("The state is the principal guarantor of people's rights"). In both models union exposure also increases the probability of a pro-state answer, as does being a Peronist sympathizer (model 1).

Role of the State in the Economy

On the issue of the state's role in the economy the effects of zone are significant (table 6.10). Living in either Villa 20 (zone 1) or in Barrio General Savio (zone 2), as opposed to living in Old Town (zone 3), increases the probability of having an interventionist view of the state.

TABLE 6.7. OLS Regression on Local Political Mistrust

Independent Variables	Model 1	Model 2
(Constant)	-.336	-.395
	(.297)	(.289)
Female	.096	.125
	(.095)	(.096)
Manual worker	.103	.128
	(.131)	(.131)
Informal worker	.097	.122
	(.130)	(.129)
Hostile	.112	.094
	(.101)	(.100)
Union exposure	.090	.106
	(.119)	(.118)
Activist	.373**	.367**
	(.146)	(.145)
Immigrant	.304**	.321**
	(.143)	(.140)
Education	-.098	-.097
	(.082)	(.081)
Peronist	.072	
(PJ)	(.133)	
Radical		.436**
(UCR)		(.187)
Zone 1	-.180	-.180
Shantytown	(.146)	(.145)
(Villa 20)		
Zone 2	.054	.048
Housing project	(.114)	(.113)
(Barrio G. Savio)		
No. of observations	472	472
R-square	.035	.045
F-change		
(zones 1 and 2)	1.241	1.228

Note: Standard errors are between parentheses. Tolerance levels are above .561 for model 1 and .567 for model 2.

*p < .1; **p < .05; ***p < .01.

TABLE 6.8. Ordered Logit on State Size

Independent Variables	Model 1	Model 2
Female	.269	.247
	(.187)	(.189)
Manual worker	.281	.266
	(.259)	(.260)
Informal worker	-.173	-.195
	(.255)	(.256)
Hostile	-.440**	-.425**
	(.197)	(.197)
Union exposure	.687***	.677***
	(.243)	(.242)
Activist	-.282	-.288
	(.287)	(.285)
Immigrant	.221	.012
	(.283)	(.278)
Education	.269*	.270*
	(.159)	(.158)
Peronist	-.076	
(PJ)	(.262)	
Radical		-.344
(UCR)		(.372)
Zone 1	.382	.378
Shantytown	(.288)	(.286)
(Villa 20)		
Zone 2	-.107	-.108
Housing project	(.222)	(.222)
(Barrio G. Savio)		
No. of observations	496	496
-2Log likelihood	589.774	558.742
Chi-square	24.592***	25.331***
Pseudo R-square		
(Nagelkerle)	.057	.059
(Cox & Snell)	.048	.050

Note: Standard errors are between parentheses.

*p < .1; **p < .05; ***p < .01.

TABLE 6.9. Ordered Logit on State Role in Society

Independent Variables	Model 1	Model 2
Female	-.022	-.049
	(.172)	(.174)
Manual worker	.071	.064
	(.236)	(.237)
Informal worker	-.278	-.292
	(.234)	(.235)
Hostile	.056	.072
	(.181)	(.182)
Union exposure	.424*	.469**
	(.217)	(.215)
Activist	-.203	-.165
	(.264)	(.263)
Immigrant	**1.068***	**.946***
	(.268)	(.263)
Education	.062	.021
	(.147)	(.145)
Peronist	.465*	
(PJ)	(.243)	
Radical		-.297
(UCR)		(.343)
Zone 1	.033	.102
Shantytown	(.264)	(.263)
(Villa 20)		
Zone 2	.154	.145
Housing project	(.205)	(.205)
(Barrio G. Savio)		
No. of observations	495	495
-2Log likelihood	813.722	779.335
Chi-square	**27.136***	**24.509**.
Pseudo R-square		
(Nagelkerle)	.058	.052
(Cox & Snell)	.053	.048

Note: Standard errors are between parentheses.

*p < .1; **p < .05; ***p < .01.

Gender and level of education are also significant predictors. Being female increases the probability of having an interventionist view (at the 0.01 level), while higher levels of education decrease the probability (at the 0.05 level).

In sum, place-based effects are present only for the variable of state role in the economy. This suggests that perceptions of the state are not an insurmountable obstacle for framing activities at the grassroots in Villa Lugano.

On Activists

Activists are the principal agents of grassroots movements' organizational and framing activities. It is worth exploring their political orientations, particularly if there are salient cleavages among them across zones. This is another important piece of the puzzle for understanding how movements may (or may not) be able to solve the discursive dilemmas they face in complex political-cultural environments. In this section I discuss the political orientations of Villa Lugano activists. I am interested in exploring, fi st, if activists' political orientations were territorially divided and, second, the degree of similarity between activists' political orientations and those of their potential followers in each zone of Villa Lugano.

Activists versus Nonactivists

The models I discussed previously tested for the effects of being an activist compared to not being an activist in Villa Lugano, disregarding the zone in which activists operated. As I showed, activists scored lower than nonactivists on their preference for autonomy in local participation: they preferred, more than nonactivists did, to work more closely with political parties and/or government officials. Interestingly, activism was negatively correlated with liberal democracy and positively correlated with delegative democracy. Activists also had a more positive perception of local politicians than nonactivists did, which correlated with being more willing to accept that popular organizations should work closely with political parties and the government on local issues.

TABLE 6.10. Ordered Logit on State Role in the Economy

Independent Variables	Model 1	Model 2
Female	.637***	.622***
	(.195)	(.197)
Manual worker	.269	.258
	(.269)	(.270)
Informal worker	-.004	-.018
	(.264)	(.265)
Hostile	-.117	-.108
	(.203)	(.204)
Union exposure	-.156	-.145
	(.241)	(.239)
Activist	-.049	-.024
	(.303)	(.301)
Immigrant	.118	.066
	(.298)	(.295)
Education	-.407**	-.423**
	(.168)	(.168)
Peronist (PJ)	.158	
	(.275)	
Radical (UCR)		-.245
		(.374)
Zone 1 Shantytown (Villa 20)	1.098***	1.120***
	(.306)	(.305)
Zone 2 Housing project (Barrio G. Savio)	.557**	.555**
	(.227)	(.227)
No. of observations	485	485
-2Log likelihood	506.229	490.212
Chi-square	55.204***	55.283***
Pseudo R-square		
(Nagelkerle)	.131	.131
(Cox & Snell)	.108	.108

Note: Standard errors are between parentheses.

*p < .1; **p < .05; ***p < .01.

Activists by Zone

To compare the political opinions of activists while taking into account their place of residence, I used the same two basic models presented previously. Across zones, the political orientations of activists differed on three issues (table 6.11). First, compared to activists from Old Town (zone 3), Barrio General Savio (zone 2) activists scored lower on mobilization; they tended to prefer to channel neighborhood demands through formal and informal contacts with state officials rather than to resort to neighborhood mobilization (0.1 level of significance). In this aspect of local participation, activists from Villa 20 (zone 1) held similar preferences to those of Old Town (zone 3). On the other hand, in terms of autonomy of participation, all activists held similar preferences, regardless of zone of residence. Yet activists' preferences differed on the settlement or displacement of shantytown dwellers. As one might expect, compared to activists from Old Town (zone 3), activists from Villa 20 (zone 1) were more favorable toward the settlement option than toward the eviction option (significant at the 0.1 level).

Regarding national political issues, activists differ on the variables measuring liberal democracy and the state's role in society (the question "What is the Argentine state?"). Compared to activists from Old Town (zone 3), activists from Barrio General Savio (zone 2) scored lower on the liberal democracy variable (significant at the 0.01 and 0.05 levels respectively). On the defi ition of the Argentine state or the state's role in society, being an activist in Villa 20 (zone 1) or in Barrio General Savio (zone 2) increased the probability of having a negative view of the state (significant at the 0.05 level).

In sum, for the purposes of the analysis it is worth noting that activists from Villa 20 and from Old Town held similar views on strategies of participation but differed on the settlement of the shanties and on the role of the state. Villa 20's activists supported the settlement of shantytowns and held more negative views about the state than Old Town's did. The issue of shantytown settlement (or social hostility), a divisive issue among neighbors, reappeared among activists.

TABLE 6.11. Political Orientations of Activists by Zone

Dependent Variables	Villa 20 Shantytown (zone 1)	Barrio Savio Housing Project (zone 2)	Villa Lugano Old Town (zone 3)
Mobilization vs. Clientelism			
Model 1 OLS	.198	-.543*	Reference
	(.281)	(.288)	category
Model 2 OLS	.180	-.559*	
	(.293)	(.286)	
Liberal democracy			
Model 1 OLS	-.539	-.817**	Reference
	(.369)	(.387)	category
Model 2 OLS	-.843	-.857***	
	(.312)	(.386)	
Settlement/eviction			
Model 1 OLS	**.827***	-.034	Reference
	(.299)	(.323)	category
Model 2 OLS	.655**	-.045	
	(.294)	(.308)	
State role in society			
Model 1 OLogit	-1.430**	-1.323**	Reference
	(.647)	(.692)	category
Model 2 OLogit	-1.536**	-1.430**	
	(.666)	(.702)	

Note: Standard errors are between parentheses.

*p < .1; **p < .05; ***p < .01.

MAKING SENSE OF DISCURSIVE DILEMMAS

The statistical analysis has shown that the zones have divergent views on local issues, especially on strategies for local participation. We can be certain that place-based effects are at work. For issues of national politics, place-based effects are less significant. The only divergence on national issues explained by place-based effects is the role of the state in the economy. This strongly suggests that the discursive dilemmas the CVL faced in reaching out to the whole of Villa Lugano were rooted in *local* rather than national political cleavages.

As I already mentioned, the analysis of the CVL's discourse shows a frame of meaning that included three basic aspects: the injustice caused by the inequality between the northern and southern parts of the city, the rights of citizenship based upon paying taxes, and a positive evaluation of cooperation with political parties and government officials at the local level, based upon trust in democracy. Indeed, the ideas of democracy as a set of basic freedoms and of the state as responsible for delivering basic services were the backbone of the CVL's discourse. Following Snow and Benford (1992), it can be said that the CVL's "diagnostic framing" was based upon geography and entailed the idea that Buenos Aires was a divided city. As we saw, Avenida Rivadavia separates the north of the city, where the affluent neighborhoods of Barrio Norte, Belgrano, and Recoleta are concentrated, from the south, which contains the popular neighborhoods of Villa Lugano, Villa Soldati, Mataderos, and Barracas. One CVL pamphlet of April 15, 1987, reads:

> City Hall is calling for a bid to fix the paving of Avenida del Libertador, Avenida Belgrano, Avenida de Mayo [all in the North, GIO]. These are not at all priority projects for the city. To this should be added rising taxes for services that we never receive here in Villa Lugano. We are the fourth most important neighborhood in terms of contributions to the city revenues, but we are forty-fourth when it comes to city resource allocation. Where does our money go?

According to this view, corruption, lack of accountability, and clientelism in City Hall were to blame for this injustice. In terms of prognostic framing, the CVL made clear from the start that petitioning alone was not the solution. Mobilization was crucial to reverse the course of events. Petition and mobilization, historically rooted in the urban poor's repertoire of contention, were inscribed in a language of rights as part of the guarantees of democracy. Finally, the CVL motivational framing entailed the ideas of the citizen as taxpayer and of participation as a basic right of democracy.

Yet place-based disagreements on the best strategy of participation posed a discursive dilemma for the CVL when it attempted to mobilize neighborhood zones other than Old Town. The CVL invited representatives and officials of the city and national legislature to its most important gatherings, and frequent trips to City Hall and the city legislature were a crucial part of its strategy. In discourse and practice, the CVL often proposed cooperation with the local government and all political parties. This met with resistance in other zones of Villa Lugano, such as Villa 20, that had a more autonomous view of participation. The CVL did not adjust its frame of meaning when expanding the organization beyond its demands for street paving; it relied on the same discourse in trying to reach the whole of Villa Lugano. This was revealed in my in-depth interviews with core activists. Their strategy of working closely with political parties and government officials had been successful in generating a high-resonance frame of meaning and mobilizing Old Town for getting the streets paved. So these activists fi mly believed that this same strategy would apply well to other zones of the neighborhood for the pursuit of other demands. That events would prove them wrong evinces one—but just one—of the discursive dilemmas faced by the CVL.

*   *   *

In this chapter we have seen that there are important cleavages in popular political culture among residents of Villa Lugano regarding local participation, strategies of mobilization, the meaning of democracy, political and social mistrust, and the role of the state. The existence of these cleavages is a fi ding that contradicts the common view of a homogeneous political culture among the lower classes in Argentina. As I discussed in chapter 5, such a view is unwarranted; the empirical data presented in the current chapter make clear that at least with regard to the urban poor in Villa Lugano, the politico-cultural homogeneity thesis is not true.

In the present chapter, I uncovered some of the factors that account for the existence of these cleavages. Among these factors, I was most interested in whether place-based effects were at work and, if so, how they might have posed important constraints on the CVL's framing capabilities when it tried to reach the whole of Villa Lugano. My hypothesis was that spatially based cleavages, by creating a series of discursive dilemmas, adversely affect the chances of urban movements to put forward a high-resonance frame of meaning. As the analysis presented in this chapter shows, in Villa Lugano some cleavages are indeed explained by place-based effects. These effects account for political cleavages regarding local participation and strategies of mobilization. As we saw, among these cleavages a more autonomous view of local participation in Villa 20 collided with the CVL's and Old Town's less autonomous attempts at forging coalitions with other grassroots organizations and state officials. This cleavage created one of the crucial discursive dilemmas the CVL encountered when it tried to expand to other zones of Villa Lugano.

We have reached a point in the analysis where we can return to the main question of the present work and ask once more: What prevented the CVL from mounting a movement of the whole of Villa Lugano and finally led to its dissolution? Was it only a matter of disagreement on the preferred strategies of local participation that I found in this chapter?

To answer this question in the next chapter, I turn to one of the most robust fi dings of this research, *social hostility among neighbors.* As I will show, social hostility is the most important contributing factor to explain the decline and eventual dissolution of the CVL. Social hostility, deeply rooted in territorial traditions and settlement patterns, created an insurmountable discursive dilemma for the CVL when it attempted to mobilize the entire neighborhood of Villa Lugano. To this I turn now.

APPENDIX

Strategies of Local Participation

To map out differences in strategies of collective action at the local level, I explored the following survey items using OS.

1. Should citizens meet to solve neighborhood problems? (table 5.25)
2. Which is the best participation strategy, mobilization or clientelism? (table 5.26)
3. Have you ever participated to solve a neighborhood problem?
4. Should neighborhood organizations have close or limited relationships with political parties? (table 5.27)
5. Should neighborhood organizations have close or limited relationships with government? (table 5.28).

OS yields two main dimensions of variation (or summary variables) on strategies of local participation: (1) autonomous participation and (2) mobilization versus clientelism, as shown in table 6A.1.

TABLE 6A.1. Component Loadings on Strategies of Local Participation

	Dimensions of Variation	
	Autonomous Participation	Mobilization vs. Clientelism
1. Should citizens meet to solve neighborhood problems?	-.145	.835
2. Which is the best participation strategy? Mobilization vs. clientelism	-.205	.814
3. Have you ever participated to solve a neighborhood problem?	.143	.228
4. Relations between neighborhood organizations and political parties	.869	.128
5. Relations between neighborhood organizations and government	.854	.168

Model Summary for Strategies of Local Participation

		Variance Accounted For	
Dimension	Cronbach's Alpha	Total (Eigenvalue)	Percent of Variance
1	.453	1.568	31.360
2	.391	1.456	29.116
Total	.837[a]	3.024	60.476

[a] Total Cronbach's Alpha is based on the total Eigenvalue.

On Democracy

The survey items used in OS to explore models of democracy are:

1. Which is more important when you decide your vote, the candidate or the party to which the candidate belongs? (table 5.11)
2. "Parties are all the same." Do you agree with the statement? (table 5.10)
3. "Instead of political parties, Argentina needs an able and courageous man willing to achieve national unity." Do you agree with the statement? (table 5.2)
4. Should democracy guarantee before anything a decent standard of living or just free elections? (table 5.1)
5. "If the president has to break the law to solve a serious national problem, it is better that he do it and solve the problem." Do you agree with the statement? (table 5.5)
6. "Citizens have the opportunity to participate in politics by voting in elections. Then it is the president's responsibility to rule the country the way he or she judges best." Do you agree with the statement? (table 5.24)
7. "Political parties only divide the people." Do you agree with the statement? (table 5.9)
8. "The president should not suffer interference by Congress or the courts." Do you agree with the statement?
9. Which is more important, democracy or economic development? (table 5.20)
10. Are two or more parties an important condition for saying that a country is democratic?
11. Is equal treatment by the courts an important condition for saying that a country is democratic? (table 5.14)
12. Is freedom of speech an important condition for saying that a country is democratic?
13. Are free elections an important condition for saying that a country is democratic?
14. Is freedom of association an important condition for saying that a country is democratic?

OS yields two main dimensions of variation. The table of component loadings (table 6A.2) below helps to clarify the conceptual meaning of

TABLE 6A.2. Component Loadings on Models of Democracy

	Dimensions of Variation	
	Liberal Democracy	Delegative Democracy
1. Which is more important when you decide your vote?	.164	.192
2. Parties are all the same. Agree?	.127	.522
3. Instead of political parties, Argentina needs an able and courageous man willing to achieve national unity. Agree?	.015	.667
4. Democracy should guarantee before anything a decent level of living or just free elections.	.017	.385
5. Breaking the law by the president to solve national problem. Agree?	.103	.553
6. Citizens' chances for participation are only during national election times. Agree?	.137	.399
7. Parties only divide the people. Agree?	.032	.543
8. The president should not suffe interference by Congress or courts. Agree?	.181	.550
9. Which is more important, economic development or democracy?	.133	.513
10. Are two or more parties an important condition to say that a country is democratic?	.829	-.134
11. Is equal treatment by justice an important condition to say that a country is democratic?	.727	-.133
12. Is freedom of speech an important condition to say that a country is democratic?	.767	-.065
13. Are free elections an important condition to say that a country is democratic?	.626	-.016
14. Is freedom of association an important condition to say that a country is democratic?	.846	-.146

Model Summary for Models of Democracy

		Variance Accounted For	
Dimension	Cronbach's Alpha	Total (Eigenvalue)	Percent of Variance
1	.722	3.037	21.694
2	.607	2.290	16.357
Total	.875[a]	5.327	38.050

[a] Total Cronbach's Alpha is based on the total Eigenvalue.

both dimensions. Dimension 1 summarizes what I would call attributes of liberal democracy, while dimension 2 summarizes attributes of delegative democracy according to O'Donnell's (1994) defi ition discussed in chapter 5.

Political Mistrust

The solution of OS is based upon the following questions:

1. A political party is a group of people that either a) seeks its own interests; b) tries to serve the country; or c) makes the workings of government more difficult. (table 5.12)
2. "Parties only divide the people." Do you agree with the statement? (table 5.9)
3. The Argentine state is either a) a group of bureaucrats who defend only their own interests; b) a means of oppressing the poor; c) the main guarantee for defending popular interests. (table 5.19)
4. Are you satisfied with democracy?
5. Should shantytowns be settled or evicted?
6. What do you think about the neighborhood's politicians? (table 5.13)
7. Do capitalists contribute to national development? (table 5.21)

The table of component loadings (table 6A.3) helps us clarify these results.

On the State

The survey items used in OS are:

1. The state should a) disappear; b) continue as it is; c) reduce much of its expenditures and the number of its employees; d) not reduce its expenditures or employees but improve the way it functions. (table 5.17)
2. The Argentine state is a) a group of bureaucrats who defend only their own interests; b) a means of oppressing the poor; c) the main guarantee for defending popular interests. (table 5.19)
3. To solve the economic problems of Argentina, the state should a) have a lot of control over the economy; b) intervene only in some activities of the economy; c) not intervene in the economy. (table 5.18)

An OS two-dimensional solution did not yield significant results. But a three-dimensional solution revealed that each of the three items may be considered individually as a significant dimension of variation. I decided to analyze statistically these survey items separately in an ordinal scale.

TABLE 6A.3. Component Loadings on Political Mistrust

		Dimensions of Variation	
	Political Mistrust	Social Mistrust	Political Mistrust (Local)
1. Parties are . . . ?	.651	-.171	-.129
2. Parties only divide the people. Agree?	.620	-.111	-.123
3. The Argentine state is	.602	.127	.259
4. Are you satisfied with democracy?	.506	.430	.019
5. Should shantytowns be settled or evicted?	.124	.830	-.160
6. What do you think of neighborhood politicians?	.251	-.122	.853
7. Do capitalists contribute to national development?	.481	-.386	-.415

Model Summary for Political Mistrust

		Variance Accounted For	
Dimension	Cronbach's Alpha	Total (Eigenvalue)	Percent of Variance
1	.495	1.737	24.814
2	.101	1.095	15.641
3	.027	1.024	14.628
Total	.864[a]	3.856	55.083

[a] Total Cronbach's Alpha is based on the total Eigenvalue.

CHAPTER 7

Hell Is Other People

L'enfer, c'est les autres.

Jean-Paul Sartre, La Nausée

By all accounts, the tipping point in the life cycle of the CVL was the decision of leaders and activists to expand the organization and pursue a comprehensive program of public goods for Villa Lugano. This expansion brought in new participants to the CVL, especially (but not only) from Villa 20. Some neighbors and leaders of Villa 20 had participated in the CVL's early struggles for paving, but this participation was defensive in nature: to make sure that the streets to be paved in Villa Lugano would not affect significantly the geography of the shantytown. Indeed, some houses in Villa 20 had to be removed, and in the end they were, to make way for the much-needed new infrastructure that came along with the new paved roads.

The participation of residents from Villa 20 in the CVL came at the right moment, since the survival of the organization was at stake: participation in the CVL had begun to decline as road paving neared completion. But, more importantly, the CVL's ambitious program for the whole of Villa Lugano required the participation and mobilization of all sectors of the neighborhood. While the leaders of the CVL encouraged the expansion of the organization and welcomed the new participants, many CVL activists expressed skepticism about the whole enterprise. The hidden transcript (Scott 1985) of this skepticism involved a significant dose of *social hostility* of the activists toward neighbors living in other zones of Villa Lugano, above all shantytown dwellers but also housing-project residents. This hostility expressed cleavages that are deeply rooted in Villa Lugano's housing settlement patterns and that adversely affect popular collective action independently of other existing national political-cultural cleavages. Furthermore, by adversely affecting popular capabilities for collective action, social hostility among the urban poor ultimately erodes the quality of democracy. I discuss below some of the causes of social hostility in Villa Lugano, but I fi st frame this topic within a broader perspective, that of trust and social capital and its effects on the quality of democracy.

As noted in preceding chapters, much debate has emerged around Robert Putnam's thesis on the positive effects of social capital on democracy—that civic participation generates trust among citizens and that this, in turn, makes democracy work better. Social capital refers to the "social networks and the norms of reciprocity and trustworthiness that arise from them" (Putnam 2000: 19). As mentioned earlier, Putnam's ideas can be traced back to the civic culture paradigm in political science. Gabriel Almond and Sidney Verba put forward the neo-Tocquevillian thesis that democracy is based upon a particular political culture, one with "high frequencies of political activity, of exposure to political communications, of political discussion, of concern with political affairs" (1963: 31). They called this particular type of political culture the civic culture. One central aspect of Putnam's thesis is that an engaged (and as a consequence) *trusting* citizenry makes democracy work better by generating cooperation not only among citizens but also between citizens and government regarding the provision of public services. Peter Evans (1997) has defi ed this cooperation between the citizenry and public officials more broadly as the state-society synergy required for the successful implementation of public policy and the improvement of living conditions. A second important aspect in Putnam's thesis is that an engaged citizenry also enhances the quality of democracy by making public officials more accountable.

A common criticism of the trust/democracy thesis is that the causal mechanisms that link trust and democracy are not clear. Trust can be either social or political in nature.[1] *Social trust* refers to a *horizontal relationship* between two parts or individuals. A may trust B to do X, but this happens with no intermediation (Hardin 2002). *Political trust* refers to a *vertical relationship* between citizens and their government. What are the links between horizontal (social) and vertical (political) trust? And how can one differentiate their effects on the quality of democracy? According to Putnam, interpersonal trust (A) promotes associationism (B), which in turn promotes trust in the political system (C):

$A \rightarrow B \rightarrow C$

More specifically, *horizontal* trust→ social participation → *vertical* trust → regime support → higher democratic quality.

Recently, as noted, some scholars have argued against Putnam's thesis by suggesting that political *mistrust* is what makes democracy work.[2] This skeptical tradition is philosophically rooted in political liberalism. In his discussion of James Madison's tenth Federalist paper, Hardin (1999) shows the influence of Hume and Montesquieu on Madison's skepticism. Madison mistrusted the capacity of would-be representatives to always act with patriotism or love of justice. He feared that in the end corruption, faction, and the will to power would lead representatives to betray the interests of the people. For this reason, institutional checks and balances based upon *mistrust* in government should be the cornerstone of democracy. O'Donnell (2003) has referred to this as the "legal institutionalization of political mistrust."

Note that political (mis)trust and its potential effects on democracy operate at different scales. The positive or negative effects of (mis)trust on the quality of democracy should be evaluated at three different levels of the polity: government, political regime, and state. There are several possible combinations: A can mistrust government X, but at the same time A can trust the workings of the democratic regime as well as of the state institutions to correct the flaws of X. This is one possible combination among many and, I assume, a positive one for making democracy work. But if vertical mistrust happens at two or more levels of the polity, we expect mistrust to have a negative effect on the quality of democracy. So when arguing for or against vertical mistrust one has to keep in mind the *scale* at which it operates.

(Mis)trust either vertical (political) or horizontal (social) is also a question of varying degrees of intensity or *thresholds*. High-intensity social mistrust I defi e as social hostility. Social hostility can be either inter- or intragroup. I argue that both types are detrimental to the quality of democracy by precluding social cooperation of the type suggested by Putman's thesis. Taken to the extreme, high-intensity social hostility not only is detrimental to democracy but can lead to mass killings and genocide, as in the case of Kenya, Bosnia, Rwanda, and Sudan. In the same vein, high-intensity political mistrust turns into political alienation and affects the chances of collective claim making and eventually the quality of democracy. If people intensely mistrust government officials, the workings of a democratic regime, and state institutions, then the probability of cooperation between society and the state or for state-society synergy is minimal.

If one conclusion can be drawn from this discussion, it is that how much social and/or political (mis)trust is beneficial for the quality of democracy is an empirical matter operating at different scales and degrees of intensity. All in all, it is a matter of thresholds: too much of a good thing may turn into a bad thing, and perhaps vice versa.

In what follows I discuss the complex roots of social hostility in Villa Lugano. I argue that social hostility among the urban poor is primarily place based and that it adversely affects their capabilities for collective action.

THE GEOGRAPHY OF SOCIAL HOSTILITY

Place of residence matters. Besides the many economic reasons that make it matter, especially for the urban poor, place of residence in Buenos Aires has a strong stereotyping force. Chapter 3 discussed that city's north-south divide and the negative images about the poor, distant, and underdeveloped southern neighborhoods. But residence particular types of habitat within the city may also draw attributions of contrasting moral, psychological, and political characteristics to residents who would otherwise belong, socioeconomically, to census categories quite similar to those of the people stereotyping them.[3] Place-as-location and habitat should be seen as social ordering categories. Shantytown and public housing residents have historically had a "bad reputation" in Buenos Aires, regardless of whether they live in the northern or southern part of the city. Residents of shantytown Villa 31 in Retiro (one of the most exclusive upper-class neighborhoods in the city) have the same bad reputation as those of Villa 20 in Villa Lugano. By the same token, residents of the housing project Fuerte Apache in the periphery of Buenos Aires are considered to be as "unreliable" as residents of Barrio General Savio. Type of habitat (shantytown, housing project, *conventillo*, etc.) adds another dimension to the basic north-south divide in the city of Buenos Aires.

Stigmatizing others by their neighborhood and by the type of housing they inhabit is by no means a propensity of a particular social sector or class. While one might intuitively think of stigmatization of the poor by the rich (or in geographical grammar of the south by the north), popular neighborhoods like Villa Lugano also deploy contested images of people's worth and human dignity that are linked to the location and characteristics of their respective habitats.

Stigmatization happens in the population at large in Argentina. It also happens in public discourse. Stanley (2003, 2005) has extensively documented how public discourse in Argentina in the last two decades has construed the poor (especially shantytown dwellers or *villeros*) as criminals, shantytowns as places of crime, and the war on crime as a "war on the poor." For example, Stanley refers to a speech of the Peronist candidate Carlos Ruckauf during the gubernatorial campaign of the province of Buenos Aires in 1999: "It is necessary to enter the *villas* with all the [police] agents necessary to put an end to crime. The police are capable, it's simply necessary to give them instructions and combat decisions. But let us give them the norms they need: we can't have a situation where a policeman enters one of these places and kills someone and then some lawyer of the criminal appears and says it's the policeman who is the murderer."[4]

Shantytowns and public housing projects are often portrayed in the media as places of crime and moral perversion, inhabited by lazy people of dubious backgrounds. In the end, the argument goes, these people have gained access to those places either through *usurpación* (illegal land occupation) or through clientelistic arrangements with local party bosses. The two actions (*usurpación* and clientelism) are perceived as equally improper and even unlawful. The common thread is that "these people" do not deserve to live in the city of Buenos Aires, a city that still is perceived by most Argentines to be the locus of "civilization versus barbarism."[5] They are the "outsiders."[6] This perception, I argue, is a function of territorial traditions historically rooted in distinctive urban settlement patterns in the city of Buenos Aires. As noted in chapter 3, these settlement patterns are mostly the by-product of state intervention (or nonintervention) through housing policy.

In Villa Lugano, one of the most populated popular neighborhoods of Buenos Aires, one can see the placed-based stigmatization of the disadvantaged at close range. While the CVL core activists publicly favored the participation of people from all sectors of Villa Lugano, the in-depth interviews and the analysis of local press materials that I conducted reveal otherwise. I argue that social hostility was the decisive contributing factor that led to the decline of the CVL and, with it, the many hopes it had raised for fully democratizing urban space and improving the quality of democracy.

FRAMING THE OTHER

Representations of the Poor in the Local Press

In chapter 2 we saw through the lens of social history the importance of the printed press (both national and local) in the formation of a public sphere and in the emergence of popular contentious politics in Buenos Aires around the time of its federalization in 1880. Printing has been a critical component in the formation of all social movements, not only in Buenos Aires but also worldwide. Pamphlets and the popular press have been vital in many revolutionary events. In turn, revolutionary events have further promoted the spread of the presses, magazines, newspapers, and the like. According to Tarrow (1998), print and associations make a complementary and explosive combination for the development of social movements and other forms of popular contention. Local newspapers and magazines especially may not only work in favor of popular contention but also reflect (and reinforce) core themes of collective action framing.

Villa Lugano has several local newspapers, magazines, and, more recently, radio stations. The most important periodicals in terms of circulation at the time of this research were the weekly *Centro Informativo* and *Semanario Lugano* and the monthly *Enfoques*. All provided general information on the neighborhood, commercial advertisements, and editorials. Content analysis of these publications, especially of the editorials during the time span of this research, reveals a series of representations of the other that bring to the fore the profound local cleavages and social hostility present in Villa Lugano and show how place and habitat (mainly the modalities of access to housing) help explain the emergence and durability of those cleavages.

The Noncitizens: Profiling the Villeros

One common theme that immediately appears in local press editorials is the lack of interest shown by city and national authorities regarding everything that happens in the south of Buenos Aires. This is especially the case, according to the editorials, in relation to illegal land occupations. Indeed, the national press, above all the conservative newspaper *La Nación,* usually reports on land occupations only when they happen in the north of the city or in areas with high real estate values. The now (in)famous shantytown Villa 31 in Retiro is a recurrent theme in the news. There have been many attempts to eradicate this shantytown, based on the argument that the value of the land makes the existence of a land invasion preposterous in this northern, rich enclave of the city. The concern is not at all the living conditions of Villa 31 inhabitants but the place-as-location where they live, a place "naturally" reserved for those who can afford it: the upper classes. This naturalization of spatial inequality has high resonance in Villa Lugano. It is striking that the local press in this popular neighborhood has also adopted a place-based view of inequality. Editorials suggest that to live in Villa Lugano is a privilege for shantytown dwellers: the neighborhood is within the jurisdictional limits of the city of Buenos Aires and this implies better schools, transportation, health services, and federal police surveillance. These are all high-quality public goods compared to the ones provided outside Buenos Aires, in the periphery or *conurbano bonaerense*. These high-quality public goods are also costly; their provision is maintained by high taxes.

In this context, the *villeros* are seen, not as individuals in need, but as people who take advantage of others, free-riding on other neighbors who duly pay their taxes and services. Paying taxes is seen as a condition for being a citizen and, even more important, for being a person of moral standing. "For many years, we have been proclaiming that the shantytowns and their inhabitants, *the villeros,* are not disadvantaged people, not even people with economic difficulties; in fact, if that is the case, these are the same difficulties faced by any citizen who pays electricity, who pays gas, and who is hardly able to save money to pay rent, etc., etc.; in sum, they have no greater problems than those citizens that make the effort to live decently."[7]

The editorials also reflect a particular image of immigration, one that is rooted in the ideas of Argentina's founding fathers on this issue. While in their writings Juan Bautista Alberdi and Domingo Faustino Sarmiento promoted northern against southern European immigration, nowadays southern European immigration is seen as vastly preferable to immigration from neighboring Latin American countries. Furthermore, an image projected by the editorials is that most shantytowns' inhabitants are of immigrant origin. This partially contradicts census data and at least in the case of Villa 20 is simply not true: as noted, at the time of my research half of that neighborhood's household heads were natives of Argentina (CMV 1988). However the local press insists:

It is one thing to be solidaristic and another to be stupid. It is one thing to be an immigrant (Spaniard, Italian, German, etc., etc.) but another is the fact that all the countries of Latin America send us their delinquents, prostitutes, and all their *lacra social* [social trash] . . . , because in our country the Argentine citizen is not well defended by guarded frontiers. Nowadays, the criminals from all South America enter our country as "immigrants" because criminal activity has high returns and also because there are laws that defend these criminals. We should thank our representatives in Congress for this.[8]

Immigrant origin is just one stereotypical characteristic frequently invoked in the profiling of shantytowns. The *villeros,* Argentines or otherwise, are also accused of being linked to illegal economic activities, clientelism, and social resentment. Of the illegal activities, two predominate in the editorials: drug trafficking and real estate dealings. *Semanario Lugano,* for instance, comments regarding a drug raid in Ciudad Oculta (Hidden City), one of the most famous shantytowns of Buenos Aires City and the biggest in the Villa Lugano area, that although "drug trafficking can happen anywhere a raid in Ciudad Oculta, carried out by the men (the police) who care about the lives and order of citizens, should be no surprise to us"; the neighborhood "has become a place of drug smuggling and use, one need only see the list of detained, indicted, and sentenced on these matters that live there."[9]

In the same article, which goes on to describe how police conducted the raid *Semanario Lugano* delves into the "antisocial" behavior of the *villeros,* a recurrent theme in other editorials dealing with the shantytowns.

> Everything was prepared so the policemen could take by surprise the dealers in the *casilla* (shack), communications among policemen were well coordinated, and if everything went as planned, expectations were that no innocent persons would be in danger. Ambulances (used as a camouflage in the *operativo* [police operation]), are a normal feature of this shantytown, since fi hts among the *villeros* cause all sorts of damages and injuries; and in spite of all the collaboration and work for the well-being of the *villeros,* often the doctors and nurses that accompany the ambulance are stoned without justification.

The local press also claims that shantytown dwellers commonly engage in illegal land transactions in the neighborhood. Editorials refer to the existence of a shantytown real estate mafia with close links to politicians.

> The shantytowns are promoted by political power, they do not result from misery or lack of work. When President Alfonsín took office in 1983, people from shanties in Buenos Aires and greater Buenos Aires were already prepared to take over [usurpar] apartments in the housing project Samoré in Villa Lugano. The police had to protect the place for months, but this was not an attempt at getting an apartment so as to live better, as anyone could assume; there is something we have been denouncing for the last four years in this newspaper, the existence of a

true real estate Mafia *villera*. Some *villeros* own one lot in each one of the several shantytowns of the city, and as if this were not enough, they have the support of City Hall. In sum, misery and promiscuity are financially supported with the taxes paid by honest citizens. . . . As soon as President Alfonsín took office in 1983, the shantytowns tripled the number of their inhabitants, without any complaints by any Radical Party member.[10]

Centro Informativo goes on to link the shantytowns to vote buying and political parties.

With increasing freedom of the press, the truth becomes apparent; today, almost nobody doubts the fact that the shantytown is a hiding place for criminals and for people that want to live out "the ribs of others," and as if this were not enough, the shantytowns are promoted by the politicians in order to increase their voting shares in their party primaries so as to be elected as candidates for city councilmen or neighborhood advisors. This is not only carried out by the Justicialistas [Peronists] and the Radicals; the left- ing parties get an important share of the vote, and believe it or not, also the [right-wing] UCD, especially in electoral district 22 [Villa Lugano], 80 percent of the party members come from the shanties, especially from Villa 20 and its surroundings, since when are there so many capitalists-liberals in the shantytowns?[11]

Another recurrent issue is the injustice of social expenditures for the *villeros*. *Semanario Lugano*'s editorials insistently complain that state-sponsored food programs and housing assistance go mostly to illegal immigrants living in the shanties. The Plan Arraigo during the Menem administration was singled out as the most clientelistic plan in history because "it takes into account all kinds of benefits for maintaining the villas. . . The PAN box [National Food Plan, launched by the Alfonsín administration] is another one of the corruption events that keep on going on and are used to feed the *villeros* who are 70 percent illegal immigrants and not just 30 or 40 percent as the media suggests and authorities choose to hide."[12] Also of concern are the provision of health care for poor immigrants and these immigrants' use of public hospitals.

Villeros are often stereotyped in the press as lazy and resentful. Yet editorials simultaneously suggest that the shantytowns are very well organized. This "organization" has negative connotations: *villeros* organize mainly to take advantage of other people and to free-ride on public goods. What is even more infuriating for the editorialists is the *villeros'* stand that society has an obligation to help them improve their situation, an outrageous demand for tax-paying and law-abiding citizens.

Representations of the residents of housing projects are not quite as damning but still highly negative. Housing projects are often portrayed as examples of "good things happening to bad people." The editorials suggest that these nicely built and in some cases almost luxury apartment complexes are often inhabited by people who do not deserve them.[13] One example of this "tragedy" is Barrio Copello, one of the nicest housing projects of Villa Lugano. Several problems plague the project, the most important one being the allocation of apartments by clientelistic means through the Municipal Housing Council (Comisión Municipal de la Vivienda). Actually, this problem is common to all housing projects of Villa Lugano. Furthermore, many apartments have been illegally occupied. There are no official statistics, but in Barrio General Savio the property status of around 30 percent of the apartments is uncertain. Consequently, most housing project residents are (somehow) suspected of not being the true legal owners of their apartment. According to *Semanario Lugano,* "Barrio Copello was an attempt at improving the zone with high-quality building, but this deeply contrasts with many of its residents, many of whom are employees of the Municipal Commission for Housing who abused their institutional power at the expense of others truly in need."[14] The residents of Barrio Copello are described as having in common with other housing project residents an inability to organize themselves (unlike the supposedly "hyperorganized" shantytown dwellers), and the buildings' management is said to be corrupt. Thus "Barrio Copello could be one of the model neighborhoods of the City of Buenos Aires, but surprisingly we fi d there people who prefer to live in the dirt [mugre], disorder, rather than getting together to solve common problems."[15]

All these local press representations of the *villeros* and housing project residents in Villa Lugano resemble those in the national press,

and some are partially true. There is drug trafficking in many shantytowns and housing projects, as in other parts of the city, north and
south. There is also a real estate market in the shanties. When I asked
interviewees in Villa 20 how they had gained access to their home,
46 percent responded, "I bought the parcel or the house."

It was also true that some housing projects were in bad shape and
that many apartments were *tomados* (illegally occupied) or allocated in
a clientelistic way to people that did not truly need them. Clientelism
and vote buying are well documented, especially in the shantytowns,
and constitute a strategy used by all political parties, regardless of ideology. Many people in Villa 20 reported that they had joined the right-
wing UCD just before elections and that they had done so to get some
material benefits. But this should not overshadow the fact that most
of Villa 20 and Barrio General Savio residents are hardworking people
who suffer from the criminal activity, clientelism, and police corruption
in their midst. They know this very well; when I asked Villa 20 and
Barrio General Savio residents how they thought they were perceived
by the other neighbors, negative answers predominated. Examples of
responses were: "They are afraid of us," "We have ruined the landscape
of Villa Lugano," "They ignore us," and "They think we are the worst."
One interesting response in Barrio General Savio was "They think we
are like Villa 20"!

Were these images of the "other" portrayed by local newspapers
shared by neighbors in Old Town? Were they shared by CVL core activists? If so, what conclusions may be drawn regarding human dignity,
collective action capabilities, and solidarity among the urban poor? Let
me fi st delve into the minds of the CVL core activists and ask them
their opinions about "others" in Villa Lugano.

The Hidden Transcript of the CVL

Even though most CVL core activists supported the leaders' proposal to
expand the CVL's program to include issues such as better health care,
housing, and transportation, as soon as meetings to discuss these issues
began and new people, especially from shantytown Villa 20, started to
participate in the CVL, social cleavages began to emerge. These cleav-

ages were social and place based. The data below also reveal how clientelism increases social hostility and how it adversely affects collective action and ultimately the prospects of democratization of urban space.

What were the opinions of the CVL leaders and core activists about shantytown residents? How did they evaluate their participation in the CVL? How did this affect the workings of the CVL? Let me turn fi st to the ethnographic data.

On Villa 20 Participation in the CVL

It was not easy to explore the issue of social hostility among CVL core activists. Above all, they perceived themselves as democratic, law-abiding, tolerant, and participatory citizens. They said that their main motivation was the development of the whole Villa Lugano, and they were full of good intentions. But through answers to various open questions these activists expressed contrasting opinions on these matters. I asked fi st how the participation of Villa 20 residents in the CVL began. Isabel responded in this way:

> I don't know why those people from Villa 20 who showed up at CVL meetings rather quickly disappeared. They acted by themselves. I think they got houses nearby . . . They were not interested in the CVL per se, they participated to see if they could get something out of it. They always acted alone. They are organized, very well organized, I should say. They came to the CVL to try, from another angle, to make advances for their own goals and nothing else. They were not committed to the neighborhood.

Isabel was one of the core activists who was openly hostile toward Villa 20 participants. She was distrustful of their intentions, believing that they were not interested in the development of the neighborhood as such and were just looking for material benefits. In her account the *villeros* defi itely received something: houses nearby. Isabel, like some other core activists, also expressed anger toward clientelism. During the interview she insisted that it was unfair for shantytown people to receive material benefits such as free housing while others had to work hard to get a mortgage from a private bank. Isabel mentioned several times that her parents, of Polish background, were *decent* immigrants who had worked hard to buy their land and build their home. This same story was told by other core activists, some of them from an Italian background. Villa Lugano has been par excellence an immigrant community, built up from scratch. The original settlement patterns involved private ownership of land and petitions to authorities for infrastructure. Isabel also complained about the *ñoquis* she had seen during visits to City Hall and to the Buenos Aires City Council. *Ñoquis* (gnocchi) is an Italian pasta dish that is traditionally served on the twenty-ninth of each month. Public employees linked to machine politics are called *ñoquis* since they are reputed to show up at work only on the twenty-ninth of each month to collect their salary check.

Eduardo, another core activist, held similar views. He expressed the remote possibility of working with shantytowns to improve Villa Lugano but shared with Isabel very negative opinions about the people of Villa 20. He believed that they did not have a comprehensive view on how to improve the neighborhood for everybody's advantage:

With Villa 20 there was no rapport, no appeal. But I'm not saying there would never be a possibility of acting all together for the neighborhood. They came to the CVL with a well-developed plan, they came to us for their problems and just for their problems. They tried to use us as a springboard. I remember that when we began the struggle for the paving they set up many conditions. There were times when some of them did not want to move their houses or open the streets. They tried to use our contacts to get information or to advance their own demands with the city officials we were dealing with and nothing else. All this was carried out with a lot of stipulating of conditions on their part, their lawyers, their strategies, their law articles, that was it. They have a very strong movement in terms of strategy. The problem is that they tried to use the CVL, a very honest organization, formed with neighbors and with great support throughout all areas of the neighborhood, of Villa Lugano as a whole. We did very good things without hurting anybody. They started participating in CVL and everything became a confusion of issues, which at the end would provoke the breakdown of the CVL, and that is what fi ally happened. Those who were just neighbors left the movement of the CVL because of that.

Hector, a Radical Party sympathizer and one of the founding CVL core activists, had a different view than Isabel and Eduardo. But he insisted several times that he did not know Villa 20 participants well. As we saw in chapter 4, this type of "local knowledge" is a crucial asset for a social movement's networking activities. In the case of the CVL, many of the founding participants had known each other since childhood even though they held different political preferences. There was a *minimum threshold of trust* among CVL participants that was lacking with people from Villa 20.

> People from Villa 20 came to the CVL invited by Victorio and Omar [the main leaders of the CVL]. For my part, I did not reject these people because they were *villeros,* but I did not know them at all. Some of them are very well prepared in terms of participation skills and are highly educated. I remember Rafael, he was from Chile, a highly capable and well-educated man.

Betty, a core activist, summarized better than anyone the general feeling of CVL core activists about Villa 20 and Barrio General Savio.

> Our goal was the paving of the roads, the neighbors wanted that so badly . . . There was no quorum for other issues. For example, regarding the opening of health centers in Villa 20 and Barrio General Savio, I asked why not in Villa Lugano properly speaking [referring to Old Town]? We had a health center in Somellera Street many years ago. And because we do not live in a housing project or in a shantytown it was closed down and never reopened! And we have lived for so long in the neighborhood . . . We do not need a health center here too? If I had an emergency or if I needed a vaccine, I had to go to the very end of shantytown number 6 [Villa Cildañez, a smaller shantytown also located in Villa Lugano]. Why did I have to take my son there? There must be a health center here, in Old Town, as I demanded during the meetings, and as we did when we demanded a stoplight close to the school in Old Town.

Them and Us

I asked CVL core activists if there were any significant differences between Villa 20 and Old Town residents. As the following interview excerpts show, there were plenty.

They Live Differently

The fi st representation of Villa 20 residents was that they lived differently from other people in Villa Lugano. The proffered explanations cited many causes, biological, social, cultural, and political. Here are Betty's opinions:

> They cannot or they do not want to be integrated into society. They live differently. I see that regarding children. They have many, and then they send them to the streets. You are not supposed to have ten babies and then expect the state to take care of them. Here in Villa Lugano [referring to Old Town] things are completely different. This is not pejorative, it might be that it comes to them as a legacy, a cultural thing. I remember when I worked in the TV factory [Philco] once we gathered toys for the villa, and when we visited them they told us to go to hell; they did not understand that we were also poor and workers and that those toys implied a lot of sacrifice on our part. They are very *desconfiados* [mistrustful], they get together among themselves and think other people try to hurt them. Some of them did not want the paving because some streets pass by the middle of the shantytown. I'm not saying they are bad people, to the contrary. A lot of people must be subjugated so that others can use the villa as an *aguantadero* [criminal hideout]. Everybody can tell you that when there are robberies in the neighborhood the criminals run into the villa and hide there, when the police search Villa Oculta they run into Villa 20, and so on and so forth. We have always had shantytowns in Buenos Aires and in Villa Lugano also, but it has never been this bad.

They Are Free Riders

Shantytown residents were also seen as free riders, people who take advantage of other neighbors. The resettlement of Warnes made a deep impression on most CVL core activists and was mentioned several times during my interviews. Warnes was an empty, never-fi ished, hospital building where many homeless people lived. City Hall, under the Peronist administration of Mayor Carlos Grosso during the Menem government, decided to evacuate this dangerous building. People living in Warnes received houses nearby. This generated a clash with neighbors and reinforced the idea of injustice and the free-riding of the *usurpadores*. According to Eduardo,

> There are a lot of differences between shantytown residents and us. They do not pay services or taxes. They live in strategic areas: for example, on an avenue with wide access, something that I cannot afford. They have everything for free, nobody pays for what they consume. I think they should have the same benefits I have from life, but by paying their bills. There are bad people there, it is like an infectious disease. There must be good people there too. But they are not interested in integrating with the neighborhood either. They get benefits for living that way. The people that came to our area from Warnes are now selling the houses they got for free from the government for $2,000. One of them exchanged his house for a television set. If they felt the neighborhood was their own, they would be willing to improve their home and living conditions.

They Are Outsiders

A crucial perception of Villa 20 residents among Old Town CVL activists was that they were "outsiders." This fi ding in many ways resembles the work of Norbert Elias and John Scotson (1994) on the English working-class community of Winston Parva. These scholars found that the oldest residents of the neighborhood stigmatized the "just arrived" as immoral and criminal, in what amounted to attributing less human worth to them. In Elias and Scotson's work, stigmatization was based on *time,* the old versus the new in the neighborhood. In the case of Villa Lugano, stigmatization was a function of *space,* Old Town versus Villa 20 and, to a significant extent, versus Barrio General Savio too. This was Isabel's response to the question "What is your opinion of shantytown Villa 20?"

I would like them to disappear! They should not exist. People in Villa 20 are not integrated into the neighborhood, they think only about themselves, they live among themselves. We have nothing to do with them. I think it is wrong to give them everything just because they live in the shantytown. It is a *comodidad* [convenience] on their part. The Warnes residents got a whole brand-new neighborhood, and now they are selling the houses and coming back to the shantytown. This means you cannot give these people a house because they are simply "not interested in it." Ah! and they also complained about the type of houses they got for free! Maybe the houses had several deficiencies, but you have to fix your own house, paint it and other things, otherwise it deteriorates like anything else. Everybody has to invest time and work on their own house, but if you want to sit down and do nothing, then that's another matter.

Not all CVL core activists held such opinions. Hector thought otherwise, but he was a minority voice.

Villa Lugano was divided by housing area. And each area has received a name, that is why some people do not feel part of Villa Lugano. I think that people from Villa 20 feel very isolated. I talk to some of them a lot, and they think that people do not like them, but it is not like that . . . The problem is that there are indeed people of *mal vivir* [criminals] in the shantytown. You see two or three kids together and you are ready to think that something bad can happen to you, you fear they can rob you, and perhaps they have nothing to do with something like that. But we have that image fi ed in our minds: this is the big problem. They are human beings too. I know also that you cannot give a house to whomever, but to those who are "workers." Indeed, I believe that the difference is that we are kind of *racist.*

Blame It on Clientelism

Amalia was one of the CVL's core activists. At the time of her participation in the CVL she was a member of the Communist Party. Today she supports former Buenos Aires mayor (currently city councilman) Aníbal Ibarra, who ran his campaign on the center-left Alianza coalition ticket. Ibarra was a member of the youth branch of the Communist

Party. Amalia was Chilean and never became an Argentine citizen, even though her husband and two daughters were.

> There was a lot of resistance to the *villeros* in the CVL. It is understandable somehow. The shantytown problem is plain clientelism. Nobody wants to mess up with the clients. People still vote for a *choripán* [sausage sandwich]. I do not think we should solve all the *villeros'* problems, but we should have done something altogether to improve the neighborhood. It is like the movie *Juan Moreira* . . . , just for some wine or a *choripán,* political parties secure their clients. It is the same with housing. But we should not give the *villeros* a gift! They have to pay as much as they can. Nobody gave anything for free to the Old Town residents of Villa Lugano, and it should not be that way for the *villeros* either.

Omar was one of the two most important members of the CVL. He was its fi st organizer. As we saw in chapter 3, he had been and still was a Communist Party member. Omar had been in charge of negotiations with Villa 20 leaders during the early struggles for the paving, when some streets within the shantytown needed to be opened for infrastructure. He had a positive attitude toward *villeros,* and during the CVL meetings he insisted that they had the right to a decent living, whether they were Argentines or not. However, Omar had a complex view of the shantytown question.

> Well, in the shantytowns there are an overwhelming number of *asistencialistas* [providers of social goods], local bosses . . . It is a mix of truly poor people and those who make profits from their shanty. There are guys in Villa 20 who are building little rooms and then they rent them . . . These are the ones that bring the Bolivians. Then there are the others, the ones that do not build the rooms but can give you or sell you some space. Furthermore, there is a political business that includes mobilization and votes and that is linked to the soup kitchens. Right now, the soup kitchen within the shantytown is a kind of populism and *asistencialismo*. There are many businesses running at the same time in the shanties. This is a very different situation than that of the 1960s or 1970s, when *villeros* were harshly repressed and sent to jail.

Spatial Injustice

In his account of the shantytown situation, Victorio (one of the two main leaders of CVL) suggested that spatially based injustice had two aspects. Residents of Old Town perceived the material benefits obtained by shantytown residents through state policies, clientelism, or nonpayment of taxes and services as a basic injustice. Yet many residents of Villa 20 were people in need, with no other housing options. The situation then turned into a noncooperative game in which all neighbors of Villa Lugano were trapped and ended up worse off han before.

> Residents of Old Town see things about Villa 20 that they understandably dislike: some of those living in the shantytown have a car, and a house out in the countryside, yes, yes, yes, like a weekend house! They are not the majority of those living in the shantytown, but they do exist and are also very visible. Then you have the ones who have small factories inside the shanty, like the Koreans and others. Seeing this situation, the neighbor in Old Town reasons, "I kill myself working and paying for the house, and I pay all the services and taxes, why should I participate to benefit them?" They cannot tolerate the usurpation. They do not realize that Argentina owes a social debt to these people, not to all of them, but to the majority that live there, in those conditions. In the 1960s, you could still buy a piece of land in the city of Buenos Aires to be paid over twenty years, the way my father did, and then on the weekends you were supposed to build your house. That is no longer possible.

How can we make sense of social hostility in Villa Lugano? What factors at the individual level can help us explain it?

MODELING SOCIAL HOSTILITY

The sieve diagram below highlights the pattern of association between social hostility toward neighbors and neighborhood zone. Social hostility is an additive index that measures open hostility toward neighbors living in other zones of Villa Lugano (excluding the respondent's own). I used two open questions to gather opinions about neighbors living in the other zones of Villa Lugano. I coded responses into "hostile" and "nonhostile" categories. Examples of hostile responses were "They are all thieves [*chorros* in Argentine slang]"; "They are lazy people"; "They do not want to pay taxes"; "They are dirty people"; or simply "They are bad people." Nonhostile responses included statements such as "They are people like us"; "They are poor people"; and "They are also Argentines, but with no luck." Expressing hostility toward neighbors in at least one zone of Villa Lugano other than one's own classified the respondent as hostile.

The main purpose of a sieve diagram is to graphically represent frequencies in a two-way contingency table in relation to expected frequencies under the assumption of independence (Friendly 2000).[16] We see in the sieve diagram of graph 7.1 a clear pattern of association by the density of shading and by the solid and dotted lines in the rectangles representing frequency cells. Cells with greater than expected frequency are shown with solid lines. Thus the hypothesis of independence between the two variables, social hostility and zone, can be rejected. Furthermore, the density of shading and the solid lines in the upper third rectangle indicate that in Old Town of Villa Lugano, the place where the CVL initiated its activities, social hostility predominated. To further explore this association, table 7.1 shows the results of a logistic regression for social hostility. I tested the same two models used in the previous chapter on political orientations. The results showed that zone was the most powerful predictor of social hostility when all other predictors were held constant. Living in Villa 20 (zone 1) or in Barrio General Savio (zone 2) decreased the odds of being hostile toward people in neighboring zones (always compared to the reference category, Old Town). More precisely, the odds of "being hostile toward neighbors" of a resident of Villa 20 decreased by a factor of .107 (i.e., were 90 percent lower) when compared to a resident in the Old Town (again zone 3 was the reference category). For a resident of Barrio General Savio the odds of being hostile also decreased when compared to the odds of Old Town residents (by a factor of .221, or 78 percent lower).

We can express the association between hostility and zone in another way, by switching the reference category to the shantytown Villa 20 (zone 1). Doing so increased the odds of being hostile for both Barrio General Savio (zone 2) and Old Town (zone 3). The odds of

GRAPH 7.1. Hostility by zone.

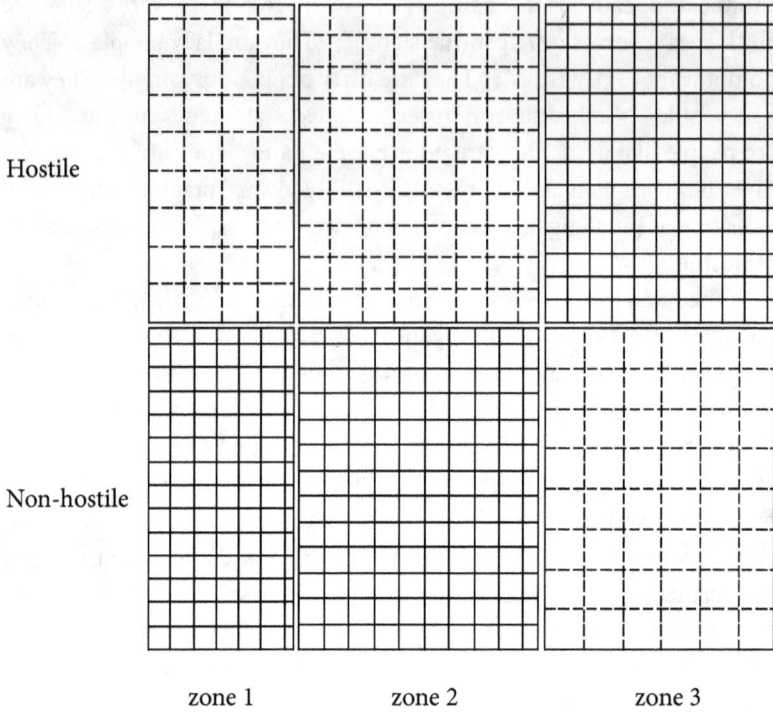

zone 1   zone 2   zone 3

Summary Model for Hostility by Zone

Test of Independence

DF	CHISQ	PROB
2 G.F.	82.304	0.0000
L.R.	85.532	0.0000

Expected Frequencies

	zone1	*zone2*	*zone3*
Hostile	59.5	97.7	93.8
Non-Hostile	60.5	99.3	95.2

Standardized Pearson Deviates

	Villa 20	*Barrio General Savio*	*Old Town*
Hostile	−3.44	−2.20	4.98
Non-Hostile	3.41	2.18	−4.94

TABLE 7.1. Logistic Regression on Hostility

Independent Variables	Model 1	Exp(B)	Model 2	Exp(B)[a]
(Constant)	1.122*	3.071	.969	2.636
	(.616)		(.605)	
Female	-.171	.843	-.124	.884
	(.205)		(.208)	
Manual worker	-.387	.679	-.348	.706
	(.280)		(.281)	
Informal worker	.025	1.025	.060	1.062
	(.282)		(.283)	
Union exposure	.098	1.102	.103	1.108
	(.253)		(.251)	
Activist	.678**	1.969	.643**	1.903
	(.323)		(.321)	
Migrant	.420	1.521	.460	1.584
	(.323)		(.316)	
Education	-.185	.832	-.173	.841
	(.174)		(.172)	
Peronist (PJ)	.018	1.018		
	(.291)			
Radical			.723*	2.061
Zone 1 Shantytown (Villa 20)	-2.232***	.107	-2.230***	.108
	(.311)	(.310)		
Zone 2 Housing project (Barrio G. Savio)	-.1.511***	.221	-1.512***	.221
	(.233)		(.233)	
-2Log likelihood	605.653		602.663	
R-square (Cox & Snell)	.170		.175	
(Nagelkerle)	.227		.234	
X2 Block	80.032***		79.986***	
Model	94.376***		97.366***	
No. of observations	505		505	

Note: Standard errors are between parentheses.

[a] Exp(B) = factor change in odds for unit increase in x.

*p < .1; **p < .05; ***p < .01.

TABLE 7.2. Logistic Regression on Activists' Hostility

Independent Variables	Model 1	Exp(B)	Model 2	Exp(B)
(Constant)	1.101*	3.007	.923	2.518
	(.643)		(.630)	
Female	-.260	.771	-.212	.809
	(.189)		(.191)	
Manual worker	-.724***	.485	-.689***	.502
	(.259)		(.260)	
Informal worker	.033	1.034	.068	1.071
	(.255)		(256)	
Union exposure	-.017	.983	-.027	.973
	(.235)		(.234)	
Immigrant	.107	1.113	.185	1.203
	(.269)		(.265)	
Education	-.047	1.048	.073	1.076
	(.152)		(.150)	
Peronist	-.160	.852		
(PJ)	(.266)			
Radical			.746*	2.109
(UCR)			(.405)	
Activists zone 1	-.414	.661	-.493	.611
Shantytown	(.661)		(.665)	
(Villa 20)				
Activists zone 2	-.1.317*	.268	-1.374**	.253
Housing project	(.233)		(731)	
(Barrio G. Savio)				
-2Log likelihood	682.163		678.921	
R-square (Cox & Snell)	.035		.041	
(Nagelkerle)	.046		.055	
Model	17.866*		21.108**	
No. of observations	505		505	

Note: Standard errors are between parentheses.

*p < .1; **p < .05; ***p < .01.

being hostile in Old Town were 9.3 times higher than in Villa 20. In Barrio General Savio the odds of being hostile were twice those for Villa 20. Furthermore, the models in table 7.1 also show that the odds of being hostile were twice as high for activists as for nonactivists (significant at 0.05).

Hostility and Activism

We have seen that being an activist increased the odds of being hostile. It is also important to look into activists by zone. Were activists equally hostile regardless of their zone of residence? Table 7.2 shows the results of a logistic regression for activists only. As we see, activists from Villa 20 and from Old Town held similar levels of hostility. On the other hand, activists from Barrio General Savio were less hostile when compared to the reference category (zone 3, Old Town). Being an activist in Barrio General Savio (zone 2) decreased the odds of being hostile by a factor of .268 in model 1 and .253 in model 2 (about 70 percent lower). A significant fi ding, however, was that being a manual worker decreased the odds of being hostile among activists by about 50 percent.

Activists' versus Nonactivists' Level of Hostility by Zone

How did activists differ from nonactivists on level of social hostility for each of the three zones of Villa Lugano? Many hypotheses could be raised: for example, if activists had higher levels of hostility than their potential followers they might be the biggest impediment to mounting collective action. They could also activate and raise the level of hostility

GRAPH 7.2. Hostility by activism by zone.

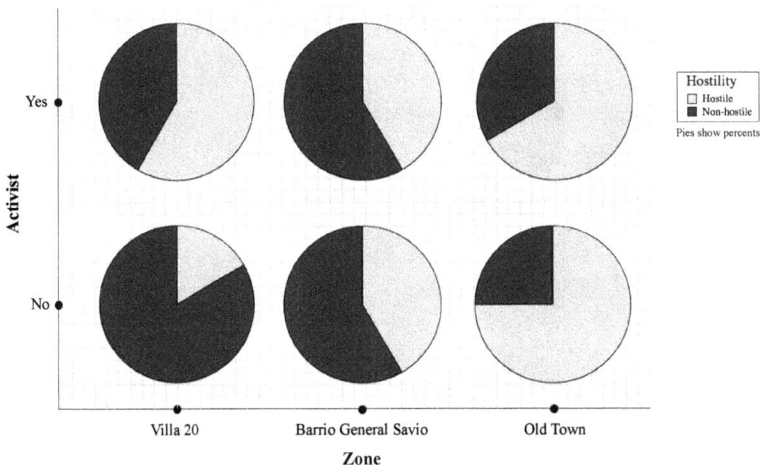

among people who otherwise were not hostile to neighbors of other zones. And if potential followers were more hostile than activists, then activists and leaders might be able to do little to reduce their hostility and mobilize the whole neighborhood to pursue public goods. Graph 7.2 shows a plotted pie chart graphing the three-way cross-tabulation for hostility by activism by zone.

The pie chart anticipates many of the results of the logistic regression below. Among activists, those from Barrio General Savio were the least hostile, followed by Villa 20. What is striking at fi st sight and without any modeling assumptions is that the widest discrepancy in hostility was between Villa 20 leaders and their potential followers in the shantytown. While activists and their potential followers in Barrio General Savio and Old Town had basically the same distribution of opinions regarding hostility, in Villa 20 activists were overwhelmingly more hostile than their potential followers. Below I report the results of a logistic regression for activists' versus nonactivists' social hostility according to zone (table 7.3). Recall that when neighborhood zone was disregarded the odds of being hostile for activists were twice those for nonactivists. However, it is interesting to note once again that in Villa 20 shantytown, activists showed a higher level of hostility than shanty-

TABLE 7.3. Logistic Regression on Activists' versus Nonactivists' Hostility by Zone

Independent Variables	Model 1	Exp(B)	Model 2	Exp(B)
Activists Shantytown Villa 20 (zone 1)	1.607*** (.552)	4.987	1.570*** (.557)	4.806
Activists Housing Project Barrio General Savio (zone 2)	.070 (565)	1.073	.100 (.567)	1.105
Activists Villa Lugano Old Town (zone 3)	.056 (.544)	1.057	-.111 (.526)	.895
No. of observations	505		505	

Note: Standard errors are between parentheses.

*p < .1; **p < .05; ***p < .01.

town dwellers did. Indeed, the odds of being hostile for activists in Villa 20 were five times higher than the odds for nonactivists in the same zone (significant at the 0.01 level).

We can thus conclude that social hostility was strongly placed based among residents of Villa Lugano, especially in Old Town. Hostility was also present among activists and leaders, mainly in shantytown Villa 20 and Old Town. It was rooted in settlement patterns or, more broadly, territorial traditions. This, in turn, was intertwined with the politics of clientelism, in relation to vote buying through the provision of access to government housing and other state social services. Different settlement patterns had different effects on social cohesion. For this reason, placed-based social hostility created the most important discursive dilemma for the leaders and activists of the CVL committed to mobilizing the whole of Villa Lugano to make it a more democratic and egalitarian urban space. The CVL achieved a high-resonance frame of meaning during the struggle for street paving by propounding the idea that residents of southern Buenos Aires, as taxpayers, had the same rights to the city as those living in the north; after all, their parents and then they themselves had bought land and gradually built their homes and their neighborhood. As the in-depth interviews revealed, Old Town residents felt they had to work hard and pay taxes to have decent conditions. This frame of meaning was highly successful for mobilizing people, especially during and just after the transition to democracy in Argentina in the early 1980s. But later it would work against the CVL's attempts to incorporate into the movement the illegal residents of Villa 20 *(usurpadores)* and public-housing residents (suspicious tenants). Both of these groups were perceived as having had easy if not illegal access to housing, which most residents of Old Town and their ancestors did not have. Rampant clientelism made things even worse. The perception that clientelism was at work in the shantytowns and in the housing projects generated in Old Town a sharp sense of injustice that constantly reinforced social hostility. While on the shop floor or at the office workers might attain solidarity regardless of their residence, at the neighborhood level differing settlement patterns and consequent perceptions of injustice acted as a centrifugal force that undermined collective action. Place-based social hostility plus its further activation by clientelism posed an insurmountable discursive dilemma for the CVL.

Conclusion

Contentious collective action occurs frequently, yet it never loses its ability to surprise. From the southernmost and poorest corner of Buenos Aires City, a group of highly committed leaders and activists convinced others to join forces and demand their citizenship rights by reclaiming urban space. They encountered resistance and skepticism from fellow citizens in the beginning, but they fi mly held to their course and obtained some important goals. Several lessons, some positive and others negative, can be drawn from the experience of the CVL in Villa Lugano and could plausibly apply to similar urban settings of Argentina and beyond. During five long years of struggle, from 1983 to 1988, the CVL achieved important material goals. A total of 220 roads were paved, with concomitant improvements in neighborhood infrastructure (potable water and city sewage). As a result, sanitary conditions improved significantly. But perhaps more importantly, the CVL achieved a symbolic goal: it instilled in most of its participants the conviction that they were full citizens of Buenos Aires and that democracy was to be realized not only by voting in elections but also by reclaiming urban space in local struggles.

In spite of the cyclical nature of urban popular movements, one general conclusion that can be drawn from the CVL experience is that pervasive free riding is not inevitable. As we saw through the CVL's rise and fall, contentious collective action may happen and yields important returns for the democratization of urban space.

The fi st theoretical concern of this study was to assess the role of civil society in democratization. As I argued, scholars and policy makers have disagreed on the effects of an active civil society on the quality of democracy and people's well-being. While some argue that an "organized civil society" is good for democratic stability, others suggest—on the basis of the experience of Latin America and eastern Europe—that a "rebellious civil society" is necessary for pushing democratization forward. At the root of this disagreement is the role of political contention in democratization. Historically, political contention is at the core of most democratization processes. Even though it does not always lead to democratization, in most democratization advances it has been present in one form or another. The experience of the CVL seems to confi m my hypothesis that a *contentious* civil society is a necessary condition for the expansion of democracy and citizenship rights. By acting collectively and challenging power holders, the CVL was able to reclaim urban space and, in so doing, to affirm the status of Villa Lugano's residents as full citizens of Buenos Aires.

Yet the CVL experience also suggests that a contentious civil society is a necessary but not a sufficient condition for democratization. Indeed, as I discussed in chapter 4, the "open-door" policy of Mayor Saguier toward the dispossessed south of Buenos Aires was crucial for the early successes of the CVL, while the "closed-door" policy of Mayor Suárez Lastra significantly helped its collapse. It follows that in democratic polities without a minimally receptive state (at the national and/ or local level) contentious collective action becomes hard to sustain. This is an important aspect for understanding the role of civil society vis-à-vis the state in democratization. It was the "synergy" (Evans 1997) between a receptive state and a contentious civil society that opened the road to paving and with it better environmental conditions for the urban poor of Villa Lugano. We can conclude, then, that both a contentious civil society and the existence of receptive state officials are necessary preconditions for the democratization of urban space—for making urban space equally available and livable to all.

A second theoretical concern of this study referred to the effectiveness of citizenship rights among the urban poor and how this may affect the quality of democracy. I argued that voting is a basic right of citizenship but is just one of them. Other citizenship rights are equally important, and without them the very act of voting is undermined. In spite of disagreements about the multiple meanings of democracy, nobody can deny that free and fair elections are at its core. But even a narrow (procedural) defi ition of democracy as no more than the holding of free and fair elections needs to include other rights, such as the rights of associational autonomy and of free expression. As noted, these are some of the "surrounding freedoms" of the political regime, without which voting is less than meaningful (O'Donnell 2004). Among these rights, associational autonomy is of foremost importance for those disadvantaged members of society who practically have only this resource to make their voices heard in the political process (Fox 1994). As Amy Gutmann (1998: 3) has stressed: "Without access to an association that is willing and able to speak up for our views and values, we have a very limited ability to be heard by many other people or to influence the political process, unless we happen to be rich or famous."

In this respect, the experience of the CVL, successful in many ways as it was, provides fertile ground for understanding some of the main obstacles poor people face to fully exercise their right of autonomous association and mount contentious collective action. Among these obstacles, political clientelism stands out. While patron-client relationships have been historically endemic to political life in Argentina as well as in many other countries of Latin America, since the transition to democracy in the 1980s they seem to have further expanded and become even more entrenched. Some scholars have already referred to this paradox: the democratization of formal political institutions in Latin America has come hand in hand with the expansion and strengthening of "informal" institutions such as clientelism (O'Donnell 1996; Helmke and Levitsky 2002). Today, thanks to extensive fieldwork, we know well the intricacies and internal logic of political clientelism. For example, there is significant empirical evidence that parties and candidates often channel public resources to mobilize electoral support (Auyero 2000; Levitsky 2003). There is also evidence that not all parties benefit equally from clientelistic practices (Calvo and Murillo 2004) and that poor, rather than better-off, citizens are mostly the target of these practices (Brusco, Nazareno, and Stokes 2004). Regardless of some nuances in approach, these recent studies focus on clientelism only as a strategy of electoral mobilization and on citizens as voters. In spite of these important advances for understanding the functioning of clientelism in the new democracies of Latin America, a full evaluation of its effects on people's well-being and on the quality of democracy is still lacking. Drawing on the experience of the CVL, I argue that political clientelism, understood broadly as the exchange of material rewards for political support, negatively affects the quality of democracy by precluding the effectiveness of two fundamental rights of citizenship: voting and association. It violates not only the freedom of voting (by pressing "clients" to vote for candidates that offer handouts) but also the autonomy of association. In so doing, political clientelism undermines the realization of the full-fledged political citizenship that is entailed by democracy.[1]

Generally speaking, clientelistic practices by state officials and party bosses interfere with the right of associational autonomy of poor citizens and prevent them from mounting collective action, fi st, by co- ercing and/or co-opting grassroots leaders and activists, and second, by creating incentives for zero-sum competition among popular organi- zations in a context of scarce resources. The experience of the CVL also points to a third and less explored way by which clientelistic practices interfere with the right of associational autonomy: generating (as well as reinforcing already present) *social hostility* among poor citizens, often due to perceived unfairness in the distribution of clientelistic re- wards. Some scholars have suggested that the extension of clientelistic practices in Argentina has been overrated (Brusco, Nazareno, and Stokes 2004). In any case, the data presented in chapter 7 show that the *perception* that clientelistic practices were widespread in Villa Lugano sufficed to (re)create resentment and ultimately social hostility among different segments of the population of this neighborhood. Injustice in the distribution of resources was at the base of this social hostility. As we saw, most Villa Lugano residents in Old Town believed that their tax payments were being used clientelistically to benefit shantytown and state-built condominium dwellers (especially but not only) regarding access to housing. To make things worse, in the shantytowns most of those seen as benefiting from clientelism were believed to be foreigners from neighboring countries.

The CVL clashed with this deeply rooted social hostility when it tried to move beyond a narrow defi ition of citizens as taxpayers and articulate a frame of meaning for the whole of Villa Lugano. How could the CVL mobilize followers for improving health and housing in Villa Lugano if this would also benefit those who did not pay taxes and who, as a consequence, were not perceived as deserving citizens? By the same logic, the experience of the CVL in Villa Lugano suggests that social hostility hinders the formation of the minimum level of (horizontal) trust required for broad-based collective action to happen. As we saw in chapter 4, most members of the CVL expressed the view that a minimum of social trust (based upon face-to-face contacts and longtime settlement in Old Town) was important for each person's decision regarding whether to participate in the struggle for paving. This is an important issue, at odds with some scholars' assertion that clientelism entails some kind of "trust" between the parties involved (Auyero 1999; Lazar 2004). This assertion disregards not only the many coercions implicit in clientelistic exchanges but also the externalities of social hostility they generate. In any case, if clientelism entails some kind of interpersonal trust, it is defi itely not of the kind required for autonomous collective action, as the experience of the CVL makes evident.

We have learned from Elias and Scotson (1994) that hostility to others can emerge even in the absence of any apparently relevant political, socioeconomic, or ethnic cleavage(s). As Moore (2000) has argued, to understand the way hostility operates one must look into its historical causes and the factors that may reinforce it. While hostility does not automatically entail discrimination or persecution of the other, when it is acted upon it always involves some conception of moral (im)purity. The historical roots of social hostility in Argentina are complex. They can be traced back to the founding fathers' ideas of nation building and desirable immigration. But as the data presented in chapter 7 suggest, social hostility among the urban poor is primarily place based: it is defi ed by place of residence and, equally important, by the way people gain access to it—through land invasion, clientelism, or the market. This makes clear the relevance of geography and settlement patterns in the formation of social identities. In this sense, as I discussed in chapter 3, social hostility is a direct consequence of highly fragmented and residual state housing and urban policies, which have segregated and divided, instead of integrating, the urban poor.

We can thus conclude from the experience of the CVL that the right of associational autonomy, crucial for the realization of democracy, is adversely affected by political clientelism. Whether or not clientelism is widespread, the perception that such is the case exacerbates place-based social hostility. This perception hindered the framing capabilities of the CVL and prevented it from mounting a movement to improve the whole of Villa Lugano.

A third concern of this study was to answer why the study of the dynamics of contentious collective action is at all relevant from the perspective of the urban poor. If we adopt Amartya Sen's defi ition of economic development as freedom, the "expansion of the capabilities of people to lead the lives they value—and have reason to value" (1999: 18), the successes and failures of popular collective action become a central component of development. In Sen's development framework, the expansion of people's capabilities depends upon the elimination of oppression and the provision of some basic services. Yet, as I noted, Peter Evans persuasively argues that the expansion of individual capabilities crucially depends on the achievement of *collective capabilities*. The ability of an individual to choose the life he or she has reason to value depends upon the possibility of acting with others who have reason to value similar things (2002: 56). As a consequence, for the poor it is even truer that "dense, diverse, organized collective action is necessary to exploit the opportunities created by elections and civil rights, and complement the dispersed efforts of groups and individuals. Public policy that explicitly acknowledges the importance of collective action, public mores that are open to contestation and collective struggles, and focused efforts to stimulate and sustain organizations that transcend primordial and parochial interests are all necessary components in the quest for development as freedom" (2002: 57).

In sum, collective capabilities are crucial to achieve development as freedom as well as to improve the quality of democracy by giving effective voice to the poor in the political process. This is their main chance to influence policies that may improve their living conditions.

As we saw in chapter 2, in the repertoire of contention of the urban poor in Buenos Aires, historically union action has the longest tradition and has overshadowed the more ephemeral and fragmented actions of grassroots organizations. Indeed, in Argentina the two decades that preceded Peronism were decisive for the separation in the urban poor's consciousness of the realms of work and home. Innovations in strategies of contention came out of struggles in both realms, but from that period on, demands over production and social reproduction often took, as I argued, divergent roads. Urban demands for better environmental and living conditions became disentangled from work-related demands. This split between the realms of residence and work is not peculiar to Buenos Aires.[2]

Since the 1970s, the dramatic decline of unions as a result of repression by the 1976–83 military regime and neoliberal economic restructuring has left the urban poor in Buenos Aires and other important cities of Argentina with few resources to struggle for their citizenship rights, especially their right to the city. Grassroots mobilization, fragmentary and ephemeral as it has been, is one of the very few organizational options still available to the disadvantaged living in the popular neighborhoods of Buenos Aires. In this context, knowledge of the factors affecting the dynamics of contentious collective action among the urban poor is of foremost importance, not only for the improvement in the quality of democracy and for the generalized effectiveness of the rights of political citizenship, but also for the progressive realization of development as freedom. Thus the experience of the CVL provides important lessons for similar neighborhoods of southern Buenos Aires and, hopefully, for other Latin American cities.

The last—but central—concern of this study was to bring to the fore the relevance of geography, space, and territory for understanding the dynamics of contention. Indeed, no single factor can explain why popular movements succeed or fail. In this study, political opportunities, organization, leadership, and cognitive frames of meaning converged in one specific space—Villa Lugano—to give birth to the CVL. As I discussed in chapter 1, in spite of a recent "spatial" turn in the study of politics, among social scientists geography has been rather absent from the study of popular movements and organizations. However, as the experience of the CVL shows, geography is a constitutive part of collective action and should be analyzed as such. As William Sewell Jr. (2001: 55) has argued, we should pay special attention to the ways that "spatial constraints are turned to advantage in political and social struggles and the way that such struggles can restructure the meanings, uses, and strategic valence of space."

Geography, as we saw in chapter 4, was present in the organization and mobilization of the CVL, especially in the formation of networks of activists by areas. It was also present in the formulation of frames of meaning that referred to the north-south inequities of Buenos Aires. Furthermore, in chapter 6 we saw that geography explained disparities of opinion on strategies of local participation; this turned out to be one of the main cleavages affecting the organization of mobilization in Villa Lugano. Finally, the analysis in chapter 7 showed that geography was at the root of social hostility—the most robust contributing factor to the dissolution of the CVL. All in all, the ultimate goal of the CVL was the constitution of spatial agency as I have defi ed it: reshaping urban space by reclaiming it. This, I would claim, is also true of most popular mobilization attempts at the grassroots level in other urban settings in Latin America and probably elsewhere. In attempting to reach this goal, movements' participants affirm their right to the city and their status as full citizens.

*   *   *

There is no magic formula for successfully mounting contentious collective action. However, in a worldwide context of sustained urbanization and shantytown population growth (UN-Habitat 2006), the experience of the CVL in Villa Lugano suggests several aspects to be taken into account by both scholars and organizers of urban popular movements.

In this study we witnessed the dynamic emergence of an autonomous social movement of the urban poor in a neighborhood of the city of Buenos Aires. This movement not only took up the opportunities provided by the democratic opening and a receptive state but also appropriated a language of rights of citizenship that was sincerely held by its participants. Yet we have also witnessed the crisis and the disappearance of this movement. As the literature abundantly shows, this is not unusual for popular movements. In this particular case, the analysis of the various data I gathered showed that the decline of the CVL could be to a great extent explained by historically rooted place-based social hostility among different residential sectors of Villa Lugano. Social hostility was exacerbated by increasing political clientelism once the transition to democracy began in the 1980s, which greatly helped to generate for the CVL an unsolvable discursive dilemma when, encouraged by its initial successes, it tried to scale up its hopes and demands for the whole of Villa Lugano. The welfare of the entire neighborhood and the full enjoyment of their rights consequently suffered from this failure.

This is a rather sad ending to a complex, and initially hopeful, story. Yet I believe this story is worth telling because the factors that fi ally hindered the CVL (the negative effects of clientelism on popular collective action and the fragmented patterns of settlement and habitat of the urban poor) seem to be also operating in similar geographies elsewhere: in the southern neighborhoods of Buenos Aires and its periphery, in other cities of Argentina, and in Latin America. Hopefully, future research will substantiate this assertion that may have important implications for the strategies to be undertaken by popular urban social movements and organizations. The quality of our fledging democracies and people's well-being depend in no small measure on it.

APPENDIX A

Survey Demographics

Gender

	Frequency	Percent
Females	261	51.5
Males	245	48.5
Total	506	100

Housing Area

	Frequency	Percent
Villa 20	70	13.8
Barrio G. Savio	193	38.2
Old Town	243	48.0
Total	506	100

Age

	Frequency	Percent
18–24	65	12.9
25–34	98	19.4
35–44	122	24.1
45–54	77	15.2
55–64	90	17.8
65–74	43	8.5
75 and over	11	2.2
Total	506	100

Citizenship

	Frequency	Percent
Natives	442	87.3
Foreigners	64	12.7
Total	506	100

Type of Employment

	Frequency	Percent
Manual	104	20.5
Nonmanual	155	30.7
Housewife	142	28.0
Professional	6	1.1
Pensioners	52	10.3
Unemployed	47	9.5
Total	506	100

Type of Employment (of Those Employed)

	Frequency	Percent
Formal	153	57.0
Informal	116	43.0
Both	1	0.3
Total	270	100

Education

	Frequency	Percent
Elementary (incomplete)	40	8.0
Elementary	178	35.2
High school (incomplete)	85	16.8
High school	125	24.7
Technical (incomplete)	10	1.9
Technical	20	4.0
College (incomplete)	26	5.2
College	9	1.8
Nursing school	10	1.9
Military school	1	0.2
Never attended	2	0.3
Total	506	100

Schooling Type

	Frequency	Percent
Public	470	92.9
Private	33	6.5
DA	3	0.6
Total	506	100

Household Size (Number of Persons)

	Frequency	*Percent*
1–3	240	47.5
4–6	240	47.4
7–9	24	4.7
10 and over	2	0.4
Total	506	100

Head of Household

	Frequency	*Percent*
Female	40	7.9
Male	437	86.4
One person	24	4.7
DA	5	1
Total	506	100

Household Income

	Frequency	*Percent*
Low	168	33.2
Medium-low	158	31.2
High	44	8.7
Varies monthly	111	21.9
DA	25	5.0
Total	506	100

Class Self-Identification

	Frequency	*Percent*
Lower class	284	56.1
Middle lower class	98	19.4
Middle class	117	23.2
DA	7	1.4
Total	506	100

Survey Questionnaire

Encuesta #:
Nombre del encuestador:
Fecha:
Área:
de sorteo y dirección:
Nacionalidad:

1. Sexo:
_____ 1) Femenino
_____ 2) Masculino

2. ¿Dónde hace habitualmente sus compras?
_____ 1) Mercado central
_____ 2) Jumbo
_____ 3) Supermercados
_____ 4) Negocios minoristas (almacén, carnicería, etc.)
_____ 5) Otros (especificar):

3. ¿Concurre Ud. o algún miembro de su familia a alguno de los parques que le voy a mencionar?
SI   NO   ¿Por qué?
_____ 1) Parque Roca
_____ 2) Parque de la Ciudad
_____ 3) Club de Golf
_____ 4) Parque de Las Victorias
_____ 5) Zoofitogeográfico

4. ¿Ud. cree que alguno de esos parques está desaprovechado y que, en su lugar, debería instalarse otra cosa? (especificar para cada parque sí o no. Si responde no, pasar a #6)

SI   NO
_____ 1) Parque Roca
_____ 2) Parque de la Ciudad
_____ 3) Club de Golf
_____ 4) Parque de Las Victorias
_____ 5) Parque Zoofitogeográfico

5. ¿Ud. que instalaría en su lugar? (Las opciones no son excluyentes, aceptando un máximo de tres)
_____ 1) Parque Roca
_____ 2) Parque de la Ciudad
_____ 3) Club de Golf
_____ 4) Parque de Las Victorias
_____ 5) Parque Zoofitogeográfico

[Códigos de respuesta:

1) Hospital
2) Escuela
3) Plaza
4) Vivienda
5) Industria
6) Comercio
7) Otro (especificar):_____]

6. ¿Pertenece a algún sindicato? ¿Cuál? (Si no pertenece, pasar a #9)

7. ¿Tiene algún cargo sindical? ¿Cuál?

8. ¿Qué opina de su sindicato?

9. ¿Perteneció a algún sindicato en el pasado? ¿Cuál? (Si no perteneció, pasar a #11)

10. ¿Tuvo algún cargo en dicho sindicato?

11. (Para todos) ¿Cuál es su opinión sobre los sindicatos en general? (Si el entrevistado no responde espontáneamente, preguntar): ¿Ud. cree que los sindicatos deberían existir?

12. ¿Está afiliado a algún partido político? ¿Cuál?

SI   NO

_____ 1) PJ

_____ 2) UCR

_____ 3) UCD

_____ 4) MAS

_____ 5) PO

_____ 6) PSP

_____ 7) DC

_____ 8) MODIN

_____ 9) Otro (especificar):_____

_____ 98) No sabe

_____ 99) No respondió

13. Si no es así, ¿simpatiza con algún partido político?

SI   NO

_____ 1) PJ

_____ 2) UCR

_____ 3) UCD

_____ 4) MAS

_____ 5) PO

_____ 6) PSP

_____ 7) DC

_____ 8) MODIN

_____ 9) Otro (especificar):_____

_____ 98) No sabe

_____ 99) No respondió

14. ¿Ha votado regularmente por algún partido?

SI   NO

_____ 1) PJ

_____ 2) UCR

_____ 3) UCD

_____ 4) MAS

_____ 5) PO

_____ 6) PSP

_____ 7) DC

_____ 8) MODIN

_____ 9) Otro (especificar):_____

_____ 98) No sabe

_____ 99) No respondió

15. (Si está afiliado, simpatiza o ha votado regularmente por algún partido preguntar): ¿Por qué le gusta ese partido (o por qué es peronista o radical)?

16. ¿Ud. recuerda a quién ha votado en las elecciones nacionales para presidente desde que tiene edad para votar?:
1946:_____
1952:_____
1958:_____
1963:_____
1973:_____
1983:_____
1989:_____

17. (Pregunte por las elecciones que el entrevistado no recordó espontáneamente, teniendo en cuenta su edad)
1946 (Perón):_____
1952 (Perón):_____
1958 (Frondizi):_____
1963 (Illia):_____
1973 (Perón):_____
1983 (Alfonsín):_____
1989 (Menem):_____

18. ¿Cómo consiguió su primera vivienda en Villa Lugano?
_____ 1) Tomó el terreno o la casa
_____ 2) Compró el terreno o la casa a su anterior dueño
_____ 3) Alquiló
_____ 4) Compró un departamento o una casa a través de un programa de vivienda del gobierno
_____ 5) Compró o está por comprar su vivienda a través del plan de radicación de barrios de emergencia del gobierno
_____ 6) Compró a través de un crédito del Banco Hipotecario Nacional
_____ 7) Otra (especificar):_____
_____ 8) No sabe
_____ 9) No respondió

19. ¿Cómo consiguió su actual vivienda en Villa Lugano?
_____ 1) Tomó el terreno o la casa
_____ 2) Compró el terreno o la casa a su anterior dueño
_____ 3) Alquiló
_____ 4) Compró un departamento o una casa a través de un programa de vivienda del gobierno

_____ 5) Compró o está por comprar su vivienda a través del plan de radicación de barrios de emergencia del gobierno
_____ 6) Compró a través de un crédito del Banco Hipotecario Nacional
_____ 7) Otra (especificar):_____
_____ 8) No sabe
_____ 9) No respondió

20. ¿Qué otro tipo de viviendas tuvo y en que barrios? (Seguir la clasificación
anterior, alquilada, comprada, etc.)
Tipo de Vivienda   Barrio
a) _____   _____
b) _____   _____

21. ¿Para conseguir el lugar donde vive actualmente, necesitó pedir ayuda a
alguna persona?
SI   NO
_____ 1) Pariente
_____ 2) Vecino
_____ 3) Alguien del sindicato
_____ 4) Compañero de trabajo
_____ 5) Político o alguien ligado a un político
_____ 6) Policía
_____ 7) Cura o religiosa
_____ 8) Alguien de la sociedad de fomento del barrio
_____ 9) Patrón
_____ 10) Otra (especificar):_____
_____ 11) No precisó recurrir a nadie
_____ 98) No sabe
_____ 99) No respondió

22. ¿Qué cobertura médica tiene Ud. en la actualidad?
(Leer códigos hasta #5)
_____ 1) Privada
_____ 2) Sindical (obra social)
_____ 3) Comunitaria (centro de salud o sala de barrio)
_____ 4) Hospital público
_____ 5) PAMI
_____ 6) Otra (especificar):_____
_____ 7) Ninguna
_____ 8) No sabe
_____ 9) No respondió

23. ¿Y durante los últimos diez años?
(Leer códigos hasta #5)
_____ 1) Privada
_____ 2) Sindical (obra social)
_____ 3) Comunitaria (centro de salud o sala de barrio)
_____ 4) Hospital público
_____ 5) PAMI
_____ 6) Otra (especificar):_____
_____ 7) Ninguna
_____ 8) No sabe
_____ 9) No respondió

24. Frente a un problema serio en su barrio, que perjudique a todos, ¿Ud. cree que los vecinos deben reunirse para buscar juntos una solución o dejar que las autoridades cuiden del problema?
_____ 1) Los vecinos se deben reunir
_____ 2) Dejar que las autoridades resuelvan el problema
_____ 3) No vale la pena hacer nada
_____ 4) Otra (especificar):_____
_____ 8) No sabe
_____ 9) No respondió

25. ¿Cómo cree Ud. que se obtienen mejores resultados para lograr los reclamos del Barrio? a través de: (Leer códigos hasta #3)
_____ 1) Trámites legales iniciados por la Sociedad de Fomento o Comisión Vecinal
_____ 2) La movilización vecinal para plantear el problema a las autoridades
_____ 3) Los contactos personales con funcionarios o dirigentes políticos
_____ 4) No vale la pena hacer nada
_____ 5) La combinación de algunas de las estrategias anteriores (espontánea):
_____ 6) Otros medios (espontánea):
_____ 8) No sabe
_____ 9) No respondió

26. ¿Ud. participó en alguna manifestación vecinal para mejorar el barrio? ¿Cuándo y con qué objetivo?

27. ¿Participó o participa en alguna organización vecinal? ¿De qué tipo? (si no participa o participó pasar a #29) (Leer códigos hasta #4)
_____ 1) Sociedad de fomento (especificar):_____
_____ 2) Comisión vecinal (especificar):_____

___ 3) Club deportivo
___ 4) Organización religiosa
___ 5) Cooperadora escolar
___ 6) Otra (especificar):_____
___ 7) Ninguna
___ 8) No sabe
___ 9) No respondió

28. ¿Tiene o tuvo algún cargo en dicha organización? ¿Cuál?

29. (Si participó en alguna manifestación u organización vecinal preguntar) ¿Por qué decidió participar? (Si no participó nunca pasar a #32)

30. (Si participó en alguna manifestación u organización vecinal preguntar): ¿Qué experiencia le queda (o qué aprendió) de su participación vecinal?

31. (Si participó en alguna manifestación u organización vecinal pero ya no participa preguntar): ¿Por qué dejó de participar?

32. (Para todos) ¿Por qué cree Ud. que los vecinos participan poco?

33. De acuerdo a su opinión, las relaciones entre los partidos políticos y las organizaciones barriales deberían ser:
(Leer códigos hasta #3)
___ 1) Estrechas
___ 2) Limitadas
___ 3) No deberían tener ninguna relación
___ 8) No sabe
___ 9) No respondió

34. De acuerdo a su opinión las relaciones entre el gobierno y las organizaciones barriales deberían ser:
(Leer códigos hasta #3)
___ 1) Estrechas
___ 2) Limitadas
___ 3) No deberían tener ninguna relación
___ 8) No sabe
___ 9) No respondió

35. ¿Qué es más importante cuando Ud. decide a quién votar, el candidato o el partido al cual pertenece?
___ 1) La persona en si
___ 2) El partido al que pertenece

_____ 3) Los dos son igualmente importantes (espontánea)
_____ 4) Ninguno de los dos
_____ 5) Otra (especificar):_____
_____ 8) No sabe
_____ 9) No respondió

36. Cuando se habla de política se utilizan expresiones tales como "izquierda," "centro" y "derecha." En esta tarjeta hay una serie de números que van de izquierda a derecha, ¿en cuál de ellos Ud. ubicaría a los siguientes partidos? (Leer de a uno por vez): PJ, UCR, UCD, MODIN, MAS.

01 02 03 04 05 06 07 08 09 10

izquierda   derecha

_____ De 01 a 10
_____ 11) Centro (espontánea)
_____ 12) No entiende la pregunta
_____ 13) No le parece importante
_____ 98) No sabe
_____ 99) No respondió

37. (Mostrar tarjeta #2) ¿Dónde se ubicaría a Ud. mismo?

01 02 03 04 05 06 07 08 09 10

izquierda   derecha

_____ De 01 a 10
_____ 11) Centro (espontánea)
_____ 12) No entiende la pregunta
_____ 13) No le parece importante
_____ 98) No sabe
_____ 99) No respondió

38. Dígame que tres cosas cambiaría para que la Argentina fuera el país que Ud. sueña:

39. Ud. está de acuerdo o en desacuerdo con la siguiente frase:
"En el fondo, los partidos políticos son todos iguales."
_____ 1) Está de acuerdo totalmente
_____ 2) Está de acuerdo en parte
_____ 3) Indeciso

_____ 4) Desacuerda en parte
_____ 5) Desacuerda totalmente
_____ 8) No sabe
_____ 9) No respondió

40. Los partidos políticos son en general (aceptar varias respuestas):
(Leer hasta #3)
_____ 1) Un grupo de personas que sobre todo busca su propio beneficio
_____ 2) Un grupo de personas con vocación de servir al país
_____ 3) Un grupo de personas que solo hacen más difícil la tarea del gobierno
_____ 4) Otra (especificar):_____

41. De acuerdo a su opinión, ¿cuál es el problema más grave de la Argentina actualmente?

42. ¿Y el segundo problema más grave?

43. Últimamente, mucha gente discute sobre que debería hacerse con el Estado. De acuerdo a su opinión el Estado debería:
_____ 1) Desaparecer
_____ 2) Seguir como está
_____ 3) Achicar mucho sus gastos y el número de empleados
_____ 4) No achicarse, pero mejorar la manera como funciona
_____ 8) No sabe
_____ 9) No responde

44. De acuerdo a su opinión, el estado argentino es:
_____ 1) Un conjunto de funcionarios que solo defiende su propio interés
_____ 2) Un medio de opresión de los que más dinero tienen sobre los pobres
_____ 3) La principal garantía para que los intereses del pueblo sean respetados
_____ 4) Otra (espontánea):_____

45. De acuerdo a su opinión, ¿Cuáles son, de la lista que voy a leerle, las funciones que deberían estar principalmente a cargo del Estado? (Lea cada opción y pregunte si o no)
SI   NO
_____ 1) Salud
_____ 2) Desarrollo económico
_____ 3) Vivienda
_____ 4) Educación
_____ 5) Control de la inflación
_____ 6) Seguridad

____ 7) Empleo para todos
____ 8) Garantizar un nivel de vida adecuado a los jubilados y pensionados
____ 9) Otra (especificar):_____
____ 10) Ninguna
____ 98) No sabe
____ 99) No respondió

46. De acuerdo a su opinión el poder político de los siguientes sectores debería:
1-expandirse   2-mantenerse igual   3-reducirse
____ 1) Iglesia
____ 2) Fuerzas armadas
____ 3) Empresarios
____ 4) Sindicatos
____ 5) Partidos políticos
____ 6) Grupos vecinales
____ 7) El presidente de la nación
____ 8) Radio, TV, y diarios
____ 9) La policía
____ 10) Los jueces
____ 11) El Congreso
____ 12) El Partido Justicialista
____ 13) La Unión Cívica Radical
____ 14) Otros (especificar):_____

47. En su opinión, ¿para qué sirve la democracia?

48. Dígame si está de acuerdo o no con la siguiente frase:
"En vez de partidos políticos, lo que hace falta es que el pueblo siga a un hombre capaz y decidido que haga la unidad nacional."
____ 1) Está de acuerdo totalmente
____ 2) Está de acuerdo en parte
____ 3) Depende (espontánea)
____ 4) Desacuerda en parte
____ 5) Desacuerda totalmente
____ 8) No sabe
____ 9) No respondió

49. ¿Qué esperaba Ud. de la democracia en 1983?

50. ¿Lo que Ud. esperaba de la democracia se ha cumplido?
SI   NO   ¿Por qué?

51. Considerando una escala de 1 a 10 puntos, ¿Qué nota le daría al Gobierno del Presidente Carlos Menem?

52. Dígame, ¿Cuál de los siguientes sectores que le voy a leer es el más culpable de los problemas que la Argentina enfrenta hoy?
_____1) El gobierno actual
_____2) El gobierno de Alfonsín
_____3) Los gobiernos militares
_____4) La democracia
_____5) El Congreso y los partidos políticos
_____6) La burocracia del estado
_____7) Los empresarios
_____8) Los intereses extranjeros
_____9) Otro (espontánea):_____
_____98) No sabe
_____99) No respondió

53. En su opinión, ¿cuáles de las siguientes cosas que voy a leerle son o no importantes para decir que un país es democrático?
_____1) Que existan dos o más partidos políticos
_____2) Que la justicia trate a todos igualmente
_____3) Que todos puedan decir libremente lo que piensan
_____4) Que todos ganen lo suficiente para llevar una vida decente
_____5) Que los gobernantes sean electos por el voto del pueblo
_____6) Que todos puedan participar en sindicatos y organizaciones comunitarias
_____7) Otra (espontánea):_____
_____8) No sabe
_____9) No respondió

54. Dígame, ¿Con cuál de las siguientes frases Ud. está más de acuerdo?:
_____ 1) "La democracia debe, antes que nada, asegurar la libertad de la población para elegir el gobierno a través del voto."
_____ 2) "La democracia debe, antes que nada, asegurar un nivel de vida decente para toda la población."
_____ 3) Está de acuerdo con las dos frases (espontánea)
_____ 8) No sabe
_____ 9) No respondió

55. ¿Ud. cree que en la Argentina la ley es aplicada a todos por igual?
_____ 1) Si
_____ 2) No

_____ 8) No sabe
_____ 9) No respondió

56. Ud. está de acuerdo o en desacuerdo con las siguientes afi maciones:
"Si para resolver un grave problema nacional, el Presidente tuviera que violar las leyes, es mejor que lo haga y que resuelva el problema."

57. Está de acuerdo/desacuerdo:
"La ocasión que tienen los ciudadanos para participar en política es votando en las elecciones. Después, corresponde al Presidente gobernar el país de la manera que él juzgue mejor."

58. Está de acuerdo/desacuerdo:
"Los partidos políticos solo sirven para dividir al pueblo."

59. Está de acuerdo/desacuerdo:
"Una vez electo, el presidente debe gobernar de la manera que le parezca mejor para el país, sin aceptar interferencias del Congreso o los Jueces."

60. ¿Ud. cree que los empresarios argentinos tratan de contribuir para la riqueza y el desarrollo del país, o solo intentan obtener benefi ios personales?
_____ 1) Intentan contribuir
_____ 2) Solo intentan obtener beneficios personales
_____ 3) Otra (espontánea):_____
_____ 8) No sabe
_____ 9) No respondió

61. ¿Con cuál de las siguientes frases Ud. concuerda más?
_____ 1) Lo importante es que haya desarrollo económico, aunque sea sin democracia, o
_____ 2) Lo importante es que haya democracia, aunque con poco desarrollo económico
_____ 7) Ninguna de las dos (espontánea)
_____ 8) No sabe
_____ 9) No respondió

62. La mejor forma de resolver los problemas económicos de la Argentina es a través de:
_____ 1) Que el Estado tenga mucho control sobre la economía
_____ 2) Que el Estado deje de intervenir en la economía
_____ 3) Que el Estado intervenga solamente en algunas actividades de la economía

____ 4) Otra (espontánea):_____

____ 8) No sabe

____ 9) No respondió

63. ¿Qué clases sociales cree Ud. que existen en la Argentina?

64. ¿A qué clase social cree Ud. que pertenece?

65. En comparación a la vida que tuvieron sus padres, ¿Ud. cree que su vida es mejor, igual o peor?

66. ¿Pensando en sus hijos o los hijos de sus amigos, lo más probable es que tengan una vida mejor, igual o peor que la suya?

67. ¿Cuáles son a su criterio los principales problemas de la zona en la que Ud. vive?

68. ¿Cuál es su opinión sobre los políticos del barrio?

69. Muchos vecinos de Lugano opinan que uno de los principales problemas de la zona es la falta de seguridad. ¿Ud. está de acuerdo o no?

70. (Si está de acuerdo en # 69, preguntar): ¿A qué se debe la falta de seguridad?

Villa Lugano (Old Town):

71. Su casa, como muchas otras de Villa Lugano, está muy cerca de la Villa 20. Como Ud. sabe, hay distintas opiniones sobre la gente que vive allí; por ejemplo, se dice que si bien hay muchas personas que quieren progresar y salir de la villa, hay otras que, por el contrario, se dedican a actividades ilegales, como la droga y el juego. Dígame, Ud. que tiene un mejor conocimiento por vivir cerca de la Villa 20, ¿qué opina sobre las personas que viven en ella?

72. ¿Ud. cree qué los habitantes de la Villa 20 se sienten integrados a Villa Lugano? ¿Por qué?

73. ¿Por qué cree Ud. que viven en la villa?

74. ¿Ud. ha participado en alguna organización vecinal o reclamo colectivo junto con personas que viven en la villa? (Si responde si, aclarar en que organización y para que demanda)

75. Durante muchos años, distintos gobiernos han intentado resolver el problema de las villas sin éxito. Ud. cree que el problema de las villas debe resolverse radicándolas, es decir fi anciando la construcción de casas en el mismo terreno, o erradicándolas, es decir, trasladando a sus habitantes a otras áreas de la ciudad.

____ 1) Radicando

____ 2) Erradicando

____ 3) Otra(espontánea):_____

____ 8) No sabe

____ 9) No respondió

76. Su casa se encuentra muy cerca también del barrio General Savio, comúnmente llamado Lugano I y II. Dígame, ¿cuál es su opinión sobre las personas que viven allí?

77. ¿Ud. ha participado en alguna organización vecinal o reclamo colectivo con personas que viven en alguno de los monoblocks del barrio? (Si responde si, aclarar en que organización y para que demanda)

78. ¿Ud. cree que los habitantes de Lugano I y II (Barrio General Savio) se sienten integrados a Villa Lugano?

Barrio General Savio:

71. Su casa, como muchas otras de Villa Lugano, está muy cerca de la Villa 20. Como Ud. sabe, hay distintas opiniones sobre la gente que vive allí; por ejemplo, se dice que si bien hay muchas personas que quieren progresar y salir de la villa, hay otras que, por el contrario, se dedican a actividades ilegales, como la droga y el juego. Dígame, Ud. que tiene un mejor conocimiento por vivir cerca de la Villa 20, ¿qué opina sobre las personas que viven en ella?

72. ¿Ud. cree qué los habitantes de la Villa 20 se sienten integrados a Villa Lugano?

73. ¿Por qué cree Ud. que viven en la villa?

74. ¿Ud. ha participado en alguna organización vecinal o reclamo colectivo con personas que viven en la villa? (Si responde si, aclarar en que organización y para que demanda)

75. Durante muchos años, distintos gobiernos han intentado resolver el problema de las villas sin éxito. ¿Ud. cree que el problema de las villas debe resolverse radicándolas, es decir fi anciando la construcción de casas en el mismo terreno, o erradicándolas, es decir, trasladando a sus habitantes a otras áreas de la ciudad?

_____ 1) Radicando

_____ 2) Erradicando

_____ 3) Otra(espontánea):_____

_____ 8) No sabe

_____ 9) No responde

76. Su casa se encuentra también muy cerca del sector más viejo de Villa Lugano. Dígame, ¿cuál es su opinión sobre las personas que viven allí?

77. ¿Cómo cree qué ellos se sienten con respecto a barrios como Lugano I y II?

78. ¿Ud. ha participado en alguna organización vecinal o reclamo colectivo con personas que viven en el sector más viejo del barrio? (Si responde si, aclarar en que organización y para que demanda)

79. Hay vecinos del barrio que dicen que los habitantes de Lugano I y II no se sienten parte de Villa Lugano. Dígame, ¿Ud. cree que tienen razón? ¿Por qué?

80. ¿Ud. se siente parte de Villa Lugano o solo de Lugano I y II? ¿Por qué?

Villa 20:

71. ¿Cuál es su opinión sobre la gente que vive bordeando la Villa 20?

72. ¿Y de los habitantes de los departamentos de aquí enfrente (Lugano I y II)?

73. Hay vecinos del barrio que dicen que los habitantes de la Villa 20 no se sienten parte de Villa Lugano. Dígame, ¿Ud. cree que tienen razón? ¿Por qué?

74. ¿Ud. se siente parte/vecino de Villa Lugano o solo de Villa 20? ¿Por qué?

75. Como Ud. sabe, se dicen muchas cosas, que no son siempre verdaderas o justas, sobre las personas que viven en barrios humildes como la Villa 20. Sin embargo, siempre hay gente con malas intenciones que trata de marginar a la gente que vive aquí. Por esa razón me gustaría que me dijera: ¿Qué es lo que Ud. percibe que los vecinos de Villa Lugano piensan de las personas que viven en la Villa 20?

76. ¿Por qué cree Ud. que piensan así?

77. ¿Ud. ha participado en alguna organización vecinal o reclamo colectivo con personas que viven en el sector más viejo del barrio? (Si responde si, aclarar en que organización y para que demanda)

78. ¿Y con personas que viven en los edificios de departamentos como Lugano I y II? (Si responde si, aclarar en que organización y para que demanda)

79. Ahora, para resumir nuestra charla sobre el Barrio, describa en tres (3) palabras, como por ejemplo bueno, malo, etc., lo que Ud. piensa de sus vecinos de la Villa 20.

80. Durante muchos años, distintos gobiernos han intentado resolver el problema de las villas sin éxito. ¿Ud. cree que el problema de las villas debe resolverse radicándolas, es decir fi anciando la construcción de casas en el mismo terreno, o erradicándolas, es decir, trasladando a sus habitantes a otras áreas de la ciudad?
_____ 1) Radicando
_____ 2) Erradicando
_____ 3) Otra(espontánea):_____
_____ 8) No sabe
_____ 9) No responde

81. Si le ofrecieran un departamento en Lugano I y II, ¿Ud. se mudaría de aquí?
SI   NO   Por qué?

82. ¿Por qué vive Ud. en Villa 20?

Todas las Zonas (all zones):

83. Año de nacimiento:_____

84. Lugar de nacimiento (Si nació en Capital Federal, pase a #86):

85. Si no nació en Capital Federal, ¿desde cuándo vive en Capital Federal?

86. ¿Cuándo llegó a Villa Lugano?

87. Tipo de empleo actual (especificar por cuenta propia o dependiente)

88. ¿En qué barrio/zona trabaja?

89. Empleo previo (especificar, por cuenta propia o dependiente, y por qué lo dejó)

90. Estudios cursados:

91. ¿Ud. como diría que es su situación económica: mejor, igual o peor que hace diez años?

92. ¿Cómo está compuesta su familia? (especificar quien es el jefe de la familia)

93. Ingreso personal y familiar mensual aproximado:_____

NOTES

———

Introduction

1. Collier and Mahoney (1996) provide a good summary of this topic, as do King, Keohane, and Verba (1994).

Chapter 1.   Contentious Politics in Space

1. Thompson (1971) used the expression "collective bargaining by riot."

2. New developments in methodology, particularly in survey techniques, further contributed to the characterization of protesters as rational actors and of protest as a form of expressing demands rather than as dysfunctional behavior. For example, survey data showed that protesters of the 1960s in the United States were not "marginal" individuals: rather, they were mostly students raised in families with liberal or left- ing political backgrounds (Tarrow 1989).

3. Gamson's (1975) pioneering research focused on the effects of various organizational features on protest success. He concluded, fi st, that the more bureaucratized organizations were more likely to achieve success, and second, that the combined effects of both centralization and bureaucratization reinforced the chances of movement success. Factionalism was the best predictor of movement failure. Gamson's fi dings were later contested by Goldstone (1980) and Gerlach and Hine (1970), who argued in their study of the Pentecostal and Black Power movements in the United States that decentralized, multicellular organizations whose units possess partial autonomy can carry out tasks more effectively. For a comprehensive discussion, see Tarrow (1989).

4. Among the most influential contributions are those of Piven and Cloward (1979), Tilly (1978), and Tarrow (1989).

5. For example, Paris residents tend to use street barricades because these are inscribed in the history of Parisian contention (Tarrow 1989).

6. It is well beyond the scope of this review to present an assessment of populism. At the risk of oversimplification, populism can be defi ed as a political regime whose legitimation lies in the controlled incorporation of new classes that have emerged out of a process of rapid inward-oriented industrialization. Populism entails both the recognition of some citizenship rights to the

lower classes and the political creation and manipulation of the clientele born out of these sectors. See Weffort (1980).

7. See Perlman (1976) for a review.

8. Along the same lines, see Castells (1983) and Touraine (1965, 1983).

9. It is worth noting that with very few exceptions (Radcliffe and Westwood 1996), scholars of contentious politics in Latin America have not focused on these spatial aspects.

10. I use geography, context, territory, and place as exchangeable concepts.

11. For a discussion of the concepts of space and place, see Agnew (1997, 2002).

12. The discussion of territory draws on Duffy Toft (2003)

13. For a review of recent trends, see Platt (2004).

Chapter 2.   Buenos Aires: A Contentious City

1. I use *Buenos Aires* alone to refer to the capital city of Argentina. When I am referring to the periphery of Buenos Aires (Greater Buenos Aires) or to the province of Buenos Aires, I will explicitly refer to it as such.

2. The *piqueteros* are a protest movement born out in the provinces, even though some groups protest in Buenos Aires. On the other hand, the *asambleas populares* organized in 2002 in Buenos Aires soon disappeared. For an account of the *asambleas,* see Rossi, Pérez, and Armelino (2002).

3. *Federalization* here refers to the designation of Buenos Aires as the capital of the republic. Law 1029 was sanctioned by Congress on September 20, 1880, under the presidency of Nicolás Avellaneda. For a discussion of the process that led to the federalization of Buenos Aires, see Gutman and Hardoy (1992).

4. For this purpose, I follow closely the periodization used by L. Gutiérrez and Romero (1995).

5. This section is based primarily on Sábato (1992, 2001).

6. On December 14 an "assembly of grocers, bakers, innkeepers and cigar dealers established a committee to arrange a public meeting in order to organize a popular demonstration against new taxes. The meeting took place the following date and was attended by four thousand people. Three decisions were taken: to increase the number of the committee members; to ask the governor to veto the law, and to call a popular meeting at Plaza Lorea. As the governor did not respond the organization of the protest went ahead. The newspaper published the announcement to attend the demonstration and agents were appointed in every quarter to organize the meeting" (Sábato 1992).

7. With the exception of the burning of the Salvador School in 1875. See Leandro Gutiérrez, "El incendio del Colegio del Salvador, 1875: Expresión de protesta social," Buenos Aires, n.d., quoted in Sábato (2001).

8. The historical account that follows is largely based on PEHESA (1982, 1983).

9. *Gremios,* the predecessors of formal unions, were small and noncompulsory organizations and had a high mobilization capacity.

10. *Criollos* are residents of local birth but foreign ancestry.

11. The 1902 Residence Law stipulated the deportation of any rebellious foreigner. The 1910 Social Defense Law prohibited the entry to Argentina of those suspected of anarchism and prohibited the formation of anarchist groups.

12. For a comprehensive account of their emergence, see Privitello (2003).

13. For the early development of social policies in Argentina, see Lo Vuolo (1995).

14. The discussion of *vecinazos* is based upon González Bombal (1985).

Chapter 3.   Buenos Aires: A Divided City

1. Perhaps the most recent and dramatic example of the difficulties in translating popular collective action into policies that benefit lower-class *porteños* is the short life of the *asambleas populares barriales* (popular neighborhood assemblies). During the 2001–2 crisis, which resulted in the fall of the center-left coalition government of Alianza, these assemblies emerged with the goal of improving the well-being of *porteños,* but most of them soon disappeared. See Rossi (n.d.) and Rossi, Pérez, and Armelino (2002).

2. There is an extensive literature on the spatial structuration of Buenos Aires since the late nineteenth century. See Gorelik (1998), Gutman and Hardoy (1992), Oszlak (1991), and specially Torres (1978, 2001).

3. Argentina's Human Development Index for 2004 was 0.788 (PNUD-Argentina 2006).

4. The Unsatisfied Basic Needs Index measures structural poverty in terms of lack of adequate housing, sanitary conditions, and basic education.

5. I defi e *shantytown* or *slum* as a residential urban zone inhabited by the very poor who have no access to tenured land of their own and lack access to safe water and adequate sanitation (private or public toilet). This defi ition is based upon UN-Habitat (2006).

6. Census data in this section are from Alvarez de Celis (2003).

7. *Centros de gestión y participación* (CGPs) are the newly implemented district divisions of Buenos Aires City for decentralized management of local affairs. Neighborhoods, school districts, and electoral districts are somewhat similar.

8. In 1994 the city became autonomous from the central government and elected its fi st mayor.

9. International Style was a major architectural movement of the 1920s and 1930s. Its basic design principles are identical to those of modernism, but the term *International Style* refers to the buildings and architects of the formative decades of modernism, before World War II. Adolph Loos and Peter Behrens are the two most well-known architects of this movement.

10. According to indicators used in INDEC (1990) and MCBA (1991).

11. MCBA (1991) and Alvarez de Celis (2003).

12. CMV (1988).

Chapter 4. An Analytic Narrative of Popular Contention

1. In 1978, the PRN implemented a series of policies aimed at decentralizing services but not resources. Municipal governments undertook the delivery of services for which they subcontracted private service providers, a practice that led to corruption and fi ancial imbalances in the municipal budgets. González Bombal (1985) lists the negative effects of these policies.

2. For a discussion of *basismo,* see Lehmann (1996).

3. In this respect, the development and organizational profile of Villa Lugano resemble those of the new *asentamientos* of Greater Buenos Aires, where neighborhood associations take a primary role in occupying the land and achieving basic infrastructure services. For a study of these *asentamientos,* see Lawton (1994).

4. In-depth interviews reveal that many of those neighbors who did dare to petition authorities during the PRN were physically threatened.

5. A center-left arty founded by a dissident group of the Radical Party.

6. According to Granovetter (1978), a threshold is that point where any perceived benefits of doing the activity in question exceed the perceived cost. As will become evident in what follows, for a group of highly committed neighbors and old and new party activists, the cost threshold of participation was significantly lower than for other people that later on joined the CVL movement.

7. On the use of the language of rights in social movements in Latin America, see Foweraker (1995) and Foweraker and Landman (2000).

8. From 1972 until 1999, each neighborhood elected a Neighborhood Advisory Council; the one in Villa Lugano had nine members who were supposed to "communicate" neighborhood demands to the City Council and to the mayor. Their functions were never clearly stipulated by law.

9. Until the 1994 reforms, the mayor of Buenos Aires was appointed by the president of the republic, not elected.

10. Although the legal status granted to SFs varies by province and county, in most cases SFs are explicitly denied the right to deal with or invoke partisan issues and must fulfill several formal requirements when petitioning to authorities.

11. O'Donnell (1998) has termed "horizontal accountability" the checks and balances sanctioned by law in a democratic system.

12. The CVL had divided the neighborhood into four (critical) areas according to infrastructure deficiencies. Different types of activists mobilized each of these areas: Communist Party activists predominated in the area delimited by Piedrabuena and Barros Pazos streets and Radical Party activists in the area between Tellier and Madariaga streets. In the area delimited by Chilavert and Oliden streets and the surroundings of Villa 20 shantytown, a more heterogeneous group of neighbors and other activists linked to several parties predominated.

13. Even though all petitions were signed in the name of the CVL or the "neighbors" of Villa Lugano, several grassroots organizations participated either directly or by providing monetary resources to the CVL. By reading minutes of the CVL meetings I found the participation of the following organizations in this fi st mobilization phase: Club Lomas, Club Yupanqui, Club Belgrano, Club 9 de Julio, Comisión Vecinal Almirante Brown, and Sociedades de Fomento Mariano Moreno, Escalada, Florentino Ameghino, and Soldati, as well as activists from the Communist, Radical, Peronist, and Intransigente parties.

14. Larrosa had allegedly supported the march and had promised the CVL leaders to facilitate their participation during the council session.

15. The construction company that was granted the biggest paving plan in Villa Lugano (a total of eighty streets). The other paving companies were Alegre S.A. and Sigma.

16. Larrosa was reelected but lost around eight thousand votes compared to the previous election.

17. Many CVL participants had knowledge of construction because they were construction workers or architects, or simply had built their own houses little by little. This allowed them to check on the paving projects.

18. Today there is still no hospital in Villa Lugano, although Mayor Aníbal Ibarra, just before being impeached in March 2006, announced his intention to build one. The current mayor, Mauricio Macri of the center-right party PRO (Propuesta Republicana), built a hospital in 2010, but nowadays it functions only as a modest health center.

19. The CGDs were created by an ordinance of the City Council, and City Hall soon created an undersecretariat to organize their implementation. Former council member Dallochio, who was not reelected in 1985, was appointed undersecretary.

20. The JCN emerged in 1968 among university students in the province of Santa Fe. It allied with Renovación y Cambio and the two groups together pushed for the candidacy of Raúl Alfonsín in the 1983 national elections. On the JCN, see Leuco and Díaz (1987). Several JCN members occupied key posts in the powerful Comité Capital of the party, and others were appointed to the National Cabinet, progressively taking the place of Renovación y Cambio members.

21. Several qualifications in terms of gender, age, and residence were enforced until the reform of 1918. Voting and candidacy were restricted to Argentine men at least twenty-five years old who had been residents of Buenos Aires for at least six months. Immigrants were eligible too under the same restrictions but also were required to have resided in the city for at least five years (Walter 1993).

22. All Argentine men over eighteen years old had the right and obligation to vote in elections for City Council. Women were not allowed to vote.

23. For a discussion of informal institutions and the consolidation of democracy, see O'Donnell (1996) and Helmke and Levitsky (2002).

24. Of course, candidates at all levels use clientelistic incentives to attract constituencies, but at the neighborhood level they affect, above all, the autonomous organizational capacity of the urban poor. See Fox (1994) on threats and inducements.

25. Larrosa was indicted in early 1998 under corruption charges for diverting public funds to a sports club owned by him.

Chapter 5.   Framing Collective Action

1. The poverty line is calculated by adding to the cost of a basic food basket (or "indigence line") the cost of some nonbasic food items. Poor households are those whose monetary income is below the value of the poverty line. Households living below the indigence line cannot satisfy any of their basic needs. For a discussion of these measurements, see Altimir (1979), Feres and León (1990: 136–41), and Minujín (1992: 40–41).

2. Unlike the most influential writers on the authoritarian mind-set of the working classes (Lipset 1960), Germani (1955, 1962) did not attribute to the popular sectors an inner propensity toward authoritarian political orientations; he saw such orientations as contingent upon a set of interrelated contextual, subjective, organizational, and economic factors.

3. I understand political fragmentation as the existence, within a given population, of clear-cut cleavages in dimensions involving national and/or local political issues.

4. Robert Fishman (on Spain), Lazlo Bruszt and Janos Simon (on central/eastern Europe), and the "Grupo de Política" of CEBRAP (on São Paulo) have kindly shared with me their questionnaires and data.

5. "La democracia debe, antes que nada, garantizar: a) la libertad de la población para elegir el gobierno a través del voto, b) asegurar un nivel de vida decente para toda la población." I did not include the option "Both" in this question, but I coded this response when it occurred.

6. "¿Para qué sirve la democracia?"

7. "En vez de partidos políticos, lo que hace falta es que el pueblo siga a un hombre capaz y decidido que haga la unidad nacional."

8. "Para solucionar los problemas que la Argentina enfrenta hoy, el poder político del Presidente debería a) expandirse, b) mantenerse, o c) reducirse."

9. Federal intervention is an attribution of the federal government to take control over a province under extreme circumstances (e.g., to guarantee the republican form of government, repel foreign invasions, or restore authority after the current authority has been deposed by sedition or invasion).

10. "Si para resolver un grave problema nacional el Presidente tuviera que violar las leyes, es mejor que lo haga y que resuelva el problema."

11. "¿Ud. simpatiza con algún partido político? ¿Cuál?"

12. "Cuando se habla de política se utilizan expresiones tales como 'izquierda,' 'centro,' y 'derecha.' En esta tarjeta hay una serie de números que van de izquierda a derecha, ¿en cuál de ellos Ud. se ubicaría?"

13. See Ranis (1992) for unionized workers' political preferences in Argentina, and Moisés (1993) for such preferences among the urban population in Brazil.

14. "Los partidos políticos solo sirven para dividir al pueblo."

15. "En el fondo, los partidos políticos son todos iguales."

16. "¿Qué es más importante cuándo Ud. decide a quién votar, el candidato o el partido al cuál pertence?"

17. "Los políticos son en general personas: a) que sobre todo buscan su propio beneficio, b) con vocación de servir al país, c) que solo hacen mas difícil la tarea del gobierno."

18. "¿Cuál es su opinión de los políticos del barrio?"

19. "¿Que la justicia trate a todos igualmente es una condición importante para decir que un país es democrático?"

20. "¿Ud. cree que en la Argentina la ley es aplicada a todos por igual?"

21. "Ultimamente, mucha gente discute sobre que debería hacerse con el Estado. De acuerdo a su opinión el Estado debería: a) desaparecer, b) seguir como está, c) achicar mucho sus gastos y el número de sus empleados, d) no achicarse, pero mejorar la manera como funciona."

22. "La mejor forma de resolver los problemas económicos de la Argentina es a través de que el Estado: a) tenga mucho control sobre la economía,

b) deje de intervenir en la economía, c) intervenga solamente en algunas actividades de la economía."

23. "De acuerdo a su opinión, el Estado argentino es: a) un grupo de funcionarios que solo defiende su propio interés, b) un medio de opresión de los que mas dinero tienen sobre los pobres, c) la principal garantía para que los intereses del pueblo sean respetados, d) ninguna."

24. "Lo más importante es que haya desarrollo económico, aunque sea sin democracia, o lo mas importante es que haya democracia, aunque con poco desarrollo económico."

25. "¿Ud. cree que los empresarios argentinos tratan de contribuir para la riqueza y desarrollo del país, o solo intentan obtener beneficios personales, sin preocuparse por el futuro de la Argentina?"

26. "¿Cuál es su opinión sobre los sindicatos en general?"

27. "Para mejorar los problemas que la Argentina enfrenta hoy el poder político de los sindicatos debería en su opinión: 1) expandirse, 2) mantenerse, o 3) reducirse."

28. "La ocasión que tienen los ciudadanos para participar en política es votando en las elecciones. Después, le corresponde al Presidente gobernar el país de la manera que él juzgue mejor."

29. "Frente a un problema serio en su barrio que perjudique a todos, ¿Cree Ud. que los vecinos deben reunirse para buscar juntos una solución o dejar que las autoridades cuiden del problema?"

30 "¿Como cree Ud. que se obtienen mejores resultados para lograr los reclamos del barrio, a través de: 1) trámites legales iniciados por la Sociedad de Fomento o Comisión Vecinal, 2) mobilización vecinal, 3) los contactos personales con funcionarios o dirigentes políticos, 4) no vale la pena hacer nada?"

31. "De acuerdo a su opinión, las relaciones entre los partidos políticos y las organizaciones barriales deberían ser: 1) estrechas, 2) limitadas, 3) no deberían tener ninguna relación."

32. "De acuerdo a su opinión, las relaciones entre el gobierno y las organizaciones barriales deberían ser: 1) estrechas, 2) limitadas, 3) no deberían tener ninguna relación."

Chapter 6.   Discursive Dilemmas

1. On this issue I follow Tarrow (1994).

2. I use the concept of scaling up to refer to the diffusion of contentious collective action to a higher-order spatial level (e.g., from zone to zone within a neighborhood, from neighborhood to city, or even from neighborhood to nation). For discussion of the concept, see Agnew (1997).

3. One of the goals of OS is to represent in as few dimensions as possible the "latent structure" or relationship patterns among a large set of variables. By reducing the dimensionality of the data set, OS allows for the interpretation of a few mutually uncorrelated components that represent most of the information found in the original variables (survey items in the present case). The technique is most useful when a large number of variables prohibits direct interpretation of the relationships between objects (subjects and units).The advantage of OS over similar procedures (such as linear principal components) is that it can create a "perceptual map" of survey data by mixing in the analysis variables measured at different levels (nominal and ordinal, not only interval). Furthermore, with OS one can explore underlying factors and in many cases identify what they represent conceptually. By combining survey questions on different themes one may fi d significant overlaps among items or dimensions that represent cultural, political, or social cleavages that were not evident before performing OS. In other words, one can discover the underlying attitudes that lead people to respond to survey questions as they do. OS can also be defi ed as a quantification of qualitative data, since it not only reduces the dimensionality of the data set while accounting for as much of the variation as possible but also optimally quantifies the original variables and assigns scores to object (or cases) accordingly. The resulting object scores (with 0 mean and unit variance) can then be used in combination with other more traditional statistical procedures. Optimal quantification is obtained by an iterative method called alternating least squares.

4. For the variable measuring a hostile attitude toward neighbors, in each zone the survey asked two open questions on opinions about neighbors living in other zones of Villa Lugano. The questions were "What do you think about the neighbors living in the zone A?" and "What about those living in zone B?" This variable did not reflect opinions on neighbors living in the same zone of the interviewee; consequently a score of 1 on hostility means expressing a hostile view on at least one of the other zones of Villa Lugano. The union exposure variable refers to current or past union membership. The education variable was recoded as 1 = low (no schooling and some primary school); 2 = medium (primary education, some high school, some technical education); 3 = high (high school education, technical education, some college education, and college education).

5. Note that the resulting OS object scores for each dimension of variation are normalized to have a mean of 0 and a standard deviation of 1. Accordingly, the general distribution of opinions regarding autonomous participation in local politics was quite divided (about 60 percent of respondents scored above the mean).

6. On the dimension of liberal democracy, the majority of the respondents (352 or 76 percent) scored above the mean.

7. Half of the sample scored above the mean.

8. "Settlement" of shantytowns included granting of land titles to residents and the provision of public funds for upgrading of housing.

Chapter 7.   Hell Is Other People

1. I follow here Vargas-Cullel (2005).

2. See Hardin (2002) and Cook, Hardin, and Levi (2005).

3. By *habitat* I refer to the physical conditions that surround a species or a community. See Clements and Shelford (1939) for a discussion of habitat as environment.

4. *Pagina/12*, August 5,1999, quoted in Stanley (2005).

5. The dichotomy of civilization versus barbarism refers to Domingo Faustino Sarmiento's book *Facundo: Civilización y barbarie* (1845). Sarmiento, the seventh president of Argentina, identified civilization with city life and northern European immigration and barbarism with the countryside and its *caudillos.*

6. In the case of shantytowns, the defi ition of *outsider* has also a strong nationalistic connotation, since it is wrongly believed that most shantytown residents are foreigners. While it is true that some shantytowns have a predominance of certain nationalities (e.g., Villa 7 is predominately populated by Paraguayans), this is not the case in other shantytowns. Villa 20 is a case in point: 50 percent of its residents were Argentine according to census data at the time of this study (CMV 1988; MCBA 1991).

7. *Centro Informativo,* August 3, 1993.

8. *Centro Informativo,* August 3, 1993.

9. *Semanario Lugano,* January 11, 1994.

10. *Centro Informativo,* August 3, 1993.

11. *Centro Informativo,* August 3, 1993.

12. *Semanario Lugano,* January 4, 1994.

13. See, for example, *Semanario Lugano,* January 22, 1994.

14. *Semanario Lugano,* February 22, 1994.

15. Ibid.

16. According to Friendly (2000), the sieve diagram was created by Riedwyl and Schüpbach in 1994 and later called a *parquet diagram*. In the display, a unit square is divided into rectangles, one for each cell in the contingency table. The height of each rectangle in row i is proportional to the marginal frequency in that row (f_{i+}); the width of each rectangle in column j is proportional to the marginal frequency in that column (f_{+j}). Hence, the area of each rectangle is proportional to the expected frequency,

$$e_{ij} = (f_{i+}f_{+j})/f_{++}$$

under the hypothesis that the row and column variables are independent. The observed frequency in each cell is shown by the number of squares drawn in each rectangle. The difference between observed and expected frequency appears as the density of shading, using different lines to indicate whether the deviation from independence is positive (solid lines) or negative (dotted lines). The original sieve diagram uses color, blue for a positive deviation and red for a negative one.

Conclusion

1. See also Ippolito-O'Donnell (2008).
2. As we saw, Katznelson (1981) portrays a similar process in New York City.

WORKS CITED

Adorno, Theodor, Else Frenkel-Brunswik, Daniel J. Levinson, and Nevitt R. Sanford, eds. 1950. *The Authoritarian Personality.* New York: W. W. Norton.

Adrogué, Gerardo. 1999. "¿Militares en las urnas? ¿A quiénes representan?" *Ciudad Futura* (1999): 7–8.

Agnew, John. 1996. "Mapping Politics: How Context Counts in Electoral Geography." *Political Geography* 15 (2): 129–46.

———. 1997. "The Dramaturgy of Horizons: Geographical Scale in the 'Reconstruction of Italy' by the New Italian Parties, 1992–95." *Political Geography* 16 (2): 99–121.

———. 2002. *Place and Politics in Modern Italy.* Chicago: University of Chicago Press.

Almond, Gabriel, and Sidney Verba. 1963. *The Civic Culture: Political Attitudes and Democracy in Five Nations.* Princeton: Princeton University Press.

Altimir, Oscar. 1979. *La dimensión de la pobreza en América Latina.* Cuadernos de la CEPAL 27. Santiago de Chile: CEPAL.

———. 1993. "Income Distribution and Poverty through Crisis and Adjustment." *CEPAL Review* 52 (April): 7–31.

Altimir, Oscar, Luis Beccaria, and Martín González Rosada. 2002. "La distribución del ingreso en la Argentina, 1974–2000." *Revista de la CEPAL* 78: 55–85.

Alvarez de Celis, Fernando. 2003. *El Sur en la ciudad de Buenos Aires. Caracterización económica territorial de los barrios de La Boca, Barracas, Nueva Pompeya, Villa Riachuelo, Villa Soldati, Villa Lugano y Mataderos.* Buenos Aires: CEDEM.

Arendt, Hannah. 1968. *The Origins of Totalitarianism.* New York: Harcourt, Brace and Jovanovich.

Armory, Ariel. 2004. *The Dubious Link: Civic Engagement and Democratization.* Stanford: Stanford University Press.

Auyero, Javier. 1999. "'From the Client's Point of View': How Poor People Perceive and Evaluate Political Clientelism." *Theory and Society* 28: 297–334.

———. 2000. "Los estallidos en provincia: Globalización y confl ctos locales." *Punto de Vista* 67: 41–48.

———. 2001. "Glocal Riots." *International Sociology* 16 (1): 33–54.

Baily, Samuel J. 1967. *Labor, Nationalism, and Politics in Argentina*. New Brunswick, NJ: Rutgers University Press.

Bates, Robert, Avner Greif, Margaret Levi, Jean-Laurent Rosenthal, and Barry Weingast. 1998. *Analytic Narratives*. Princeton: Princeton University Press.

Bell, Daniel. 1960. *The End of Ideology: On the Exhaustion of Political Ideas in the 1950s*. New York: Free Press.

Bellardi, Marta, and Aldo De Paula. 1986. *Villas miseria: Origen, erradicación y respuestas populares*. Buenos Aires: Centro Editor de América Latina.

Bendix, Reinhardt. 1961. "The Lower Classes and the 'Democratic Revolution.'" *Industrial Relations* 1 (1): 91–116.

Berger, Susanne. 1979. "Politics and Antipolitics in Western Europe in the Seventies." *Daedalus* 108 (Winter): 27–50.

Booth, Jerome, and Mitchell Seligson. 1984. "The Political Culture of Authoritarianism in Mexico: A Reexamination." *Latin American Research Review* 19 (1): 106–24.

Botana, Natalio. 1979. *El orden conservador*. 2nd ed. Buenos Aires: Sudamericana.

Bridges, Amy. 1986. "Becoming America: The Working Classes in the United States before the Civil War." In *Working-Class Formation: Nineteenth-Century Patterns in Western Europe and the United States*, edited by Ira Katznelson and Aristide R. Zolberg. Princeton: Princeton University Press.

Brusco, Valeria, Marcelo Nazareno, and Susan Carol Stokes. 2004. "Vote Buying in Argentina." *Latin American Research Review* 39 (2): 66–88.

Brysk, Alison. 1994. *The Politics of Human Rights in Argentina: Protest, Change, and Democratization*. Stanford: Stanford University Press.

Burdman, Julio. 1998. *Los porteños en las urnas, 1916–1997*. Buenos Aires: Editorial Centro de Estudios para la Nueva Mayoría.

Bustelo, Eduardo, and Alberto Minujín. 1991. "Entre pobres y ajustados." *Pagina/12*, October 10.

Caballero, Victorio. 1985. "Lugano: Una aproximación a su urbanidad." *Nueva Lugano* 1 (1985).

Calvo, Ernesto, and María Victoria Murillo. 2004. "Who Delivers? Partisan Clients in the Argentine Electoral Market." *American Journal of Political Science* 48 (4): 742–57.

Carden, Maren Lockwood. 1978. "The Proliferation of a Social Movement: Ideology and Individual Incentives in the Contemporary Feminist Movement." *Research in Social Movements, Conflicts and Change* 1: 179–96.

Cardoso, Ruth. 1989. "Popular Movements in the Context of the Consolidation of Democracy." Working Paper 120, Kellogg Institute, University of Notre Dame.

Carnota, Fernando, and Esteban Talpone. 1995. *El palacio de la corrupción: Drogas, negociados y enriquecimiento en el Concejo Deliberante*. Buenos Aires: Sudamericana.

Castells, Manuel. 1983. *The City at the Crossroads: A Cross-cultural Theory of Urban Social Movements*. Berkeley: University of California Press.

Cavarozzi, Marcelo, and Vicente Palermo. 1995. "State, Civil Society, and Popular Neighborhood Organizations in Buenos Aires: Key Players in Argentina's Transition to Democracy." In *New Paths to Democratic Development in Latin America: The Rise of NGO-Municipal Collaboration*, edited by Charles A. Reilly. Boulder, CO: Lynne Rienner.

Clements, Frederic, and Victor Shelford. 1939. *Bio-Ecology*. New York: John Wiley and Sons.

CMV. See Comisión Municipal de la Vivienda.

Collier, David, ed. 1979. *The New Authoritarianism in Latin America*. Princeton: Princeton University Press.

Collier, David, and James Mahoney. 1996. "Insights and Pitfalls: Keeping Selection Bias in Perspective." *World Politics* 48: 56–91.

Comisión Municipal de la Vivienda. 1988. *Diagnóstico socio-económico de la Villa 20*. Buenos Aires: CMV.

Consejo de Planeamiento Estratégico, Ciudad de Buenos Aires. 2000. "Análisis FODA para la ciudad de Buenos Aires." Report. December. http://estatico.buenosaires.gov.ar/areas/buenosaires2010/insumos-tecnicos/publicaciones/informesPE/Analisis_Foda.pdf.

Cook, Karen, Russell Hardin, and Margaret Levi. 2005. *Cooperation without Trust?* New York: Russell Sage Foundation.

Coordinación del Plan Estratégico de la Ciudad de Buenos Aires. 2001. "Plan Estratégico de la Ciudad de Buenos Aires." November. www.scribd.com/doc/16676064/Plan-Estrategico-de-Buenos-Aires.

CPE. See Consejo de Planeamiento Estratégico, Ciudad de Buenos Aires.

Cravino, María Cristina. 2001. "La propiedad de la tierra como un proceso: Estudio comparativo de casos en ocupaciones de tierras en el área metropolitana de Buenos Aires." Paper presented at the Society for Latin American Studies Conference, "Land Tenure Issues in Latin America," April 6–8, 2001, Birmingham, UK.

Delamata, Gabriela. 2002. "De los 'estallidos' provinciales a la generalización de las protestas en Argentina: Perspectiva y contexto en la significación de las nuevas protestas." *Nueva Sociedad* 182: 121–38.

Del Brutto, Viviana. 1989. *Partidos políticos y gestión urbana en la capital federal*. Buenos Aires: Centro Editor de America Latina.

DGEC. See Dirección General de Estadísticas y Censos.

Dirección General de Estadísticas y Censos. 2005. *Anuario estadístico de la ciudad de Buenos Aires, 2004*. Buenos Aires: Gobierno de la Ciudad Autónoma de Buenos Aires.

Di Tella, Torcuato. 1965. "Populism and Reform in Latin America." In *Obstacles to Change in Latin America*, edited by Claudio Véliz. Oxford: Oxford University Press.

Duffy Toft, Monica. 2003. *The Geography of Ethnic Violence: Identity, Interests, and the Indivisibility of Territory*. Princeton: Princeton University Press.

Eisinger, Peter K. 1973. "The Conditions of Protest Behavior in American Cities." *American Political Science Review* 67: 11–28.

Elias, Norbert, and John Scotson. 1994. *The Established and the Outsiders: A Sociological Enquiry into Community Problems*. London: Sage Publications.

Escobar, Arturo, and Sonia E. Alvarez 1992. *The Making of Social Movements in Latin America: Identity, Strategy, and Democracy*. Boulder, CO: Westview Press.

Esping-Andersen, Gøsta. 1985. *Politics against Markets: The Social Democratic Road to Power*. Princeton: Princeton University Press.

Evans, Peter, ed. 1997. *State-Society Synergy: Government and Social Capital in Development*. Berkeley: University of California Press.

———. 2002. "Collective Capabilities, Culture, and Amartya Sen's *Development as Freedom*." *Studies in Comparative International Development* 37 (2): 54–60.

Facultad de Arquitectura, Diseño y Urbanismo de la Universidad de Buenos Aires and Instituto Internacional de Medio Ambiente y Desarrollo— América Latina. 2008. "Programa Buenos Aires 2050." www.buenos-aires2050.org.

FADU-UBA and IIED-AL. See Facultad de Arquitectura, Diseño y Urbanismo de la Universidad de Buenos Aires and Instituto Internacional de Medio Ambiente y Desarrollo—América Latina.

Falcón, Ricardo. 1986. *El mundo del trabajo urbano*. Buenos Aires: Centro Editor de América Latina.

Farinetti, Marina. 1998. "Cuando los clientes se rebelan." *Apuntes* 2 (1): 84–103.

Feres, Juan Carlos, and Arturo León. 1990. "The Magnitude of Poverty in Latin America." *CEPAL Review* 41: 133–51.

Fireman, Bruce, and William Gamson. 1979. "Utilitarian Logic in the Resource Mobilization Perspective." In *The Dynamics of Social Movements*, edited by Mayer N. Zald and John D. McCarthy. Cambridge, MA: Winthrop.

Foley, Michael W., and Bob Edwards. 1996. "The Paradox of Civil Society." *Journal of Democracy* 7 (3): 38–52.

Foweraker, Joe. 1995. *Theorizing Social Movements*. London: Pluto Press.

Foweraker, Joe, and Todd Landman. 2000. *Citizenship Rights and Social Movements*. Oxford: Oxford University Press.

Fox, Jonathan. 1994. "The Difficult Transition from Clientelism to Citizenship." *World Politics* 46 (2): 154–84.

Friendly, Michael. 2000. *Visualizing Categorical Data*. Cary, NC: SAS.

Fromm, Erich. 1969. *Escape from Freedom*. New York: Holt, Rinehart and Winston.

Gamson, William. [1975] 1990. *The Strategy of Social Protest.* Homewood, IL: Dorsey.

García Delgado, Daniel. 1984. "Nuevos patrones de participación política en procesos de transición a la democracia: El caso argentino." In *"Proceso," crisis y transición democrática,* vol. 2, edited by Oscar Oszlak et al. Buenos Aires: Centro Editor de América Latina.

García Delgado, Daniel, and Juan Silva. 1985. "El movimiento vecinal y la democracia participativa: Participación y control en el Gran Buenos Aires." In *Los nuevos movimientos sociales,* vol. 2, *Derechos humanos. Obreros. Barrios,* edited by Elizabeth Jelín. Buenos Aires: Centro Editor de América Latina.

Geertz, Clifford. 1973. *The Interpretation of Cultures: Selected Essays.* New York: Basic Books.

Gerlach, Luther P., and Virginia H. Hine. 1970. *People, Power, Change: Movements of Social Transformation.* Indianapolis: Bobbs-Merrill.

Germani, Gino. 1955. *Estructura social de la Argentina.* Buenos Aires: Raigal.

———. 1962. "Clases populares y democracia representativa en América Latina." *Desarrollo Económico* 2 (2): 23–43.

———. 1969. *Sociología de la modernización.* Buenos Aires: Paidós.

———. 1978. *Authoritarianism, Fascism, and National Populism.* New Brunswick, NJ: Transaction Books.

Gibson, Edward, Ernesto Calvo, and Tulia Falleti. 1999. "Federalismo redistributivo: Sobrerepresentación territorial y transferencia de ingresos en el hemisferio occidental." *Política y Gobierno* 6 (1): 15–44.

Gifi, Albert. 1990. *Nonlinear Multivariate Analysis.* New York: John Wiley.

Godio, Julio. 1995. *Los caminos del poder: PJ, UCR, FREPASO.* Buenos Aires: Corregidor.

Godio, Julio, Hector Palomino, and Achim Wachendorfer. 1988. *El movimiento sindical argentino (1880–1987).* Buenos Aires: Punto Sur.

Goffman, Erving. 1974. *Frame Analysis: An Essay on the Organization of Experience.* New York: Harper and Row.

Golbert, Laura, and Emilio Tenti Fanfani. 1994. "Poverty and Social Structure in Argentina: Outlook for the 1990s." Working Paper 6, Kellogg Institute, University of Notre Dame.

Goldstone, Jack. 1980. "The Weakness of Organization: A New Look at Gamson's *The Strategy of Social Protest.*" *American Journal of Sociology* 85: 1017–42.

Gonzáles Bombal, María Inés. 1985. "Protestan los barrios (el murmullo suburbano en la política)." In *Los nuevos movimientos sociales,* vol. 2, *Derechos humanos. Obreros. Barrios,* edited by Elizabeth Jelín. Buenos Aires: Centro Editor de América Latina.

Gorelik, Adrián. 1998. *La grilla y el parque: Espacio público y cultura urbana en Buenos Aires, 1887–1936.* Bernal: Universidad Nacional de Quilmes.

Granovetter, Mark. 1978. "Threshold Models of Collective Behavior." *American Journal of Sociology* 83 (6): 1420–43.

Gurr, Ted R. 1970. *Why Men Rebel.* Princeton: Princeton University Press.

Gutiérrez, Leandro. 1983. "Los trabajadores y sus luchas." In *Buenos Aires: Historia de cuatro siglos,* edited by José Luis Romero and Luis Alberto Romero. Buenos Aires: Abril.

Gutiérrez, Leandro, and Luis Alberto Romero. 1995. "La construcción de la ciudadanía, 1912–1955." In *Sectores populares: Cultura y política. Buenos Aires en la entreguerra,* edited by Leandro Gutiérrez and Luis Alberto Romero. Buenos Aires: Sudamericana.

Gutman, Margarita, and Jorge Enrique Hardoy. 1992. *Buenos Aires: Historia urbana del área metropolitana.* Buenos Aires: Mapfre.

Gutmann, Amy. 1998. "Freedom of Association: An Introductory Essay." In *Freedom of Association,* edited by Amy Gutmann. Princeton: Princeton University Press.

Haber, Paul Lawrence. 1996. "Identity and Political Process: Recent Trends in the Study of Latin American Social Movements." *Latin American Research Review* 31 (1): 171–87.

Halperín Donghi, Tulio. 1985. *Reforma y disolución de los imperios ibéricos, 1750–1859.* Madrid: Alianza.

Hardin, Russell. 1999. "Do We Want Trust in Government?" In *Democracy and Trust,* edited by Mark E. Warren. Cambridge: Cambridge University Press.

———. 2002. *Trust and Trustworthiness.* New York: Russell Sage Foundation.

Helmke, Gretchen, and Steven Levitsky. 2002. "Informal Institutions and Comparative Politics: A Preliminary Research Agenda." Paper presented at the annual meeting of the American Political Science Association, Boston.

Hirschman, Albert. 1982. *Shifting Involvements: Private Interest and Public Action.* Princeton: Princeton University Press.

Hobsbawm, Eric. 1959. *Primitive Rebels: Studies in Archaic Forms of Social Movement in the 19th and 20th Centuries.* Manchester: Manchester University Press.

Hoffer, Eric. 1951. *The True Believer: Thoughts on the Nature of Mass Movements.* New York: Harper and Row.

INDEC. See Instituto Nacional de Estadística y Censos.

Inglehart, Ronald. 1977. *The Silent Revolution: Changing Values and Political Styles among Western Publics.* Princeton: Princeton University Press.

Instituto Histórico Ciudad de Buenos Aires. 1979. *Historiando Lugano: Revista Homenaje. 70 Aniversario.* Brochure.

Instituto Nacional de Estadística y Censos. 1984. *La pobreza en la Argentina.* Buenos Aires: INDEC.

———. 1990. *La pobreza urbana en la Argentina*. Buenos Aires: INDEC.

Ippolito-O'Donnell, Gabriela. 2008. "La subversión del espacio público en América Latina." *Metapolítica* 12 (57): 56–63.

James, Daniel. 1988. *Resistance and Integration: Peronism and the Argentine Working Class, 1946–1976*. Cambridge: Cambridge University Press.

Jenkins, Craig. 1979. "What Is to Be Done: Movement or Organization?" *Contemporary Sociology* 8: 222–28.

———. 1983. "Resource Mobilization Theory and the Study of Social Movements." *American Review of Sociology* 9: 527–53.

Katzman, Rubén. 1989. "The Heterogeneity of Poverty: The Case of Montevideo." *CEPAL Review* 17: 131–42.

Katznelson, Ira. 1981. *City Trenches: Urban Politics and the Patterning of Class in the United States*. Chicago: University of Chicago Press.

Kertzer, David. 1988. *Ritual, Politics and Power*. New Haven: Yale University Press.

Kessler, Gabriel. 2000. "Redefi ición del mundo social en tiempo de cambio: Una tipología para la experiencia de empobrecimiento." In *Desde abajo: La transformación de las identidades sociales,* edited by Maristella Svampa. Buenos Aires: Biblos.

King, Gary. 1996. "Why Context Should Not Count." *Political Geography* 15 (2): 159–64.

King, Gary, Robert Keohane, and Sidney Verba. 1994. *Designing Social Inquiry: Scientific Inference in Qualitative Research*. Princeton: Princeton University Press.

Klandermans, Bert. 1984. "Mobilization and Participation: A Social-Psychological Expansion of Resource Mobilization Theory." *American Sociological Review* 48: 583–600.

Klandermans, Bert, and Sidney Tarrow. 1988. "Mobilization into Social Movements: Synthesizing European and American Approaches." In *From Structure to Action: Comparing Social Movements Research across Cultures,* edited by Bert Klandermans, Hanspeter Kriesi, and Sidney Tarrow, 1–38. Greenwich, CT: JAI.

Kornhauser, William. 1959. *The Politics of Mass Society*. New York: Free Press.

Kriesi, Hanspeter. 1991. *The Political Opportunity Structure of New Social Movements: Impact on Their Mobilization*. Berlin: Wissenschafts entrum.

Laclau, Ernesto. 1979. *Politics and Ideology in Marxist Theory*. London: Verso.

———. 2005. *La razon populista*. Buenos Aires: Fondo de Cultura Economica.

Lawton, Judy. 1994. "Clientelist Politics and Peronism in the Squatter Settlements of Greater Buenos Aires: Squatters' Views on Politics and Society." Paper presented at the Congress of the Latin American Studies Association, Atlanta.

Lazar, Sian. 2004. "Personalist Politics, Clientelism and Citizenship: Local Elections in El Alto, Bolivia." *Bulletin of Latin American Research* 23 (2): 228–43.

Lehmann, David. 1990. *Democracy and Development in Latin America: Economics, Politics and Religion in the Postwar Period.* Cambridge: Polity Press.

———. 1996. *Struggle for the Spirit: Religious Transformation and Popular Culture in Brazil and Latin America.* Cambridge: Polity Press.

Leuco, Alfredo, and José A. Díaz. 1987. *Los herederos de Alfonsín.* Buenos Aires: Sudamericana/Planeta.

Levitsky, Steven. 2003. *Transforming Labor-Based Parties in Latin America: Argentine Peronism in Comparative Perspective.* New York: Cambridge University Press.

Lipset, Seymour Martin. 1960. *Political Man: The Social Bases of Politics.* Garden City, NY: Doubleday.

Lipsky, Michael. 1970. *Protest in City Politics.* Chicago: Rand McNally.

Lo Vuolo, Rubén. 1995. "The Welfare State in Contemporary Argentina: An Overview." Working Paper 2, Kellogg Institute, University of Notre Dame.

Lowi, Theodore. 1971. *The Politics of Disorder.* New York: Basic Books.

Lvovich, Daniel. 2000. "Colgados de la soga: La experiencia del tránsito desde la clase media a la nueva pobreza en la ciudad de Buenos Aires." In *Desde abajo: La transformación de las identidades sociales,* edited by Maristella Svampa. Buenos Aires: Biblos.

Mainwaring, Scott. 1987. "Urban Popular Movements, Identity, and Democratization in Brazil." *Comparative Political Studies* 20 (2): 131–59.

Mainwaring, Scott, and Timothy Scully. 1995. *Building Democratic Institutions: Party Systems in Latin America.* Stanford: Stanford University Press.

Mainwaring, Scott, and Eduardo Viola. 1984. "New Social Movements, Political Culture, and Democracy: Brazil and Argentina." Working Paper 2, Kellogg Institute, University of Notre Dame.

Marwell, Gerald, and Pamela Oliver. 1993. *The Critical Mass in Collective Action: A Micro-Social Theory.* Cambridge: Cambridge University Press.

McAdam, Doug, Sidney Tarrow, and Charles Tilly. 1997. "Toward an Integrated Perspective on Social Movements and Revolutions." In *Comparative Politics,* edited by Mark Irving Lichbach and Alan S. Zuckerman. Cambridge: Cambridge University Press.

MCBA. See Municipalidad de la Ciudad de Buenos Aires.

McCarthy, John, and Mayer Zald. 1973. *The Trend of Social Movements in America: Professionalization and Resource Mobilization.* Morristown, NJ: General Learning Press.

———. 1977. "Resource Mobilization and Social Movements: A Partial Theory." *American Journal of Sociology* 82: 1212–41.

Melucci, Alberto. 1980. "The New Social Movements: A Theoretical Approach." *Social Science Information* 19: 199–226.

———. 1988. "Getting Involved: Identity and Mobilization in Social Movements." In *From Structure to Action: Comparing Social Movement Research across Cultures,* edited by Bert Klandermans, Hanspeter Kriesi, and Sidney Tarrow. Greenwich, CT: JAI.

———. 1996. *Challenging Codes: Collective Action in the Information Age.* Cambridge: Cambridge University Press.

Merklen, Denis. 2000. "Vivir en los márgenes: La lógica del cazador. Notas sobre la sociabilidad y cultura en los asentamientos del Gran Buenos Aires." In *Desde abajo: La transformación de las identidades sociales,* edited by Maricella Svampa. Buenos Aires: Biblos.

Michailidis, George, and Jan de Leeuw. 1998. "The Gifi System of Descriptive Multivariate Analysis." *Statistical Science* 13 (4): 307–36.

Miller, Byron. 2000. *Geography and Social Movements: Comparing Antinuclear Activism in the Boston Area.* Minneapolis: University of Minnesota Press.

Minujín, Alberto, ed. 1992. *Cuesta abajo: Los nuevos pobres. Efectos de la Crisis en la sociedad argentina.* Buenos Aires: UNICEF-Losada.

Moisés, José Alvaro. 1993. "Elections, Political Parties and Political Culture in Brazil: Changes and Continuities." *Journal of Latin American Studies* 25 (3): 575–611.

Moore, Barrington, Jr. 1966. *Social Origins of Dictatorship and Democracy: Lord and Peasant in the Making of the Modern World.* Boston: Beacon Press.

———. 1978. *Injustice: The Social Bases of Obedience and Revolt.* New York: M. E. Sharpe.

———. 2000. *Moral Purity and Persecution in History.* Princeton: Princeton University Press.

Morris, Aldon. 1984. *Origins of the Civil Rights Movement.* New York: Free Press.

Munck, Ronaldo. 1998. "Mutual Benefit Societies in Argentina: Workers, Nationality, Social Security and Trade Unionism." *Journal of Latin American Studies* 30 (3): 573–90.

Municipalidad de la Ciudad de Buenos Aires. 1991. *La población residente en las villas de la ciudad de Buenos Aires: Su magnitud, localización y características. Transformaciones en el período 1960–1991.* Buenos Aires: Dirección de Estadísticas y Censos.

Murmis, Miguel, and Juan Carlos Portantiero. 1971. *Estudios sobre los orígines del peronismo.* Buenos Aires: Siglo XXI.

Oberschall, Anthony. 1973. *Social Conflict and Social Movements.* Englewood Cliffs, NJ: Prentice-Hall.

———. 1980. "Loosely Coupled Collective Confl ct: A Theory and an Application." In *Research in Social Movements, Conflict and Change,* Vol. 3, edited by Louis Kriesberg. Greenwich, CT: JAI.

O'Donnell, Guillermo. 1972. *Modernization and Bureaucratic-Authoritarianism: Studies in South American Politics.* Berkeley: University of California, Institute of International Studies.

———. 1988. *Bureaucratic-Authoritarianism: Argentina, 1966–1973 in Comparative Perspective.* Berkeley: University of California Press.

———. 1993. "On the State, Democratization, and Some Conceptual Problems: A Latin American View with Glances at Some Post-communist Countries." *World Development* 21 (8): 1335–69.

———. 1994. "Delegative Democracy." *Journal of Democracy* 5 (1): 55–69.

———. 1996. "Illusions and Conceptual Flaws." *Journal of Democracy* 7 (4): 160–68.

———. 1998. "Horizontal Accountability and New Polyarchies." In *The Self-Restraining State: Power and Accountability in New Democracies,* edited by Andreas Schedler, Larry Jay Diamond, and Marc F. Plattner. Boulder, CO: Lynne Rienner.

———. 2003. "Horizontal Accountability: The Legal Institutionalization of Mistrust." In *Democratic Accountability in Latin America,* edited by Scott Mainwaring and Christopher Welna. Oxford: Oxford University Press.

———. 2004. "Human Development, Human Rights, and Democracy." In *The Quality of Democracy: Theory and Applications,* edited by Guillermo O'Donnell, Jorge Vargas Cullel, and Osvaldo M. Iazzetta. Notre Dame: University of Notre Dame Press.

O'Donnell, Guillermo, and Philippe Schmitter. 1986. *Transitions from Authoritarian Rule.* Vol. 4. *Tentative Conclusions about Uncertain Democracies.* Baltimore: Johns Hopkins University Press.

Offe, Claus. 1985. "New Social Movements: Challenging the Boundaries of Institutional Politics." *Social Research* 52 (4): 817–26.

Oliver, Pamela. 1984. "'If You Don't Do It, Nobody Else Will': Active and Token Contributors to Local Collective Action." *American Sociological Review* 49: 601–10.

O'Loughlin, John. 2002. "Spatial Analysis in Political Geography." Unpublished paper. Boulder: University of Colorado, Department of Geography.

Olson, Mancur. [1965] 1982. *The Logic of Collective Action: Public Goods and the Theory of Groups.* Cambridge, MA: Harvard University Press.

Oszlak, Oscar. 1991. *Merecer la ciudad: Los pobres y el derecho al espacio urbano.* Buenos Aires: CEDES.

Oxhorn, Philip. 1995. *Organizing Civil Society: The Popular Sectors and the Struggle for Democracy in Chile.* University Park: Pennsylvania State University Press.

Palermo, Vicente. 1986. *Democracia interna en los partidos: Las elecciones partidarias de 1983 en el radicalismo y el peronismo.* Buenos Aires: IDES.

Panettieri, José. 1967. *Los trabajadores.* Buenos Aires: Jorge Alvarez.

Pásara, Luis, Nena Delpino, Rocío Valdeavellano, and Alonso Zarzar. 1991. *La otra cara de la luna: Nuevos actores sociales en el Perú*. Lima: CEDYS.

PEHESA. 1982. "¿Dónde anida la democracia? La participación popular y sus avatares." *Punto de Vista* 15 (August): 6–10.

———. 1983. "La cultura de los sectores populares: Manipulación, inmanencia o creación histórica." *Punto de Vista* 6 (18): 11–14.

Perlman, Janice. 1976. *The Myth of Marginality: Urban Poverty and Politics in Rio de Janeiro*. Berkeley: University of California Press.

Perreault, Tom. 2008. "Latin American Social Movements: A Review and Critique of the Geographical Literature." *Geography Compass* 2 (5): 1363–85.

Pírez, Pedro. 2005. "La confi uración metropolitana de Buenos Aires: Expansión, privatización y fragmentación." *Realidad Económica* 208: 111–34.

Piven, Frances, and Richard Cloward. 1979. *Poor People's Movements: Why They Succeed, How They Fail*. New York: Vintage Books.

Pizzorno, Alessandro. 1978. "Political Exchange and Collective Identity in Industrial Confl ct." In *The Resurgence of Class Conflict in Western Europe since 1969*, edited by Colin Crouch and Alessandro Pizzorno. London: Macmillan.

———. 1986. "Some Other Kinds of Otherness: A Critique of 'Rational Choice' Theories." In *Development, Democracy, and the Art of Trespassing*, edited by Alejandro Foxley, Michael S. McPherson, and Guillermo O'Donnell. Notre Dame: University of Notre Dame Press.

Platt, Gerald. 2004. 'Unifying Social Movement Theory." *Qualitative Sociology* 22 (1): 107–16.

Plotkin, Mariano Ben. 2003. *Mañana es San Perón*. Wilmington, DE: SR Books.

PNUD-Argentina. See Programa de Desarrollo de las Naciones Unidas-Argentina.

Podalsky, Laura. 2004. *Specular City: Transforming Culture, Consumption, and Space in Buenos Aires, 1955–1973*. Philadelphia: Temple University Press.

Popkin, Samuel. 1979. *The Rational Peasant: The Political Economy of Rural Society in Vietnam*. Berkeley: University of California Press.

Portes, Alejandro. 1989. "Latin American Urbanization in the Years of Crisis." *Latin American Research Review* 24 (3): 7–44.

———. 1998. "Social Capital: Its Origins and Applications in Modern Sociology." *Annual Review of Sociology* 1998: 1–24.

Portes, Alejandro, and Bryan Roberts. 2005. "The Free-Market City: Latin American Urbanization in the Years of the Neoliberal Experiment." *Studies in Comparative International Development* 40 (1): 43–82.

Privitello, Luciano de. 2003. *Vecinos y ciudadanos: Política y sociedad en la Buenos Aires de entreguerras*. Buenos Aires: Siglo Veintiuno.

Programa de Desarrollo de las Naciones Unidas-Argentina. 2006. *Informe de desarrollo humano 2005: Argentina después de la Crisis. Un tiempo de oportunidades*. Buenos Aires: PNUD-Argentina.

Putnam, Robert D. 2000. *Bowling Alone: The Collapse and Revival of American Community.* New York: Simon and Schuster.

Putnam, Robert D., with Robert Leonardi and Raffaella Y. Nanetti. 1993. *Making Democracy Work: Civic Traditions in Modern Italy.* Princeton: Princeton University Press.

Radcliffe, Sarah, and Sallie Westwood. 1996. *Remaking the Nation: Place, Identity and Politics in Latin America.* London: Routledge.

Ranis, Peter. 1992. *Argentine Workers: Peronism and Contemporary Class Consciousness.* Pittsburgh: University of Pittsburgh Press.

Reich, Wilhelm. 1970. *The Mass Psychology of Fascism.* New York: Farrar, Straus & Giroux.

Roberts, Kenneth. 1997. "Beyond Romanticism: Social Movements and the Study of Political Change in Latin America." *Latin American Research Review* 32 (2): 137–51.

Romero, Luis Alberto. 1995. "Participación política y democracia, 1880–1984." In *Sectores Populares, Cultura y Política. Buenos Aires en la entreguerra,* edited by Luis Alberto Romero. Buenos Aires: Sudamericana.

Rossi, Federico. n.d. "La crisis de la república delegativa en la Argentina: Oportunidades políticas y marcos interpretativos en la constitución del 'Movimiento Social Asambleario.'" Unpublished paper. National University of Buenos Aires.

Rossi, Federico M., Germán Pérez, and Martín Armelino. 2002. "Modelos de asamblea: Entre el autogobierno y la representación." Paper presented at the Jornadas de Sociología, Universidad Nacional de Buenos Aires, Buenos Aires.

Rudé, George. 1964. *The Crowd in History: A Study in Popular Disturbances in France and England, 1730–1848.* New York: John Wiley and Sons.

———. 1980. *Ideology and Popular Protest.* New York: Pantheon.

Sábato, Hilda. 1992. "Citizenship, Political Participation and Formation of the Public Sphere in Buenos Aires, 1850s–1880s." *Past and Present* 136: 139–63.

———. 2001. *The Many and the Few: Political Participation in Republican Buenos Aires.* Stanford: Stanford University Press.

Sábato, Hilda, and Ema Cibotti. 1986. "Inmigrantes y política: Un problema irresuelto." *Estudios Migratorios Latinoamericanos* 4 (December): 475–82.

Sábato, Hilda, and Elias Palti. 1990. "¿Quién votaba en Buenos Aires? Práctica y teoría del sufragio, 1850–1880." *Desarrollo Económico* 119 (30): 395–66.

Sarmiento, Domingo Faustino 1845. *Facundo: Civilización y Barbarie.* Santiago de Chile: Imprenta del Progreso.

Schneider, Cathy L. 1995. *Shantytown Protest in Pinochet's Chile.* Philadelphia: Temple University Press.

Scott, James. 1985. *Weapons of the Weak: Everyday Forms of Peasant Resistance.* New Haven: Yale University Press.

————. 1990. *Domination and the Arts of Resistance*. New Haven: Yale University Press.

Secretaría de Planeamiento Urbano y Consejo del Plan Urbano Ambiental, Ciudad de Buenos Aires. 2000. "Plano Urbano Ambiental de La Ciudad de Buenos Aires 2000." http://estatico.buenosaires.gov.ar/areas/med _ambiente/coordinacion/archivos/plan_urbano_ambiental.pdf.

Seligson, Amber. 2001. "When Democracies Elect Dictators: Electoral Support for Former Authoritarian Rulers in Argentina." Paper presented at the annual meeting of the American Political Science Association, August–September, San Francisco.

Sen, Amartya. 1999. *Development as Freedom*. New York: Alfred A. Knopf.

Sewell, William, Jr. 2001. "Space in Contentious Politics." In *Silence and Voice in the Study of Contentious Politics*, edited by R. Aminzade, Jack A. Gladstone, Doug McAdam, Elizabeth J. Perry, William H. Sewell Jr., Sidney Tarrow, and Charles Tilly. New York: Cambridge University Press.

Smelser, Neil. 1963. *Theory of Collective Action*. New York: Free Press.

Smith, William. 1991. "State, Market, and Neoliberalism in Post-transition Argentina: The Menem Experiment." *Journal of Interamerican Studies and World Affairs* 33 (4): 45–82.

Smulovitz, Catalina, and Enrique Peruzzotti. 2000. "Societal Accountability in Latin America." *Journal of Democracy* 11 (4): 147–58.

Snow, David, and Robert Benford. 1988. "Ideology, Frame Resonance, and Participant Mobilization." In *From Structure to Action: Comparing Social Movement Research across Cultures*, edited by Bert Klandermans, Hanspeter Kriesi, and Sidney Tarrow. Greenwich, CT: JAI.

————. 1992. "Master Frames and Cycles of Protest." In *Frontiers in Social Movement Theory*, edited by Aldon D. Morris and Carol McClurg Mueller. New Haven: Yale University Press.

Snyder, Richard. 1999. "After Neoliberalism: The Politics of Reregulation in Mexico." *World Politics* 51 (2): 173–204.

————. 2001. *Politics after Neoliberalism: Reregulation in Mexico*. Cambridge: Cambridge University Press.

SPU and CoPUA. See Secretaría de Planeamiento Urbano y Consejo del Plan Urbano Ambiental, Ciudad de Buenos Aires.

Stanley, Ruth. 2003. "Policing Argentina: Citizenship and Coercion." Habilitationsschrift, Freie Universitat Berlin.

————. 2005. "Controlling the Police in Buenos Aires: A Case Study of Horizontal and Social Accountability." *Bulletin of Latin American Research* 24 (1): 71–91.

Stark, David, and Laszlo Bruzst. 1998. *Postsocialist Pathways: Transforming Politics and Property in East Central Europe*. Cambridge: Cambridge University Press.

Stinchcombe, Arthur. 1987. Review of *The Contentious French: Four Centuries of Popular Struggle,* by Charles Tilly. *American Journal of Sociology* 92 (5): 1248–49.

Stokes, Susan. 1995. *Cultures in Conflict: Social Movements and the State in Peru.* Berkeley: University of California Press.

Suriano, Juan. 1984. "La Huelga de Inquilinos de 1907 en Buenos Aires." In *Sectores populares y vida urbana,* edited by CLACSO. Buenos Aires: CLACSO.

Svampa, Maristella, ed. 2000. *Desde abajo: La transformación de las identidades sociales.* San Miguel: Biblos.

Tarrow, Sidney. 1989. *Struggle, Politics, and Reforms: Collective Action, Social Movements, and Cycles of Protest.* Ithaca: Cornell University, Center for International Studies.

——. 1994. *Power in Movement: Social Movements, Collective Action, and Politics.* Cambridge: Cambridge University Press.

——. 1998. *Power in Movement: Social Movements and Contentious Politics.* 2nd ed. New York: Cambridge University Press.

Thompson, E. P. 1971. "The Moral Economy of the English Crowd in the Eighteenth Century." *Past and Present* 50: 76–136.

——. 1975. *Whigs and Hunters: The Origins of the Black Act.* New York: Pantheon Books.

——. 1993. *Customs in Common.* London: Merlin.

Tiano, Susan. 1986. "Authoritarianism and Political Culture in Argentina and Chile in the Mid-1960s." *Latin American Research Review* 21 (1): 73–98.

Tilly, Charles. 1978. *From Mobilization to Revolution.* Reading, MA: Addison-Wesley.

——. 1986. *The Contentious French.* Cambridge, MA: Harvard University Press.

——. 1995. *Popular Contention in Great Britain.* Cambridge, MA: Harvard University Press.

——. 1998. *Spaces of Contention.* New York: Columbia University, Lazarsfeld Center.

——. 2004. *Contention and Democracy in Europe, 1650–2000.* Cambridge: Cambridge University Press.

Torres, Horacio. 1978. "El mapa social de Buenos Aires en 1943, 1947 y 1960: Buenos Aires y los modelos urbanos." *Desarrollo Económico* 18 (70): 1–50.

——. 2001. "Cambios socioterritoriales en Buenos Aires durante la década de 1990." *EURE (Santiago)* 27 (80): 1–25.

Touraine, Alain. 1965. *Sociologie de l'action.* Paris: Editions du Seuil.

——. 1983. *Solidarity: The Analysis of a Social Movement. Poland, 1980–1981.* Cambridge: Cambridge University Press.

UN-Habitat (United Nations Human Settlements Programme). 2006. *State of the World's Cities, 2006/2007.* New York: United Nations Human Settlements Programme.

Van de Geer, John P. 1993a. *Multivariate Analysis of Categorical Data: Applications.* Newbury Park, CA: Sage Publications.

———. 1993b. *Multivariate Analysis of Categorical Data: Theory.* Newbury Park, CA: Sage Publications.

Vargas-Cullel, Jorge. 2005. "Citizen Support for Democracy in Costa Rica and Latin America: An Inquiry into Its Foundations, Nature, and Consequences for Political Stability." PhD diss., University of Notre Dame.

Walter, Richard J. 1993. *Politics and Urban Growth in Buenos Aires, 1910–1942.* Cambridge: Cambridge University Press.

Weffort, Francisco. 1980. *O populismo na política brasileira.* 2nd ed. Rio de Janeiro: Paz e Terra.

Wilson, James. 1961. "The Strategy of Protest: Problems of Negro Civic Action." *Journal of Conflict Resolution* 5: 291–303.

Zald, Mayer, and Robert Ash. 1966. "Social Movement Organizations: Growth, Decay, and Change." *Social Forces* 44: 327–40.

Zald, Mayer N., and John D. McCarthy. 1987. *Social Movements in an Organizational Society.* New Brunswick, NJ: Transaction.

Ziccardi, Alicia. 1983. "Villas miseria y favela: Sobre las relaciones entre las instituciones del estado y la organización social en las democracias de los años setenta." *Revista Mexicana de Sociología* 45 (1): 45–67.

———. 1984. "El tercer gobierno peronista y las villas miseria de la ciudad de Buenos Aires." *Revista Mexicana de Sociología* 46 (4): 145–72.

Zimmermann, Eduardo. 1995. *Los liberales reformistas: La cuestión social en la Argentina, 1810–1916.* Buenos Aires: Sudamericana.

INDEX

The letter *f* following a page number denotes a fi ure, *g* a graph, *m* a map, and *t* a table.

GABRIELA IPPOLITO-O'DONNELL
is professor in the School of Politics and Government at the Universidad Nacional de San Martín in Argentina.